From COBOL to OOP

From COBOL to OOP

Markus Knasmüller
BMD Business Software

ELSEVIER

AMSTERDAM • BOSTON • HEIDELBERG • LONDON
NEW YORK • OXFORD • PARIS • SAN DIEGO
SAN FRANCISCO • SINGAPORE • SYDNEY • TOKYO

Morgan Kaufmann is an imprint of Elsevier

MORGAN KAUFMANN PUBLISHERS

Publishing Director	Diane D. Cerra
Senior Editor	Tim Cox
Publishing Services Manager	Simon Crump
Production Editor	Justin Palmeiro
Editorial Assistant	Richard Camp
Project Management	Graphic World Publishing Services
Cover Design	Monty Lewis
Technical Illustration	Graphic World Illustration Studio
Composition	SNP Best-set Typesetter Ltd., Hong Kong
Copyeditor	Graphic World Publishing Services
Proofreader	Graphic World Publishing Services
Indexer	Graphic World Publishing Services
Cover Printer	Phoenix Color Corporation
Interior Printer	The Maple-Vail Book Manufacturing Group

Morgan Kaufmann Publishers is an imprint of Elsevier
500 Sansome Street, Suite 400, San Francisco, CA 94111

This book is printed on acid-free paper.

Copyright © 2001 by dpunkt.verlag GmbH, Heidelberg, Germany.
Title of the German original: Von COBOL zu OOP
ISBN: 3-932588-95-9
Translation Copyright © 2004 by Elsevier, Inc. All rights reserved.

Library of Congress Control Number: Application submitted.

ISBN: 1-55860-822-2

For information on all Morgan Kaufmann Publications
visit our website at *www.mkp.com*

Printed in the United States of America

07 06 05 04 03   5 4 3 2 1

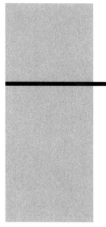

Preface to the German Version

It was Tuesday, May 15, 1990, 10.20 AM—my first contact with object-oriented programming. When I made my first experiences with this programming form as a student back then, I did not even have a compiler for it, so the only way to do my exercises was on paper. Nevertheless, I was impressed by this new concept, and later, I wrote various programming projects and even my degree and dissertation about this topic. Together with Professor Mössenböck, himself a developer of the object-oriented programming language Oberon-2, at the Johannes Kepler University of Linz, Austria, I introduced hundreds of students to the art of object-oriented programming. In 1997, BMD Systemhaus GmbH, Austria's leading manufacturer of accounting software, offered me a chance to manage their software development division with the main responsibility of converting their current COBOL development to object-oriented programming—a great challenge for me. The experiences I gained in this project, and the technique applied to convey object-oriented techniques to COBOL programmers, formed the basis for this book.

Consequently, this book addresses not only all COBOL programmers but also all other programmers interested in making a switch from conventional to object-oriented programming. It is also addressed to project managers who are interested in implementing larger projects with the use of object-oriented techniques. This means that this book has a fairly large target group—there are no doubt hundreds of thousands of programmers all over the world who have yet made this transition.

This book is aimed at facilitating exactly this for all these people. In this book, we try to show one possible, efficient way, including experiences we

vi ■ Preface to the German Version

gained and well-known errors we found, so that our readers may benefit from what we already went through and (hopefully) avoid the same errors.

I remember when I began working on that project with BMD; a book like this would have helped a great deal. Unfortunately, there was no such book, a fact that I found equally surprising and disappointing, because it would have been a useful guideline for so many people. Since then, I have had the idea of writing such kind of a book, and now, after many privations and spending almost every spare minute on it, it is finally finished.

The fact that I am the only author of this book is a little misleading; like most textbooks, this book involved some group effort, and it would probably not have come into being without the help of so many people. First and foremost, I would like to give credit to Professor Mössenböck, who extended me his invaluable support, both in his book [Mös99] and in his lectures on object-oriented programming, showing me a meaningful way to teach and learn object-oriented programming. Together with Bruno Schäffer, Professor Mössenböck also read the manuscript and made suggestions, enabling me to improve the quality of the book considerably. I owe great thanks to the staff of BMD; all of them supported my efforts to introduce object-oriented programming throughout the project and when I wrote this book. Representative for all employees of BMD, my special thanks goes to the so-called NTCS (New Technology Commercial Software) team, namely Günther Freudenthaler, Horst and Sylvia Hagmüller, Franz Pfeiler, and Robert Zeiml. Last, but not least, I would like to thank BMD managing director, Ferdinand Wieser, for his encouragement and continued support. This NTCS project was sponsored by the Austrian Innovation and Technology Fund (ITF) under project number 801813.

Also, I am thankful to my trainee student, Matthias Rumplmaier, who is the author of a large number of figures included in this book. Ursula Zimpfer proofread the manuscript to (hopefully) find any remaining typos. I also appreciate the assistance of Christa Preisendanz of dpunkt.verlag, who put a lot of organizational work in making this book happen. Sigrid Haberkorn of Borland made it possible for us to add test versions of Delphi and JBuilder to the CD attached to this book.

Finally, I would like to thank my beloved wife, Ulrike, although it will not make up for all those hours we would otherwise have spent together.

Markus Knasmüller

Preface to the English Edition

Two years have passed since the German edition of this book appeared. Although the computer industry made tremendous progress during these 2 years, it advanced very little (if at all) from the economic stance. Major crises have brought many IT corporations to the brink of ruin, and many programmers are unemployed today. This is the reason why excellent qualification is more important than ever. This is what this book wants to convey to traditional COBOL programmers, who will find these times especially hard.

However, this book has further developed during these 2 years. Not only the experiences gained from tutorials held about this issue at the OOPSLA in Tampa Bay [Kna01] and OOP 2002 in Munich, Germany, but also the invaluable suggestions of the four experts appointed by Morgan Kaufmann, namely Raimund K. Ege, Chien Yueh, Markku Sakkinen, and Gene Kozlowski, have made this English edition much more extensive than the original German version.

We appreciate the input of these experts and are grateful to Stacie Pierce and Tim Cox of Morgan Kaufmann for their patience during the past 2 years. Gudrun Wilhelm of Borland made it possible that this book now includes new demo versions of Delphi and JBuilder.

Last but not least, we would like to thank our translator, Angelika Shafir, who contributed to making the rare case happen where the translated version seems to be better than the original.

Markus Knasmüller

Contents

1

Introduction

1.1 Motivation

Y2K problem The third millennium has begun, and with it a new information technology age. Fast developments have to be expected, because together with the new millennium, a new age began without the Y2K problem. The Y2K problem involved huge manpower capacities to solve a simple but very costly problem with date formats. The removal of the Y2K problem was not creative—as we can see, for instance, in the following example of a letter written by a software development manager, probably not meant to be taken all too seriously:

Y2K taken literally Dear Boss,
Our staff has completed the 18 months of work on time and on budget. We have gone through every line of code in every program in every system. We have analyzed all databases and all data files, including backups and historic archives, and modified all data to reflect the change.

We are proud to report that we have completed the "Y2K" date change mission and have now implemented all changes to all programs and all data to reflect your new standards: Januark, Februark, March, April, Mak, June, Julk,

August, September, October, November, December. As well as Sundak, Mondak, Tuesdak, Wednesdak, Thursdak, Fridak, Saturdak.

I trust that this is satisfactory, because to be honest, none of this "Y to K" problem has made any sense to me. But I understand it is a global problem, and our team is glad to help in any way possible.

And what does the year 2000 have to do with it? Speaking of which, what do you think we ought to do next year, when the two-digit year rolls over from 99 to 00? We'll await your direction.

Joan Duh
Senior Programer

Although this change of programs brought little progress, it tied up a lot of resources—the more so as a new currency, the Euro, also had to be built into many programs. This situation paved the way for programmers, particularly those of the old school, to find suitable jobs. Because most of the programs that had to be rewritten were old programs, most of them in COBOL, COBOL programmers were suddenly in demand, although the situation had looked grim for them only a few years before the turn of the century, as new and more comfortable programming languages emerged.

The Y2K problem created plenty of jobs not only for existing COBOL programmers—many newcomers to the programming field were encouraged to study COBOL, and an equally large number of corporate programmers were retrained for this language. However, as an expert in the field once said, "Before January 1, software developers will make money from the Y2K problem, while only lawyers will make even more money from it after that date."

Job prospects   In this new age after the Y2K problem, everybody can now fully concentrate on progress and further development. Naturally, this will create a high demand for professionals, including programmers, in the field of information technology. But these jobs will require more creativity and performance and less tedious code writing. Also, new technologies, such as the Internet, UMTS, and WAP, are making progress. This means that today's COBOL programmers will have to evolve. A labor market study published by JOBSTATS in November 2002 *(www.jobstats.com)* shows that only 0.9% of all open IT jobs ask for COBOL. This demand is far below that for Java (8.4%) or C++ (10.4%), although there are now about three million COBOL programmers worldwide.

Alternatives: even crossopterygian species may survive

Thanks to the enormous benefits of object-oriented programming, which is discussed in the next section, it is not hard to understand why an object-oriented language is in greater demand. For this reason, it is important to learn this technique, and it should not be too difficult: You are only about 300 pages away from it. Of course, certain efforts will still have to be made, and some may be reluctant, asking themselves whether there are any alternatives.

Of course there are! Taking an analogy from natural life, although the dinosaurs are extinct, a species called crossopterygian (a large group of fishes that have paired fins suggesting limbs; Figure 1.1) have been around 250 million years longer than dinosaurs and are still here. Therefore, no doubt COBOL programmers will also survive without going to the effort of making an evolutionary adjustment.

All jokes aside, not just COBOL programmers but all programmers nowadays must evolve or become extinct. This book can be a step forward to avoid extinction.

Although learning object-oriented programming is necessary, it is a rather hard task. Therefore, it is useful to give some motivation now. We think that it is much easier for an experienced COBOL programmer to learn OOP than a newcomer. A COBOL programmer knows how to program and has to learn only the object-oriented features. This book teaches exactly that.

Former COBOL programmers have another advantage: an above-average knowledge of and experience with domains. We believe that this domain knowledge and experience in implementing such a software product are far more important than the programming knowledge itself. Therefore, an experienced COBOL programmer with some knowledge of object-oriented programming is a much better choice for a manager than a newcomer with perfect OO knowledge but no experience.

Figure 1.1 The crossopterygian: an alternative for COBOL users?

The rest of this chapter discusses the advantages of object-oriented programming. It also describes the necessary preparations and how this course is organized and gives a practical example for all those who are still in doubt. The example shows two things: first, that it is recommended to switch from COBOL to object-oriented programming, and second, that the concept covered in this book has been successfully applied in practice.

1.2	**Advantages of the New Technologies**

The most important advantages of object-oriented programming are as follows:

The advantages of OOP

- **Reusability:** Object-oriented programming allows an existing program code to be reused, even in a totally different program. This technique helps reduce development costs. A simple example is accounting functionality written only once and used by all programs.

- **Extensibility:** Not only can existing program codes be reused, they can also be extended by inheritance, as discussed in Section 5.2, without any effect on existing program codes or on programs that already use these code pieces. A simple example is a program written for British payroll software that could reuse many code parts from existing U.S. payroll accounting software.

- **Class libraries:** The possibility of reusing code takes us a step further, allowing us to group the most important program parts into libraries. The programmer can use these libraries, select program parts matching the new code, and extend it directly or by inheritance, without the need to change the existing program parts.

- **Uniform look of programs:** Class libraries not only reduce development costs but also ensure uniform design of new programs. For example, if the class library includes objects to design a graphical user interface, new programs written with these objects naturally have a similar look and feel. The user will find these programs friendlier, and the programmer will find the source code easier to handle.

- **Object-oriented thinking:** The biggest advantage is the new object-oriented thinking. Object-oriented programming views a program as a collection of loosely connected agents, termed objects. Each object is responsible for specific tasks. It is by the interaction of objects that computation proceeds. In a certain sense, therefore, programming is nothing more or less than the simulation of a model universe. Object-oriented programming is a new way of thinking about the process of decomposing problems and developing programming solutions [Bud02, p. 19].

OO techniques

All these advantages would be reason enough to switch to an object-oriented programming language. However, to make this switch as efficient as possible, it would be a good idea to learn other useful techniques in parallel. The most important of these techniques are described in this book. Briefly, two of them are as follows:

- **Object-oriented modeling:** In general, a project begins with a difficult and complex situation. The object-oriented design, with its holistic approach, considering both static structural properties and dynamic state changes, helps represent such a complex situation in a simple model. Object-oriented modeling analysis, design, and implementation of software happen under one conceptual umbrella.

- **Databases:** Databases can be thought of as an expansion of the principle of index-sequential files. They offer the benefit of providing many additional functions, such as recovery (ensuring that the database contents remain consistent even if a program crashes) or SQL (a simple query language). In addition, they allow end users to write their own evaluations, which means that individual adaptations are no longer required. Of course, databases are not really a feature of object-oriented programming—they can also be used in traditional programming languages, even in COBOL. However, most traditional COBOL programs (not the new one, of course) use index-sequential files instead of relational or object-relational databases.

1.3 Organization of This Book

Interested in perfection? This book helps you learn it

We think the aforementioned reasons represent enough motivation to get started right away—for example, by reading the next chapter, which takes you to the actual learning material. Before dealing with the nuts and bolts of object-oriented programming, however, it is worthwhile to explain how this book is organized.

This book does not attempt to train you for an object-oriented programming job nor does it concentrate on a specific development environment. Although most modern development environments are powerful, enabling you to create cute programs in almost no time (sometimes even without writing a single line of code), such an approach has inherent risks, particularly for the beginner. First of all, "creating" seems to be a better word than "programming," because this programming approach has little to do with real programming—it normally takes not much more than a few mouse clicks. Many technical books begin with exactly these mouse clicks.

The problem is that the applications built by such an approach may look nice but will somehow (and usually soon) not stand the test in practice. They will require modifications and extensions, which take more than a few mouse clicks. Instead, applications require sound basic knowledge, because code has to be modified and produced.

In fact, such an enterprise requires perfection—which has to be acquired, even in object-oriented programming. This book is aimed at helping you gain exactly this perfection. As rocky as the way to get there may be, because your first result will most likely not be a killer Windows application, the final result—the acquired perfection—will make up for every effort you made.

Another important thing to say here is that this book is about object-oriented programming and not about COBOL. So, whenever it is useful, we compare COBOL constructs with object-oriented programming structures. However, the former are not explained in detail when it is not necessary, because we assume that the typical reader knows all the COBOL details.

Preceding the tutorial sections of this book, which are about the differences between COBOL and object-oriented programming, there is first a section about software engineering. This section presents fundamental concepts without getting into the specific syntax of a language. Some basic concepts that are discussed there are, for example, names, types, procedural abstraction, and the important topic of keywords versus class libraries. This section is an introduction to the basic concepts of modern programming in general, before the similarities and differences between COBOL and object-oriented programming are presented.

When the world of traditional COBOL is compared with that of object-oriented programming, several fundamental differences are noted, shown in Table 1.1. It should be mentioned here that object-oriented COBOL

Table 1.1   Comparing COBOL with OOP

COBOL	*Object-oriented programming*
Terms (OCCURS, PERFORM, . . .)	Terms (records, arrays)
Static data types	Dynamic data types
Types	Classes
(Index-) sequential files	Databases
Terminal solutions	Graphical user interfaces

(OO-COBOL) also supports many of these functions. Section 1.5 presents more about OO-COBOL.

We took these differences between COBOL and OOP as a basis to prepare and design the following OOP course, one full chapter being dedicated to each of them. Building on these fundamental differences between COBOL and OOP, the tutorial sections are divided into seven blocks (including a total of 27 exercises).

The author's experience: practice makes perfect

Each block consists of several separate tutorial sections, which should be worked through. Each section concludes with exercises (mostly programming tasks). They should be worked through, because programming is not something that can be learned by heart and recited from memory, by attending theoretical lectures, or by reading textbooks (although it helps).

When I studied programming, there was one 90-minute lecture per week, supplemented by a practical exercise that had to be worked out at home (or rather at the university's mainframe, at that time). Each exercise took about 10 hours to complete. This was a very efficient learning method, showing that programming can be learned only at the computer.

For this reason, the tutorial sections in this book are organized so that they will take about 60 minutes each, and each is followed by exercises that require a multiple of this time. (The approximate time to allow yourself for each exercise is indicated in parentheses.) It is not necessary to work all exercises thoroughly, and a (short!) look at the sample solutions (in Appendix B and on the CD) is also allowed.

Skipping tutorial sections

Basically, this book follows a textbook approach, where the material contained in the chapters can be read sequentially, from front to back. However, advanced readers may choose to skip some sections. I recommend skimming the exercises of a tutorial section you intend to skip to find out this is a good idea.

Selecting a Programming Environment

Languages: Delphi, C++, Java—which one is the best?

One of the first decisions to be made at the beginning of an object-oriented project is which programming language to use. Many programming languages have been used for software development since SIMULA, the first object-oriented programming language. Among the most popular are the following:

- **Delphi:** This language is actually an object-oriented extension of Pascal [JeWi74], a language particularly popular both in universities and in practice. Delphi is well structured and, at least in my view, easy for former COBOL programmers to learn. It is conceived mainly for commercial applications.

- **C++:** This language is an object-oriented extension of the C programming language, conceived mainly for system programming. It is not one of the easiest to learn and leads to a somewhat unstructured programming style. Despite this drawback, it is currently the most popular OOP language.

- **Java:** This OOP language is similar to C++ and is used mainly to write Internet pages. The recent Internet boom is responsible for Java having the highest growth rate. One problem with this OOP language is that programs written in it tend to be slow, particularly for number-crunching tasks, because Java code is compiled into byte code, which must be interpreted. Although speed may not be critical on the Internet, the real bottleneck being line capacities and other network-related factors (most readers will surely have experienced the "World Wide Wait"), slow program speeds are tolerated less in business environments.

Now, while selecting a language appears to be hard enough, object-oriented programming does not let us settle for just a language. We must also select a suitable programming environment. In addition to a compiler, such a programming environment contains other tools, such as a debugger or a project management tool and a class library. As mentioned previously and discussed extensively in Section 5.4, such a library can often be more important than the programming language.

Selection criteria

Because there are so many different programming environments with different advantages and different disadvantages, it is an important and complex matter to select the right one. As mentioned, a larger project normally begins with choosing the development environment. It would appear meaningful to start by defining a list of requirements and then evaluate all potential candidates. Criteria established in such a requirement catalog could mean complete support of the object-oriented technology, Internet functionality, integration of database systems, previous experience and successful projects, service and support, or costs.

Project managers usually decide

The COBOL programmer who is about to jump into an object-oriented project will normally have to live with a decision made by the project's management. This book is therefore designed to be independent of any specific programming environment. A side benefit of this approach is that readers who intend to merely get an idea of what object-oriented programming is all about can skim the book without nailing themselves down to a specific programming language or development environment in advance.

Of course, this approach presents difficulties, particularly when it comes to the programming examples, because examples are normally written in a specific programming language. For examples that required a specific language be used, that language is indicated in the marginal note. We thought it preferable to present all examples in Delphi and Java, leaving out C++ altogether, because this language is similar to and gradually being replaced by Java.

1.5 Object–Oriented COBOL

One object-oriented programming language is missing in the preceding list: object-oriented COBOL (for example, [ArCo96]). OO-COBOL is "normal" COBOL with additional object-oriented functions, just as C++ is an object-oriented extension of C. Naturally, considering this book's main subject, you may wonder why it does not cover this language in detail or use it as a basis to teach object-oriented programming. There are several reasons:

Evaluating OO-COBOL

■ Current COBOL programmers normally join new project teams once they complete their professional switch to object-oriented programming. The problem is that most new projects do not use OO-COBOL.

■ Learning object-oriented programming involves not only the study of new concepts but also, and most important, the application of these concepts. A programmer who works with OO-COBOL may tend to continue using his or her familiar style and concentrate mainly on well-known parts. For this reason, it seems advisable to learn these techniques on the basis of a new language and use that language from the beginning.

■ Even when existing COBOL packages written in conventional programming code are converted to object-oriented programming, I consider it preferable to use another object-oriented programming language instead of OO-COBOL. If we use only OO-COBOL instead of COBOL, we run the risk that nothing might change for the better, especially in view of the fact that most programmers are urged to use these new concepts.

On the other hand, many COBOL programmers might hope they can become OO-COBOL programmers with no more effort than adding a few characters to their job titles [Bud02, p. 2]. They should consider the following sentences about object-oriented programming in Timothy Budd's excellent book: "Unfortunately, this hope is a long way from being realized. Object-oriented programming is a new way of thinking about what it means to compute, about how we can structure information and communicate our intentions both to each other and to the machine. To become proficient in object-oriented techniques requires a complete reevaluation of traditional software development."

1.6 Notation and Conventions

To avoid lengthy explanations of frequently occurring technical terms in each context throughout the book, Appendix C contains a detailed glossary of terms.

Source code   All program examples are highlighted with marginal notes that indicate the language (normally Delphi or Java) used in the example. Programming fragments, such as keywords, that occur in the text are highlighted by a different formatting style—for example, `program`.

1.7   The Book CD

This book includes a CD with all tutorial sections, in the form of Power-Point presentations, and sample solutions to all exercises, ready to be compiled. For readers who do not have a programming environment yet, the CD contains test versions of Borland Delphi and Borland JBuilder.

CD contents   The main directory of the CD includes three folders:

- **PowerPoint,** which includes tutorial sections

- **Delphi,** which includes sample solutions to the exercises in the Delphi programming language

- **Java,** which includes sample solutions to the exercises in the Java programming language

The structure underneath this folder follows the same order; that is, each chapter is in a separate folder, and each tutorial is in a subfolder.

If you want to install one of the two demo versions, open the file `borland.html` in the main directory, which explains how to proceed.

As a special feature, you will also find the OOPSLA tutorial "How to Manage the Change from COBOL to OOP" [Kna01] in the PowerPoint folder.

1.8   A Real–World Example

BMD   If you think you still need more motivation, despite the benefits of object-oriented programming outlined earlier, this section briefly introduces a practical example to encourage you to get going with this OOP course. The Austrian company BMD Systemhaus GmbH has successfully applied the approach to teaching and learning object-oriented programming introduced in this course. This company is one of the largest Austrian producers of business software, with an installed base of more than 12,000 customer sites. The course trained more than 40 of the company's COBOL programmers (some with close to 30 years of COBOL experience) in object-oriented programming. I have managed BMD's software development department since 1997.

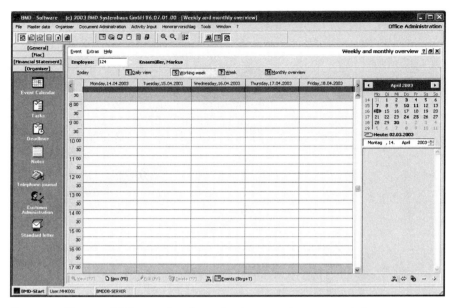

Figure 1.2 The new BMD organizer (core development time: 2 months).

Real-world experience: OOP pays off

Within the scope of this project [Kna99], the entire software development, including all existing software, has been converted from COBOL to object-oriented programming, where we are talking of more than 10 million lines of code. The practical tips for object-oriented projects given in Chapter 9 include a discussion of experiences gained from this BMD project. As another motivating argument, we note that the new object-oriented techniques helped us develop several new packages, including a document archive, a Web shop, and an organizer (Figure 1.2), within a relatively short time (each took only a few months).

2

Programming as an Engineering Discipline

Extensive experience

As mentioned in Chapter 1, COBOL programmers normally have extensive experience. Nevertheless, many of them were not lucky enough to spend years studying at a university. In fact, many often received only a brief introduction and had to start on a job and become productive immediately. This is basically nothing bad—to the contrary! Productive work is a good thing and cannot be replaced by years of studying at universities. But still, it is about time to catch up on a few things and improve systematic work.

Programming is more than coding!

This chapter deals with the process of learning these things systematically. It is aimed at improving general programming knowledge. Programming is a highly creative activity, and a complex one. In fact, it is probably more complex than many other engineering sciences. In addition, programming should not be seen as a coding task, because it involves much more, including analysis, design, development, testing, and often, commissioning (verifying whether the software solves the problem) at the customer's site.

Software engineering

All this is important and is discussed in this chapter without depending on any single language. Therefore, this chapter does not require knowledge of a specific programming language. We will come to this point in the next chapter, which briefly discusses some of the concepts explained here and then deals with language differences. Notice that we should not be talking about programming in this chapter; *software engineering* is the better and more comprehensive term.

2.1 Software Engineering Basics

Holistic approach
As mentioned, the most important thing to understand is that software engineering is a holistic approach, which means that it includes much more than the actual programming. It is a matter of professionally developing large software systems. This involves several important facts:

- **Large software:** We are talking of large software and not of small programs. This translates into high complexity, which means that many components normally have to be linked to solve the problem on hand. This complexity has to be reduced to ensure that the problem remains manageable, despite its complexity. Section 2.4 discusses a method for reducing complexity.

- **Long lifetime:** Software has a long lifetime. This is clear, because the significant effort would otherwise not pay off. Long lifetime means that versions will be built and many changes will be involved. Section 9.4.3 introduces useful versioning tools.

- **Teamwork:** Software can no longer be developed by one person. It requires developer teams, which use methods and tools to solve a problem and create software. This is possible mainly when a highly complex problem can be divided into smaller ones. Individuals can solve the smaller sets of problems, which facilitates teamwork. However, even when problems can be solved individually, frequent cooperation, including exchange of information and mutual source code revisions, is both meaningful and necessary.

- **User involvement:** Involve your (future) users in all development phases. Users look at things differently and may even have different goals, interests, experiences, and knowledge than the development team.

The following subsection begins with a reflection on software quality and then deals with the concepts involved in programming and specification.

2.1.1 Software Quality

Adaptability is important
One major problem in software development is that software cannot be perceived or understood through the senses. All we can actually perceive

are defined pieces of text in the form of reading problem descriptions or trying an existing product. Nevertheless, it is important that your software have high quality, where *quality* means all the properties needed to meet the specified requirements. Three critical factors are correctness, reliability, and adaptability. Unfortunately, the last point is often overlooked in many software development projects.

Essentially, software quality is seen on two different levels:

- **Product quality:** This view looks at how the software product was built. It mainly concerns the internal quality characteristics, such as easy readability of the program (see Section 2.2) or observing design criteria. These criteria should ensure that a piece of software is understandable, changeable, and reusable. For example, one of these design criteria is the secrecy principle (see Section 4.1), in which the components of a software system together are called black box. Only information required by the components to interact (= interface) is presented to the outside. Everything else is kept secret, in the sense of not needing to know. This approach reduces likelihood of errors and keeps changes to the implementation within local borders.

- **Usage quality:** This view is of primary importance for the use of your software. It can be determined mainly by external quality characteristics, such as appropriateness to the given tasks, transparency, controllability, and fault tolerance. Of course, a major factor is the user interface, which is discussed in Chapter 8.

2.1.2 Programming and Specification Concepts

Software development is modeling

The most important prerequisite for high-quality programs is good modeling. In addition, software systems should be modifiable, and their components should be reusable in other contexts.

Abstraction

These prerequisites are ensured by language-independent programming methodology of structured programming. The fundamental idea is *abstraction:* an approach that emphasizes the most important common features of things, events, or processes and omits unimportant differences.

Structured programming

Structured programming consists of three components: (1) abstract instructions that let you easily adapt the execution sequence of a program to the textual sequence, (2) data types that define the set of values an object or expression can take, and (3) process abstraction that lets you name and parameterize algorithms. Section 2.4 discusses process abstraction in connection with stepwise refinement.

The more complex your data structures are, the more important data abstraction becomes

Especially in object-oriented programming, data structures are often complex and dynamic, which makes it meaningful to hide the concrete representation, because this can help reduce complexity. Of particular interest are abstract data types (see details in Section 4.1), which describe sets of values exclusively by their valid operations.

2.2 Readability of a Program

We mentioned in the previous section that product quality is closely related to internal quality characteristics, of which the most important is probably easy readability of the source.

Old source code?

This section doesn't deal with anything new: COBOL also uses listings, comments, or names. The important thing to remember is that a program should be easily readable. Probably the easiest way to test this is to have a quick look at the listing after about a year from program writing and see if you still understand it. Try it, and you will find that after not seeing the code for a long time, this is often not as easy as you thought.

Source code should also be read by others!

A good exercise is to have a colleague read your source code. Simply knowing that somebody else will see the program often increases your motivation. Naturally, this method also discloses errors that might never have been discovered in a simple program test. This is an easy way to discover inefficiencies.

Returning to program readability, comments, naming conventions, and the general look of your source code have a major impact.

2.2.1 Comments

Comments are pieces of text a programmer can add to explain instructions. Such text can be laid out in arbitrary form and can extend over more than one line (or even fill several pages in extreme cases). Many modern programming environments even allow pictures and tables to be inserted in these comments, according to the maxim that a picture is worth a thousand words.

COBOL programs can be read like newspapers?

Comments can significantly improve the readability of your source code, but they should be used sparingly. Unfortunately, the number of lines in your code is often still a measure of productivity. It may be easy to measure, but it doesn't necessarily have anything to do with productivity. On the contrary, a short program may be much better than a long and complicated one that includes some dead code (that is, instructions that can never be jumped at and therefore might just as well not be there at all; for example, in the statement if 1 = 1 then print (A) else print (B), the print (B) statement is dead code because 1 = 1 will never be false).

Nevertheless, comments may even be a trifle more important in object-oriented programming than in COBOL. Because of some of their detailed commands, COBOL programs can be read like newspapers. Therefore, we can often leave out a comment that would be necessary in OOP.

Rules for writing comments

From the preceding, we can deduce the following important rules for writing comments:

- They should be short but expressive (say as much as possible in as few words as possible).

- They should be written for the maintenance programmer, not the author.

- They should be kept to a minimum. Try to write your code clearly so that comments are superfluous.

- Where they are unavoidable, lengthy comments should be written at the head and not between instructions.

2.2.2 Naming Conventions

Names

Variables, types, programs, procedures, and many other objects in the source code are given unique names; each name should be carefully selected. All of us have seen programs that include a comment right next to a variable name. This is perfectly all right, but perhaps a more descriptive name for this variable would make that comment superfluous.

Short and to the point!

These names should be short and meaningful. For example, the best name for a temporary integer counting variable has always been i. Especially in COBOL, many variable names are long, because words are separated with dashes. These dashes are not allowed in OOP. Instead, we can mix uppercase and lowercase (for example, DialogElement instead of Dialogelement) to improve readability. Many programming languages are case-sensitive, which means that two variable names are different if they differ in uppercase and lowercase letters (for example, Max and max). Still,

Table 2.1   Naming conventions

Names for	Begin with	Examples
Constants, variables	Noun, lowercase letter	`version`, `wordSize`
	Adjective, lowercase letter	`full`, `ready`
Types	Noun, uppercase letter	`File`, `TextFrame`
Procedures	Verb, uppercase letter	`WriteString`
Functions	Noun, uppercase letter	`Position`
	Adjective, uppercase letter	`Empty`, `Equal`
Modules	Noun (pl.), uppercase letter	`Files`, `TextFrames`

this functionality should not be used, because it makes programs harder to read.

Table 2.1 shows several naming conventions.

2.2.3 Source Code

Structuring   A lot can also be done for the source code if we structure it properly, which means that we should use indents. In contrast to COBOL, object-oriented programming languages are not column-oriented, so it doesn't matter whether an instruction is in column 7, column 10, or perhaps column 1.

However, considering that columns have no semantic significance, we should indent lines—for example, to distinguish the beginning and end of a loop in a loop body, as in the following example:

```
if a < b then
  while a <= b do
    Print('a was increased');
    Inc(a);
  end
else
  while b <= a do
    Print('b was increased');
    Inc(b);
  end
end;
```

2.3 Program Structure

Copies In addition to a program's readability, its structure is also important. In COBOL, you often find program parts stored in separate files, using the concept of *copies*. These copies can then be arbitrarily inserted into a new program. Although this is similar to the procedures used in OOP, it has several drawbacks. Procedures are nothing new for COBOL programmers, where this construct has increasingly been replacing "copies."

Separate types In contrast, a new feature is the ability to define separate types, because object-oriented programming lets you rebuild any arbitrary type and name it. The benefit is that you can then declare an arbitrary number of variables from that type.

This section deals with these points and the possibilities deduced from them.

2.3.1 Procedures

As mentioned earlier, the concept that extracts code parts from a program and reuses them, if applicable, is known from COBOL as *copies*. Procedures are similar to this concept, although they differ fundamentally in one point. Rather than copying and reusing the source text in another program, the procedure is only invoked and then either does that job itself or returns a result. Returning a result does not mean that a global variable is set and then read; it means that a parameter is set.

Procedures and parameters The reason is that procedures have a defined interface, called *parameters*. Values can be passed to the procedure *(input parameters)*, but the procedure can also return parameters as a result *(output parameters)*. In some cases, parameters also serve as input and output parameters and are then called *transition parameters*. For example, a procedure that determines whether a number is a prime has an input parameter (the number itself) and an output parameter, which takes a value of true or false, depending on whether the number is a prime.

Local variables Apart from this interface, there is no other communication between the calling program and the procedure. Global variables, which are commonly used in COBOL, are possible in object-oriented programming but should be avoided. They make a program harder to read and often introduce errors, because they can be modified in many different places.

In contrast, object-oriented programming prefers local variables, which means that a variable is defined within a procedure and is visible only there. It also means that using the same name for several variables in different procedures will not cause problems. The fact that they are visible only in their own procedures allows us to uniquely identify them. Indeed, identical names for different variables in different procedures can be useful. Remember that temporary integer counting variables occur almost everywhere and that they should definitely have names such as i or j, regardless of the procedure in which they occur.

Such local variables are created when the procedure is invoked, which means that their lives begin at that point. The lifetime of such a local variable ends as soon as the procedure has been completed.

2.3.2 Types

Define your own types

Each variable is of a specific type, and the same rule applies to COBOL. Many variables are of a standard type (for example, NUMERIC), but many are of a composite type (for example, for group fields). This sort of composite type occurs frequently, such as in the form of records (group fields) or arrays (OCCURS). This is why you can define your own types in object-oriented programming. Before you declare a variable, you declare a type, where a composite type can be named. The benefit is twofold: First, you do not have to restate the entire structure when you need the same type; all you have to state is the type name. Second, you can be sure that your types are compatible.

For example, two variables of the same type can be mutually assigned or tested for equality. In addition, to test for equality, you can use the default assignment operator or the default comparison operator, which means that you do not have to implement separate procedures.

This type compatibility is less important in COBOL, because COBOL lets you assign variables to other variables, regardless of their types. This is not so in the world of object-oriented programming, where assignments are permitted only if the types are compatible: Otherwise, you must do a conversion. For example, if you assign a floating-point number to an integer variable, you first have to convert the floating-point number by truncating its decimal places.

Not everything goes in OOP

We should mention at this point that OOP does not fully implement all COBOL concepts. For example, the REDEFINES keyword has no real equivalent. In theory, we could simulate it with a pointer (more about pointers in Section 3.7), but this construct doesn't really help make our programs easy to read.

Floating-point numbers
Another difference is the way OOP defines floating-point numbers. COBOL has types that specify exactly how many decimal places before and after the point should be used in computation. In contrast, OOP uses types (REAL) that compute only with a certain accuracy (to approximately 4 bytes). Consequently, inaccuracies can occur.

2.3.3 Class Libraries versus Keywords

Smaller, clearer instruction set
COBOL uses a large number of keywords—perhaps several hundred. They allow you to run many functions, but they make the language unclear and hard to manage. In contrast, object-oriented languages are characterized by a small, clear instruction set—often fewer than 50 keywords. The grammar of some object-oriented languages is even defined on a single page.

Class library
Of course, this does not mean that these languages are less powerful; in fact, the required functionalities are implemented in class libraries. A class library is a collection of functions added to a program dynamically—at runtime. This makes the components flexible and even interchangeable. For example, in a simple program you save overhead, and in a larger program, you can decide precisely which collection you need. Developers can also add optional collections of functions.

Clearly, a smaller instruction set means that the programming language is easier to learn. However, you also have to learn how to use class libraries.

2.3.4 Detailed Comparison of COBOL and OOP

To tune ourselves in to the subjects of later chapters, it is certainly meaningful to give some foretaste at this point. Table 2.2 shows the most important programming differences between COBOL and object-oriented programming, which are discussed in the following sections.

Listings 2.1, 2.2, and 2.3 show how these languages compare, based on the same simple Hello World program written in three languages: COBOL, Delphi, and Java.

Table 2.2   Comparing COBOL, Delphi, and Java

COBOL	Delphi	Java
Column-oriented	Not column-oriented	Not column-oriented
EQUAL TO	=	==
Arbitrary type assignments	Major emphasis on type compatibility	Major emphasis on type compatibility
AND	and	&&
-	Xor	^
COMPUTE, MOVE, SET	:=	=
EVALUATE	Case	Switch
PERFORM	while	while
PERFORM WITH TEST AFTER	repeat	do while
PERFORM VARYING	For	for
Many instructions in the language	Powerful class libraries	Powerful class libraries
CALL BY CONTENT	VAL parameter	Depends on parameter type
CALL BY REFERENCE	VAR parameter	Depends on parameter type
Global names	Local names	Local names
OCCURS	Arrays	Arrays
Group fields	Records	Classes
Copies	Modules	Modules

Listing 2.1. Hello World in COBOL

```
identification division.
     program-id.     hello.
***********************************
environment division.
***********************************
working-storage section.
***********************************
```

```
procedure division.
      display "----"
      display "Hello World"
      display "----"
      stop run.
```

Listing 2.2. Hello World in Delphi

```
program HelloWorld;
var
      dummy: Char;
begin
      WriteLn('----');
      WriteLn('Hello World');
      WriteLn('----');
      Read(dummy); // required to keep the result
end.
```

Listing 2.3. Hello World in Java

```
class HelloWorld {
public static void main (String args[]) {
System.out.println("----");
System.out.println("Hello World");
System.out.println("----");
}
}
```

2.4 Stepwise Refinement

How can a problem best be structured?

Now that we have introduced the most important ideas about software engineering, we will move on and describe a more algorithmic basis in this section: How can a program be structured?

To answer this question, we will introduce *stepwise refinement* [Wir71]. This is not a special technique from the object-oriented programming world but rather a general technique that could also be used in COBOL, for example. On the other hand, most COBOL programs do not have this structurization.

The frequently used COBOL keyword contributes to a lack of structure, as does the typically long lifetime of COBOL programs. During this long lifetime, different programmers with their different styles and qualities may implement modifications and/or expansions. Naturally, the structure of a program deteriorates from all kinds of different styles.

Code written by programmers who have studied COBOL in crash courses especially tends to lack structure, because fast results have been more important than quality. This was the case in recent years mainly as a result of the Y2K and Euro problems (see Chapter 1). All these reasons motivate us to dedicate a separate section to stepwise refinement.

2.4.1 General Approach

What questions come at the beginning in programming? Stepwise refinement is a general design method for algorithms. It concentrates mainly on the following questions, which are normally of interest when we start writing a program:

- Where should I start?

- Which steps should I follow, and in what sequence?

- How can the problem be split into procedures?

The intuitive way is generally to think carefully about the tasks at the beginning, before writing any code. As trivial as this may sound, designers often forget to work out a sound definition at the beginning. Normally, there is always one major problem of one sort or another, which consists of a single main task to be solved. In general, this task is complex and hard to keep in sight in its entirety, so it can usually be presented as a *black box* (Figure 2.1).

This complex task, this black box, should be split into smaller tasks in a process consisting of three steps that fulfill the following functions:

Process consisting of three steps **Step 1.** Split a complex task, A, into subtasks. Figure 2.2 shows a graphical representation.

Step 2. This step begins from the (admittedly simplified) assumption that subtasks ($B_1, \ldots, B_n$), have already been solved and are available as proce-

Figure 2.1 Black box.

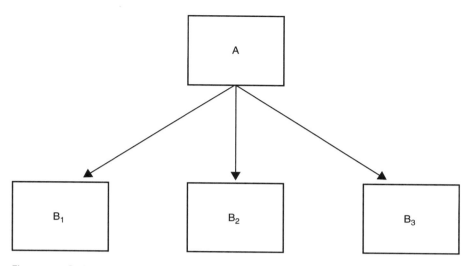

Figure 2.2 Splitting task A into subtasks.

dures. Proceeding from this basis, task A should now be implemented by calling the procedures $B_1, \ldots, B_n$.

Assumption: subtask already solved

Step 3. Study each subtask B_i in detail. More specifically, determine whether these subtasks are simple problems. If so, each one can be implemented right away. Otherwise, we have to deal with yet another problem that should be meaningfully and stepwise refined. This statement tells us how to proceed: Start from step 1 and replace task A by B_i, but only in the text.

Benefits

This method offers the following benefits:

- The problem becomes simpler, because the subtasks are easier to solve than the single big task.

- It makes working in groups easier, because different people can solve the subtasks.

2.4.2   Example

Evaluation of lottery slips

We will use a practical example in algorithm notation to better understand this technique. The task is to write a program that can be used to evaluate lottery slips (6 out of 49 possible numbers, without considering the complementary number). We will first input the six winning numbers and then the bets (that is, rows with six numbers each). Next, the number of hits (winning numbers) from each column should be output. This could look as follows:

```
3  5  7  12  17  23
3  7  12  17  26  35 => 4 hits
9  12  19  23  25  31 => 2 hits
```

To simplify this task, we assume that each group of six numbers is entered in ascending order and that all inputs are correct, which is in fact true when dealing with a lottery slip. The program is terminated by inputting the number 0.

Step 1

Determine the subtasks needed to solve the problem. A simple question we need to answer here is what commands we want to be already given to be able to implement a rough draft design. In this respect, it is important to look at the rough blocks and not the details.

When carefully studying the task, we can identify two subtasks: First, we always have to read in six numbers. Second, we have to control how many hits each of the six-number rows contains.

Which subtasks have been solved? Accordingly, we require the following procedures:

- Read the six-tuple and specify in the variable whether the input was successful (that is, result and done are output parameters).

- Compare the two six-tuples result and tup and return the number of hits in hits (that is, result and tup are input parameters, whereas hits is an output parameter).

Building on this basis, we can elaborate the following solution, where the type Tuple could stand for an array [1..6] of Integer.

```
var result, tup: Tuple; done: Boolean; hits: Integer;
. . .
ReadTuple(result, done);
ReadTuple(tup, done);
while done do begin
   CheckTuple(result, tup, hits);
   WriteLn('=>', hits, ' hits');
   ReadTuple(tup, done);
end;
```

This program looks simple and, in fact, we aren't done yet. We still have to implement the two procedures, ReadTuple and CheckTuple.

Step 2

Implementation of subtasks: trivial or not? When implementing these subtasks, we have to decide whether they can be solved the easy way or whether they have to be split further into subprocedures. Considering that neither reading six numbers nor comparing two arrays should be too difficult to solve, we could start with our implementation immediately. However, this is not always the case; in fact, subtasks can be rather complicated as well, and therefore it can be necessary to use stepwise refinement to implement them as well.

Listing 2.4 shows the procedure ReadTuple, which reads six numbers repeatedly into an array and sets the variable to TRUE if the input is correct and FALSE if it is incorrect (a number outside of 1 and 49). Listing 2.5 shows the procedure CheckTuple, which compares the two tuples a and b for a match. This procedure is relatively easy under the assumption that both tuples have already been sorted.

Listing 2.4. ReadTuple

```
procedure ReadTuple (var tup: Tuple; var done: Boolean);
   var i: Integer;
begin
   WriteLn('Please enter six numbers:');
   done := true; i := 1;
   while done and (i <= 6) do begin
      ReadLn(tup[i]);
      done := (tup[i] > 0) and (tup[i] < 50);
      Inc(i);
   end;
end;
```

Listing 2.5. CheckTuple

```
procedure CheckTuple (a, b: Tuple; var hits: Integer);
   var i, j: Integer;
begin
   i := 1; j := 1; hits := 0;
   while (i < = 6) and (j <= 6) do begin
      if a[i] = b[j] then begin
         Inc(hits); Inc(i); Inc(j);
      end
```

```
      else begin
        if a[i] < b[j] then Inc(i) else Inc(j);
      end;
   end;
end;
```

2.4.3 Summary

Stepwise refinement allows hierarchical factoring of a complex problem into gradually simpler subproblems. This systematic approach eventually takes us to the desired program to solve the task at hand. In fact, this approach enables us to implement a set of optimizations. However, do not be tempted to optimize things at any cost. Optimization is not always meaningful; it often offers little benefit and, instead, renders programs harder to understand. In these cases, it is often more useful to use appropriate tools (such as profilers) to identify areas that provide a potential for optimization and then optimize them in a targeted way.

2.4.4 Exercises

Task 1 (180 minutes): Four Wins

Practice makes perfect!

Implement the popular game "Four wins" on a game board seven fields wide and six fields high; use the stepwise refinement approach. The user should have the following options. For those not familiar with this game, following is a short explanation: There are two players, and each has different stones (for example, white and black ones). One stone is set after the other, where the players can just determine the column of the stone. The first stone in this column is set in row one, the second in row two, and so one. The player who is the first to get four stones set side by side wins. If none of the players can do this, the game ends in a tie.

■ Display the current scores.

■ Set the next stone.

■ Test whether a player has won.

■ Restart the game.

3

Basics

Core problem:
looking for exact
description

This part of our OOP course deals with general basics and the language differences as a good starting point for our study of object orientation. We provide this explanation before describing the actual object-oriented concept to ensure that we can later concentrate on this core area without dealing with less important stuff, such as loops or variable declarations. Therefore, not everything shown in this chapter is really object-oriented, but all are necessary to work with our chosen languages, Delphi and Java.

Programming means that we have to describe a problem exactly so that a computer can understand it. This holds true in the world of COBOL programming just as in the world of object-oriented programming. In this context, a program consists of data (or Data Division in COBOL lingo) and commands (Procedure Division). It is important to note that data are maintained in a memory and that this memory can be represented as a set of addressable cells. In other words, these cells can be symbolically represented by little boxes (Figure 3.1). We will frequently refer to this representation in this book.

However, as we will see in the following sections, some data and commands are unified in object-oriented programming. Initially, a program is only a gradual sequence of processes, where each step has to be precise and unambiguous (for example, "wait a little" would not meet these criteria).

No breaking
news yet

Accordingly, no breaking news is introduced at the beginning of this chapter. The concepts of COBOL are basically known, so this chapter

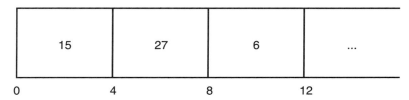

Figure 3.1 Representation of the memory as a set of cells.

focuses mainly on the differences between COBOL and the other languages. First, the symbols and data types of the Data Division are discussed and then the instructions and procedures of the Procedure Division. In particular, this chapter concentrates on procedures as well as module and pointer management. Experience has shown that pointer management is one of the most problematic areas in COBOL programming.

Environment Division　　It is worth noting at this point that object-oriented programming has no counterpart to the Environment Division of COBOL, which means that it is not necessary to describe the machine.

3.1　Replacement for the Data Division: Symbols and Data Types

In our first tutorial section, we discuss symbols, standard types, declarations, and expressions. Various exercises will help us obtain an initial entry into the programming environment used to apply the newly acquired knowledge.

3.1.1　Symbols

Symbols in a program can be names, keywords, numbers, characters and strings, special characters, and comments. Names that name the things of a program have a few fundamental differences from those in COBOL, which are independent of the language.

Delphi particularity　　In Delphi, a name has to begin with a letter, which can be followed by an arbitrary number of letters, numbers, or underscores (＿＿＿). The widely used dash in COBOL is not allowed. Also, uppercase and lowercase, as in COBOL, do not play any role; that is, Delphi is a "case-insensitive" environment.

Java particularity:
Unicode
In Java, a name can be composed of Unicode characters, which means that (in contrast to COBOL), a name can contain, for example, German umlauts. A name must begin with a letter, dollar sign ($), or underscore (____). In contrast to COBOL, names are "case sensitive"—for example the name Account is not identical to the name account. The widely used dash in COBOL is not allowed, because a dash always represents the minus operation.

Table 3.1 shows a few names and indicates the programming languages in which they are valid.

Few keywords
Keywords have the same meaning as in COBOL. They emphasize program parts (that is, they limit or introduce them), and they are reserved, which means they must not be otherwise used as names. Other languages have far fewer keywords than COBOL. For example, Java has only about 48, whereas COBOL has more than 600. This does not mean that these languages are less powerful; on the contrary. Performance is generally based on the size and quality of the class library.

Also, there are no differences worth mentioning with regard to the use of numbers, characters, strings, and special characters (for example, "+" or "–").

Column
orientation
When looking at comments—text pieces the compiler will ignore that explain the program to human readers—we notice an important difference between COBOL and object-oriented programming. COBOL uses an asterisk at the seventh position of the command line to identify a comment, which means that COBOL is a column-oriented programming language. This is something the object-oriented world has never heard of. In the object-oriented world, it does not matter at all where the symbols occur

Table 3.1   Examples of valid and invalid names

	COBOL	Delphi	Java
MR27XY	Yes	Yes	Yes
4X	Yes	No	No
aVeryLongName	Yes	Yes	Yes
a-Long-Name	Yes	No	No
10%OfSum	No	No	No
TenPercentOfSum	Yes	Yes	Yes
_MHK	No	No	Yes

within the command line. Of course, this should not prevent you from using indents to make sure your program source text maintains a neat structure.

Comments   Comments can extend over several lines and are enclosed within special symbols, or they begin at any position and occupy the remainder of the line.

Delphi   The Delphi symbols are (* and *) or //, as we can see in the following source code examples:

```
(* This text is a
   COMMENT
and the compiler will ignore it. *)
a := 25; // The comment extends to the end of the line.
```

Java   In Java, the symbols are /* and */ or //, as shown in the following source code examples:

```
/* This text is a
   COMMENT
and the compiler will ignore it. */
a = 25; // The comment extends to the end of the line.
```

Documentation comment: javadoc   Java features another particularity: the *documentation comment*. This differs from a normal comment only because it begins with the symbol /** (that is, two asterisks). A special tool called javadoc can extract documentation comments from the source text, allowing automatic creation of programming documentation. In a way, this is similar to literate programming—the representation of a program in book form [Knu84].

3.1.2 Standard Types

Value range for variables   Before you can use data items, they must be declared. The same rule applies to variables, which is the object-oriented term for data items. This means that a name and a data type are assigned to each variable. This data type defines the values the variable may contain and specifies the operators you can operate on them.

We distinguish between predefined standard types and user-defined types. Although user-defined types are also possible in COBOL, you will see during the course of this book that they are a much more robust construct in object-oriented programming. The most important standard (atomic) types are numbers (integers and floating-point numbers), characters, and Boolean variables.

Numeric types: replacement for DISPLAY, COMP, or BINARY

Numerical type definitions have important differences from COBOL. In COBOL, it is customary to use the PIC format to define how many places before and after the decimal point are essential and which other particularities apply (for example, only positive numbers, storing as dual number, and so forth). Object-oriented programming uses standard types, selected according to the value range and accuracy. Delphi and Java use similar types in similar ways, as Table 3.2 shows.

One way to influence internal storage—the DISPLAY, COMP, or BINARY formats in COBOL—is not available in object-oriented programming. Furthermore, neither Delphi nor Java has any equivalent to COBOL's fixed-point decimals. Using floating-point types instead of them is suggested—but be careful, because, unlike in COBOL, decimals cannot be represented exactly.

The character type (Char) is a single character, so it would correspond to a PIC X(1) in COBOL; examples are '7' and 'x'.

Delphi particularity

In Delphi, a variable of the type Char can be any ASCII character. Consequently, this type of variable is 1 byte long. The function ORD(ch) supplies the numerical value of a character from the ASCII character set.

Table 3.2   Standard types

Delphi	Java	Size	Value range
Shortint	byte	1 byte	−128 . . . 127
Smallint	short	2 bytes	−32768 . . . 32767
Integer	int	4 bytes	−2147483647 . . . 2147483647
Int64	long	8 bytes	−9223372036854775808 . . . 9223372036854775807
Real	float	4 bytes	Up to 10^{38}, floating-point number
Double	double	8 bytes	Up to 10^{324}, floating-point number
Char	char	1 byte (Delphi) 2 bytes (Java)	Any ASCII character; Java: Unicode!
Boolean	boolean	1 byte	TRUE or FALSE

Java particularity: support for arbitrary character sets Java was designed to be independent of any character set, so a variable of the type char can be an arbitrary Unicode character (German, Japanese, and so forth). Therefore, this type of variable is 2 bytes long.

Boolean type The Boolean type concerns truth values—something like the result of a comparative expression x < y. Boolean values can only be either TRUE or FALSE. There are no variables directly available in COBOL, but they can be simulated by the supplementary addition WHEN FALSE or by using condition names.

3.1.3 Declarations

Unique names must be defined Declarations introduce a name and link it with a type. Just as in the WORKING-STORAGE-SECTION in COBOL, which includes all variables present in the main memory, a name in object-oriented programming must also be declared before it can be used, and each name must be unique. This uniqueness must be valid only for the range of validity. Validity ranges for variables are discussed in detail in Section 3.3.

The level numbers known in COBOL are not used in object-oriented programming; in fact, the term is not known at all (although there are similar structures).

Keywords are used instead of level numbers to define constants Some of the most important declarations are those for constants and variables. Constants keep their values (which cannot be changed) across the entire program, which means each is a name for a certain value (for example, PI instead of 3.1415926). However, constant names are easier to read and often shorter to write. Most important, programs can be changed more easily with constant names than with the values themselves.

By convention, constants are written entirely in uppercase letters. Whereas COBOL uses level number 78 to declare constants, the declaration of constants in object-oriented programming is introduced by a keyword (const in Delphi, final in Java). Consequently, the name follows the constant and the value, and in Java also the type.

Example for Delphi
```
const PI = 3.1415926; // Here, the type is not implicitly determined.
```

Example for Java
```
final float PI = 3.1415926; // In Java, the type must also be stated.
```

Variables In contrast to constants, variables can be changed anytime. For example, it is possible to store inputs or results within variables. When a variable is declared, the variable name and the (explicit) type must always be stated.

Delphi   In Delphi, the variable declaration begins with the keyword var, followed by the variable name, a colon, and the type, for example, var x: INTEGER; y, z: REAL; ch: CHAR;.

Java   In Java, a variable declaration is not introduced by its own keyword. Instead, it begins with the type name and ends immediately after it with the variable name, for example, int x; float y, z; char ch;.

Initializing variables   Variables must always be initialized. Otherwise, their value (with a large number of exceptions) is undefined, which means that they can be arbitrary. For this purpose, COBOL offers the VALUE entry in a declaration. This option is also available in other programming languages, such as Java.

Java particularity   In Java, the initialization of variables can be executed directly during the declaration—for example, int count = 0;. Whether the initialization at this point contributes to easy readability is another question.

Style guidelines   By convention, variable names always begin with a lowercase letter. If a variable name consists of more than one word (for example, listSize), all the words are run together as one, and each word begins with an uppercase letter. Similarly, variables begin with a substantive or an adjective (if it is a Boolean variable).

3.1.4 Expressions

Operands and operators   Similar to COBOL, object-oriented programming uses arithmetic expressions, comparative expressions, and Boolean expressions. Each expression consists of operands (for example, variables, constants, and methods) and operators (for example, +, -, and). The operators are evaluated from left to right, and multiplication and division operations have priority over addition and subtraction operations. In doubtful cases, parentheses are used, because bracketed expressions are always evaluated first.

We assume that the arithmetic expressions +, -, and * are generally known. Similarly, division (/) and even the remainder operation of COBOL are widely known (where MOD supplies the integer remainder). However, there are minor language differences.

Delphi particularity   In Delphi, a division that uses the operator / always supplies a floating-point result. For an integer division, the keywords div and mod have to be used, which will also always supply integers (remainders are ignored).

Java particularity   In Java, division (/) and a division remainder (%) are defined both for floating-point numbers and for integers. The result always depends on the

Comparisons

type of operand. Accordingly, a division of i / j by i = 3 and j = 2 yields the result 1 in the case of integer operands or 1.5 in the case of floating-point numbers. Section 3.2.1 discusses these issues in detail.

As the name implies, comparative operators compare two values and determine the relationship between them. They always yield a Boolean result (TRUE or FALSE). The following comparative operators are available: equal to, not equal to, greater than (>), greater than or equal to (>=), less than (<), and less than or equal to (<=).

Delphi particularity

In Delphi, equality is tested by =, and inequality is tested by <>.

Java particularity

In Java, equality is tested by ==, and inequality is tested by !=.

Table 3.3 shows a summary of these operators.

Boolean expressions

Another important expression is the Boolean expression, because conditions (for example, if queries and loops) always depend on them. Both for operands and results are always a matter of a Boolean data type. Basically, the conjunction (and), disjunction (or), and negation (not) are well known from COBOL. In general, the negation has the highest priority, followed by the conjunction.

The exclusive OR—that is, either ... or ... , which actually corresponds to the human-language "or," can be expressed directly. This means, for

Table 3.3   Arithmetic and comparative operators

	COBOL	*Delphi*	*Java*
Addition	+	+	+
Subtraction	–	–	–
Multiplication	*	*	*
Division	/	/ or div	/
Remainder	MOD function	mod	%
Equality	EQUAL TO	=	==
Inequality	NOT EQUAL TO	<>	!=
Greater than	GREATER THAN	>	>
Greater than or equal to	GREATER THAN OR EQUAL TO	>=	>=
Less than	LESS THAN	<	<
Less than or equal to	LESS THAN OR EQUAL TO	<=	<=

example, that a xor b has the same meaning as (a and not b) or (not a and b) (although much easier to understand).

Table 3.4 shows how Boolean operators are syntactically expressed in the various languages of interest.

Java particularity As a Java particularity, instead of using the operators && and ||, it is also possible to use & and |. In this case, the shortcut evaluation (see Section 3.4.3) is not used, so this notation is not recommended.

Boolean algebra laws: often useful for optimization

Boolean Algebra Laws

Boolean algebra may not be on the list of the most important topics, but a programmer should have a good command of it. Nevertheless, experiences have shown that this is not always the case. The use of a few Boolean rules could help simplify expressions, making programs shorter and easier to understand. For those who think they need some brushup on this issue, the most important rules follow:

A and B ⇔ B and A, and A or B ⇔ B or A
A and (B and C) ⇔ (A and B) and C
A or (B or C) ⇔ (A or B) or C
A and (B or C) ⇔ (A and B) or (A and C)
A or (B and C) ⇔ (A or B) and (A or C)
not not A ⇔ A
not (A and B) ⇔ _____ not A or not B
not (A or B) ⇔ not A and not B
A and not A ⇔ false
A or not A ⇔ true

Building on these rules, the following example can be reshaped (or simplified):

(A > 5) and not ((A <= 0) or (A >= 10)) ⇔
(A > 5) and (not (A <= 0) and not (A >= 10)) ⇔
(A > 5) and (A > 0) and (A < 10) ⇔
(A > 5) and (A < 10)

Table 3.4   Boolean operators

	COBOL	Delphi	Java
AND	AND	and	&&
OR	OR	or	||
NOT	NOT	not	!
Exclusive OR	–	xor	^

3.1.5   Exercises

Task 1 (20 Minutes): Declarations

Give Delphi or Java definitions for the following COBOL definitions:

1. 05 ACCOUNT-NUMBER PIC 9(5)

2. 05 ACCOUNT-BALANCE PIC S9(5)V99

3. 05 CH PIC (X)

4. 05 SHORT PIC 9(2)

5. 05 EXACT-VALUE PIC S9(9)V9999

Task 2 (30 Minutes): Boolean Expressions

1. Assuming the Boolean expression (x < z) and (y < z) and (x < y) or (x >= z) and (x < y), which of the following value groups yield TRUE and which yield FALSE?
   x = 3, y = 5, z = 7
   x = 5, y = 3, z = 7
   x = 5, y = 7, z = 3

2. Write expressions that yield TRUE if
   a. ch is letter or number type.
   b. x, y, z all contain various values.

3. Simplify the expression (x <> y) or not ((y = z) and (y = x)).

Task 3 (130 Minutes): First Approach to the Programming Environment

As a first approach to the programming environment, you should walk through the material contained in Appendix A.

<table>
<tr><td>3.2</td></tr>
</table>

Replacement for the Procedure Division: Instructions

There are no divisions in OOP   As mentioned, there is no counterpart of the COBOL's "division" in object-oriented programming. On the other hand, object-oriented programming divides programs into several parts (although the division is less strict). The instruction part discussed in this section corresponds roughly to the Procedure Division. In particular, this section introduces the most important instructions: value assignment, branch instructions, and loops.

3.2.1 Assigning Values

Although COBOL uses three different types to assign one value to another—MOVE, COMPUTE, and SET—object-oriented programming has only one assignment operator. It does not matter whether the new value is a constant or an expression yet to be computed.

Delphi   In Delphi, the assignment operator is :=.
Java   In Java, the assignment operator is =.

Basically, a value assignment of the type x := y means that the left side is evaluated first (naturally in this case, but it could well be a value that would have to be determined first, for example, the *x*th element of an array). The right side is evaluated next, and finally, the value of the left side is replaced by the value of the right side. A (composite) variable must be on the left, and both sides must be compatible in terms of assignment.

Compatibility in terms of assignment or type does not necessarily mean that both variables have to be of the same type. We also speak of type compatibility when the type of the left variable is a supertype of the type of the right expression. For example, an integer can easily be assigned to a floating-point number, but the opposite can be achieved only by a type conversion (where the decimal point places are lost). The following listings show a few examples:

Delphi

```
var i, j: Integer; ch: Char; r: Real;
. . .
i := 2 * j; // Works: integer on the left, integer on the right
i := 0; // Works: integer on the left, integer on the right
r := i; // Works: real is a supertype of integer
i := r; // Doesn't work: the decimal point places would be lost
i := ch; // Doesn't work
```

Java

```
int i, j; char ch; float r;
. . .
i = 2 * j; // Works: integer left, integer right
i = 0; // Works: integer left, integer right
r = i; // Works: float is a supertype of integer
i = r; // Doesn't work: the decimal point places would be lost
i = ch; // Works: see explanation
```

We see from the last assignment that the type char of Java is assignment-compatible with short, int, and long, without the need for an explicit conversion.

Conversion: decimal point places are truncated

Even when two expressions are not assignment-compatible, we can still achieve the desired assignment. In this case, all we have to do is a type conversion. For example, by truncating the decimal point places of a floating-point number, we can convert it into an integer. Of course, we lose some information by this kind of conversion. Similarly, we have to compromise with regard to limiting the value range. Following are a few options for these type conversions.

Delphi

Floating-point numbers can be converted into integers by using the function Trunc (truncates the decimal-point places): i := Trunc (r);.

In general, a type conversion can be achieved by adding the desired type to the front, followed by the expression within parentheses—for example, i = Integer(myChar);.

Java

When an expression is to be converted into another type, we simply precede it with the desired type within parentheses—for example, i = (int) r;.

This type conversion is important when working with intermediate results, such as when assigning r = 1.5 + i1 / i2. If i1 and i2 are integers with the values 3 and 2 (that is, r = 1.5 + 3 / 2), we would intuitively assume that the result is 3. This is not the case. In fact, it would be only 2.5, because the intermediate result i1 / i2 is of type integer (as both operands are of type integer), so a result of r = 1.5 + 1 is computed.

Table 3.5   Java: shortcut assignment operators

Operator	Use	Corresponds to
+=	op1 += op2	Op1 = op1 + op2
-=	op1 -= op2	Op1 = op1 op2
*=	op1 *= op2	Op1 = op1 * op2

To avoid this, we also have to convert the intermediate result into a floating-point number—for example, r = 1.5 + (double) i1 / i2. Now we will obtain a result of 3. This maintaining the accuracy of intermediate results is naturally not known in the COBOL world.

Java particularity   In addition to the elementary assignment operator, Java offers several shortcut assignment operators that allow execution of an operation and an assignment operation in a single operator. For example, the instruction i = i + 2 can be abbreviated and expressed by i += 2. More examples are shown in Table 3.5 (from [CaWa01, page 51]).
We leave it to you to judge the readability of this type of expression.

Incremental operators are another way to abbreviate the value assignment. Instead of i = i + 1, we could write i++, or instead of i = i - 1, we could write i-.

Delphi   Delphi also offers such abbreviations—for example, instead of i := i + 1, we could use Inc(i), or instead of i := i - 1, we could use Dec(i).

3.2.2 Instruction Sequence

Instructions separated by semicolons are processed in sequence. Instructions are grouped into an instruction block, which can be compared with a paragraph in COBOL.

Delphi: semicolon as separator   In Delphi, an instruction block begins with the keyword begin and ends with the keyword end. Declarations are always before such instruction blocks and never between a begin and an end. Instructions are separated by semicolons ("separators"). A semicolon can be used after the last instruction, but this is not mandatory.

Java: semicolon as terminator   In Java, an instruction block is enclosed by braces {}, and declarations may be between instructions within a block. Each instruction is terminated with a semicolon (that is, the semicolon serves as a "terminator"), which means there must be a semicolon before the closing brace. No semicolon is required after the closing brace, even if more instructions follow.

3.2.3 The `if` Instruction

**The `if`
instruction**

The `if` instruction selects one out of two possible branches based on a condition. This instruction is well known from COBOL and is also used in object-oriented programming.

Delphi

In Delphi, the `if` instruction has the following structure:

```
if condition then instruction block1 else instruction block2
```

Delphi introduces the keyword `then` for better readability. The section `else instruction block2` can be omitted:

```
if n <> 0 then begin x := y div n; i := i + 1; end;
if x > y then max := x else max := y;
```

Java

If a branch contains only one instruction it does not have to be between `begin` and `end`; otherwise, it does. The keyword `else` must not be preceded by a semicolon.

In Java, the `if` instruction has the following structure:

```
if (condition) instruction block1 else instruction block2
```

Here, `instruction block2` may also be omitted:

```
if (n != 0) {x = y / n; i++;}
if (x > y) max = x; else max = y;
```

These `if` instructions are often nested.

3.2.4 The `switch` or `case` Instruction

Evaluate

These instruction types offer the possibility of executing one out of various instruction blocks, depending on the value of a variable. They correspond to the `EVALUATE` instruction of COBOL.

This multiple branching would also be possible by using the `if` instruction, but normally only with deep nesting so that the `switch` instruction is easier to read. In each branch of the instruction, admissible values (called *labels* or *marks*) are offered for the selected variable. If the label is equal to the variable, the instructions of this branch are executed. If none of the labels is valid, another branch will be executed. This kind of instruction can be used only if the variable is ordinal—that is, an integer and compatible (for example, character type).

Delphi particularity   In Delphi, multiple branching is introduced by the keyword case and has the following structure:

```
case variable of label list1: instruction block1;
   label list2: instruction block2;
   label list3: instruction block3;
   . . .
   else instruction blockN;
end;
```

In an example, this could look as follows:

```
case ch of
   'a'..'z', 'A'..'Z': letter := letter + 1;
   '0'..'9': digit := digit + 1;
   ' ;': semicolon := semicolon + 1;
   else other := other + 1;
end;
```

label lists   The preceding source code fragment could be used to determine how many characters, numbers, semicolons, and other characters are contained in a given text. Label lists can be used instead of a single label, such as the set of all lowercase letters ('a' . . . 'z'). Similarly, various labels can be separated by commas to form a single branch. If one of these labels is valid, the branch will be executed. However, the labels must be constants. After the end of this instruction block, branching continues to the end of the case instruction.

Java particularity   In Java, multiple branching is introduced by the keyword switch. The keyword case introduces individual labels, and the keyword default introduces the branch that is executed if none of the other labels is valid. The instruction has the following structure:

The break instruction

```
switch (variable) {
    case label1: instruction block1;
    case label2: instruction block2;
    case label3: instruction block3;
    . . .;
    default: instruction blockN
}
```

In an example, this would look as follows:

```
switch (month) {
    case 1: System.out.println ("January"); break;
    case 2: System.out.println ("February"); break;
    case 3: System.out.println ("March"); break;
    default: System.out.println ("other month");
}
```

This example outputs the names of months based on an integer. The break instruction, which causes a jump to the end of the switch instruction, is of particular importance in Java. If the break instruction were not present, all instructions following a valid label would be executed. The preceding switch instruction would look as follows with no break instructions:

```
switch (month) {
    case 1: System.out.println ("January");
    case 2: System.out.println ("February");
    case 3: System.out.println ("March");
    default: System.out.println ("other month");
}
```

For example, if the variable month had a value of 2, then the output would include not only February but also March and other month, because Java's switch always jumps to the corresponding mark. All remaining instructions are executed through the end of the switch instruction, regardless of any labels that may follow. If we want only one branch to be executed, as with EVALUATE in COBOL, we have to use break.

3.2.5　Loops

Loop types　Loops can be used to execute specific program parts several times. This corresponds to the Inline-PERFORM of COBOL. Basically, we distinguish between three different loop types: the prechecked loop (corresponds to PERFORM), the postchecked loop (corresponds to PERFORM WITH TEST AFTER), and the for loop (corresponds to PERFORM VARYING).

It is characteristic of the while loop that it may not be executed at all. This loop is executed 0 times, 1 time, or N times. A simple example shows how this loop works in Delphi:

Delphi
```
i := 1; sum := 0; // calculates the sum of 1.. n
while i <= n do begin
   sum := sum + i;
   i := i + 1;
end;
```

This example shows the structure of the while loop in Delphi:

```
while condition do begin instruction block end;
```

The same example in Java could look like this:

Java
```
i = 1; sum = 0; // calculates the sum of 1.. n
while (i <= n) {
   sum = sum + i;
   i++;
}
```

This example shows the structure of the while loop in Java:

```
while (condition) instruction block
```

The semantics of this while loop can be represented as follows:

```
L: if not cond go to end;
   instruction sequence;
   goto L;
end;
```

do-while loop   In contrast to the while loop, the postchecked loop iterates at least once. The reason is that the condition is tested only at the end of the loop iteration and not at the beginning. Accordingly, the loop iterates at least once or N times. However, there can be additional differences, depending on the programming language.

Delphi In Delphi, the keyword repeat introduces this loop type. The loop iterates repeatedly until a certain condition is met. Accordingly, this loop type is also called a repeat-until loop.

```
// shuffle the digits in the number n: 123 => 321
repeat
   write (n mod 10);
   n := n div 10;
until n = 0;
```

We can see from the preceding example that the following syntax applies:

```
repeat instruction block until condition;
```

The semantics of this repeat-until loop can be represented as follows:

```
L: instruction sequence
if not cond then goto L;
```

Java In Java, the major differences from normal while loops are that the loop begins with the keyword do, and the keyword while appears only at the end. The loop iterates repeatedly until the condition is no longer true, but it always iterates at least once.

```
do {
   c = in.read();
   . . .
} while (c != -1); // reads c repeatedly until it is not equal 1
```

Accordingly, the following syntax applies:

```
do instruction block while (condition);
```

The semantics of this do-while loop can be represented as follows:

```
L: instruction sequence
if cond then go to L;
```

for loop replaces PERFORM VARYING With the for loop, we know in advance how many times it will iterate. Also, it is similar to the PERFORM VARYING instruction of COBOL. A variable (the *iteration variable*) is initialized at the beginning of the loop and incremented in each loop iteration. The loop is terminated if the variable reaches or exceeds a certain value, that is, when the termination condition is met. This test is done before the loop iteration.

In Delphi, the for loop looks like this:

Delphi
```
for i := 0 to 10 do begin
   . . .
end
```

If the iteration variable is to be decremented by a value of 1 in each loop iteration, this is written using the downto instruction; for example, 10 downto 0. The iteration can be incremented or decremented only by a value of 1.

Java
In Java, the for loop is composed of three instruction parts, each separated by a semicolon. First, the initial value is stated, then the end condition is defined, and the third part specifies how the counter variable should be incremented or decremented in each loop iteration:

```
for (i = 0; i < 10; i++) {
   . . .
}
```

Because increments or decrements are allowed from any arbitrary instruction, it is possible to increment or decrement by an arbitrary value.

Iteration variable
The iteration variable within the for loop should not be changed and should not be used after finishing the loop; when used, it must be reinitialized.

3.2.6 Summary

Table 3.6 shows a comparative summary of the instructions presented in the previous sections.

GOTO is not supported
The GOTO instruction, frequently used by older, traditional COBOL programmers, is normally not used in object-oriented programming (although Delphi and Java offer it for special cases), because it impairs the program structure and makes the code harder to read. However, we think this is intuitive for the experienced COBOL programmer, who will most likely have had to modify such types of programs.

Table 3.6   Summary of the discussed instructions

Command	COBOL	Delphi	Java
Value assignment	COMPUTE, MOVE, SET	:=	=
if instruction	IF	if	if
case instruction	EVALUATE	case	switch
while loop (prechecked loops)	PERFORM	while	while
do-while loop (postchecked loops)	PERFORM WITH TEST AFTER	repeat	do while
for loop	PERFORM VARYING	for	for

END-IF   In contrast to COBOL, all instruction blocks terminate immediately—that is, with end—and not between END-IF, END-COMPUTE, although no distinction is made between them. However, if you want to maintain this differentiation, you can write an optional comment—something like end; // while. This can be particularly useful for long instruction blocks.

3.2.7 Exercises

Task 1 (60 minutes): Fibonacci Numbers

The term *recursion* will be explained later Fibonacci numbers are defined by the following recursion relationship:

$$F(0) = 1, F(1) = 1, F(n) = F(n-1) + F(n-2) \text{ for } n > 1$$

Write a Delphi or Java program that reads a number n and outputs the Fibonacci number F(n). Your program should not call any procedures, which means that we are looking for an iterative solution (with loops).

Task 2 (60 minutes): Book Price

Let's assume that a bookstore named Numbawan wants to purchase books from Morgan Kaufmann Publishing. The store can opt for a paperback version (at a basic price of $300.00) or a hardcover version ($400.00). Depending on the purchase quantity, Numbawan will enjoy a price discount from Morgan Kaufmann Publishing. The corresponding percentage rate follows:

	>100 copies	>200 copies	>300 copies
Paperback	0	5%	10%
Hardcover	5%	10%	15%

However, Numbawan is a fierce negotiation partner, trying to achieve the best possible deal, so they negotiate a further reduction. Provided that the store pays the invoice amount within a specific number of days, they will obtain a further discount.

	<5 days	<10 days	≥10 days
Paperback	3%	1%	0
Hardcover	5%	3%	0

Write a Delphi or Java program that reads the number of books, the book quantity ordered, and the number of days from the invoice date to the payment date and then outputs the suggested price.

3.3   Procedures

Procedures avoid duplicate code

To ensure a better program structure, you could group several instruction blocks to form a single procedure. For this purpose, we write a procedure that includes all instructions. When the functionality of the instruction block is required later on, it will be sufficient to just call this procedure. This is particularly useful when the instruction block is used more than once. Instead of permanent duplicate code, all that needs to be done is call the same procedure repeatedly.

Such procedures are also useful to ensure a good structure of your program, and they offer you an option to implement user-defined operations. Procedures are basically nothing new, because COBOL also offers the option to call "internal subprograms" by using the PERFORM function.

Java particularity

These procedures form the basis for the methods we will introduce later, which play a major role in object-oriented programming.

Java has no "real" procedures—only methods. Because this may be confusing in the beginning, we do not discuss this issue here in detail. The somehow complicated definition of a procedure as a method of a class will become clear at the latest in Section 5.1.

First overview   This subsection provides an initial overview of procedures. First, we introduce parameterless procedures, which serve to avoid duplicates. Then we discuss parameters and local names of procedures. Finally, we discuss functional procedures, which are procedures that return a result, and recursion. Subsequent sections provide additional information about procedures.

3.3.1 Parameterless Procedures

Parameterless procedures represent the simplest form of procedures. They are used mainly to avoid code duplications, as shown by the following Delphi code fragment:

```
x := 3 * y; Write(x); sum := sum + x; Write(sum);
x := 2 * x + 1; Write(x); sum := sum + x; Write(sum);
x := 3 * y + 27; Write(x); sum := sum + x; Write(sum);
```

In this example, the code `Write(x); sum := sum + x; Write(sum);` is used over and over (therefore, we speak of *code duplication*). One drawback is that the program becomes longer (which almost always means that it is more difficult to understand), and another drawback is that it is more difficult to maintain. For example, if we wanted to output a formatted x instead of just using a simple `Write`, we would have to implement that change for every occurrence.

Code savings but no runtime savings   A simple improvement would be the use of a parameterless procedure, This procedure consists of the code that is to be used over and over. Instead of writing the full code, we just call the procedure. The concept is the same in both languages, but the procedure is implemented differently.

Parameterless Procedures in Delphi

Delphi: procedure   In Delphi, procedures begin with the keyword `procedure`, followed by the procedure name and a semicolon. The instruction block after that, which must always be included between `begin` and `end` (even if it is only a single instruction), includes the instructions to be executed multiple times during the call of the procedure. The procedure has to come after the variable end definitions but before the begin of the program. The following is a simple example:

```
procedure PrintX;
begin
  Write(x); sum := sum + x; Write(sum);
end;
```

Style guidelines The naming convention says that procedure names should begin with an uppercase letter and a verb (for example, Read, SearchName).

Instead of the piece of code that has been duplicated, we can use the procedure call. When calling this procedure, it is sufficient to simply write the procedure name. The procedure call has no separate keyword (such as CALL or PERFORM in COBOL).

```
x := 3 * y; PrintX;
x := 2 * x + 1; PrintX;
x := 3 * y + 27; PrintX;
. . .; PrintX;
```

The calling program remains in memory. A variant of a procedure call similar to COBOL's CHAIN command, which overlays the calling program at the cost of losing its data, is not possible here.

Parameterless Procedures in Java

First and foremost, Java's parameterless procedures begin with the keywords static void. Later in this chapter, we present additional options that can be used to introduce parameterless procedures. Next follows the name of the procedure, a pair of parentheses, and the instruction block, which must always be included between an opening and closing parenthesis (even if only a single instruction). The following is a simple example:

```
static void PrintX () {
   System.out.print(x); sum = sum + x; System.out.print(sum);
}
```

Style guidelines The naming convention says that procedure names should begin with a lowercase letter, followed by a verb (for example, read, searchName).

Java uses methods

As mentioned, Java has no classical procedures. Instead, procedures are always embedded as methods in classes. A detailed description of Java methods and classes would go beyond the scope and purpose of this book. We refer the readers to specialized textbooks and limit ourselves to describing here just the syntactic notation:

```
class example {
   static void printX () {
      System.out.print(x);  sum = sum + x;  System.out.print(sum);
   }
}
```

We can see that the procedure is actually included within an additional construct, the *class*, introduced by the keyword class. The name example stands for an arbitrary (class) name.

In Java, we have to add a pair of parentheses after the procedure name; we discuss this issue in detail in Section 3.3.2.

Summary

To better understand how procedures are defined and called, we use Listings 3.1 and 3.2 for the preceding example to show the entire program. The points shown in these examples but not covered so far in the text will be explained later.

Listing 3.1. PrintX Implementation in Delphi

```
program ExPrintX;
var
   x, y, sum: Integer;
   ch: Char; // dummy

procedure PrintX;
begin
   WriteLn(x); sum := sum + x; WriteLn(sum);
end; // PrintX

begin
   sum := 0;
   y := 2;
   x := 3 * y; PrintX;
   x := 2 * x + 1; PrintX;
   x := 3 * y + 27; PrintX;
   Read(ch);
end.
```

Listing 3.2.
PrintX
Implementation
in Java

```java
import java.io.*;

class PrintX {
    static int sum = 0;
    static int x;
    static void printX () {
        System.out.println(x); sum = sum + x; System.out.println(sum);
    }

    public static void main (String args[]) {
        int y = 2;
        x = 3 * y; printX();
        x = 2 * x + 1; printX();
        x = 3 * y + 27; printX();
    }
}
```

3.3.2 Parameters

Data exchange:
parameters

Naturally, in most cases a call involves not only a procedure but a data exchange between the procedure and the caller. For example, in the previous example, it would surely have been useful to give the procedure a value of x and then communicate the new value of sum to the caller. Alone, this explanation shows that parameters are of two types: an input parameter and an output parameter, where, in Delphi, the output parameter is actually an input *and* output parameter.

Java particularity

In Java, there is no such thing as an output parameter. Only composite types allow a modification of the attributes in a procedure (see also Section 3.4). Simple type variables (such as int, long) have only an input parameter. This problem can be solved by using a function (see Section 3.3.4).

Whether a parameter is an input or output parameter is defined in the procedure declaration. Similarly, a parameter's type is defined in the procedure declaration, which is shown in the following examples.

Delphi

In Delphi, parameters are declared in the procedure head after the name of the procedure and between parentheses. This declaration is implemented as in normal variables (that is, by using parameterName: typeName), and several parameters are separated by a semicolon. If a parameter is to be an output parameter, you simply append the keyword var in front of it.

Table 3.7   Differences between input and output parameters: fp = formal parameter; ap = actual parameter

Input parameters	Output parameters
COBOL: CALL BY CONTENT.	COBOL: CALL BY REFERENCE.
VAL PARAMETER. Value parameter.	VAL PARAMETER. TRANSITION PARAMETER.
The caller copies the value (fp := ap).	fp is just another name for ap (both have the same address). Referring back to our small box used as a symbol that maps a variable, both can be represented by the same box (Figure 3.1).
The procedure works with copies; changes to the formal parameter have no impact on the actual parameter.	The procedure works with the original; any change to a formal parameter will also reflect in the actual parameter.
ap may be an expression (it is sufficient that it be assignment-compatible).	ap has to be a variable of the same type.

```
procedure Add (x, y: Integer; var z: Integer);
begin
   z := x + y;
end; // add
```

The input parameters in this example are the variables x and y; z is an output parameter.

Java   In Java, too, parameters are declared in the procedure head after the name of the procedure, like normal variables (separated by commas). Parentheses are used for this purpose.

The parameters, enclosed between parentheses and separated by commas, are passed on during a procedure call—for example, Add(2, a * b, result). In this respect, they can be compared with the LINKAGE SECTION of COBOL.

Table 3.7 summarizes the differences between input and output parameters. The term *formal parameter* (fp) means that parameters are declared in the procedure head. The term *actual parameter* (ap) identifies parameters stated during the call.

The following (admittedly very dirty) example (in Delphi code) highlights the difference between input and output parameters:

```
procedure Dirty (var x, y: integer)
begin
   x := 3 * x;
   y := 3 * y;
end; // Dirty
```

The following code calls the procedure:

```
a := 5; Dirty(a, a); write(a);
```

This example shows that variable a is used twice, as input and output parameter. This parameter type requires that the name of the formal parameter be different from the name of the actual parameter (see Table 3.7). For this reason, x is merely a different name for a, but similarly, y is just another name for a. This means that when x is modified, a and y will be modified. Consequently, the result is 45. The easiest way to explain this is by using a figure, representing each variable as a small box (see Figure 3.2).

Never use parameters as shown in Figure 3.2, because such programs are difficult to understand. In this teaching example, however, they show the difference between input and output parameters.

It should be mentioned that the names of formal and actual parameters are completely independent—that is, they may also be identical.

3.3.3 Local Names (Visibility, Validity)

Local vs. global names Variable declarations can also come within procedures. In this case, we speak of *local* names (as opposed to the otherwise *global* names that apply to the entire program). This is an important difference from Procedural COBOL, where definitions of the Data Division are valid within the entire program. In COBOL, only wise use of subprograms can help reduce the number of global identifiers in a system.

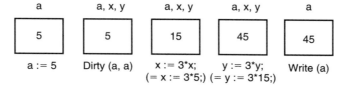

Figure 3.2 The "dirty" procedure example in graphical form.

Delphi
```
procedure PrintX (x: Integer);
   var sum: Integer;
begin
   sum := 3; Write(x); sum := sum + x; Write(sum);
end; // PrintX
```

_____

Java
```
static void printX (int x) {
   int sum = 3;
   System.out.print(x); sum = sum + x; System.out.print(sum);
}
```

The terms *visibility* and *lifetime* are important. By their nature, local variables are visible only locally, and their lifetimes differ from those of global variables.

Visibility

Visability of local names
Local names are invisible (that is, they cannot be accessed) outside the procedure in which they are declared, whereas global names are also visible in the procedure. In theory, it is conceivable that a local variable and a global variable could have the same name. In this case, the local variable has priority over the global. This means that within the procedure, only the local variable can be addressed. This situation is explained with the following Delphi example.

```
program M;
   var a, b: . . .

   procedure P;
      var b, c: . . .
   begin
      // marked position 1
   end; // P
begin
   // marked position 2
end.
```

Hiding
At marked position 1, the local variables b and c as well as the global variable a are visible—they can be accessed. The global variable b is not visible here, because it is hidden by the local b (but this does not mean that

this variable no longer exists; it is a question of lifetime, which is discussed in the next section). This example also shows that a program's readability deteriorates when local and global variables have identical names. At the marked position 2, only the global variables a and b are visible.

Java particularity Java offers an additional option to declare local variables within a block (that is, at any position between two braces). These are then valid from the position where they are declared through the end of the block in which they are declared—for example, only within one loop.

Lifetime

Local and global variables also differ with regard to their lifetimes. Global variables maintain their values (that is, they "live") over the entire program, whereas local variables live only for as long as their procedure is active. The end of the procedures causes all local variables to lose their values. If the procedure is executed a second time, the local variables are created again, and they now have nothing to do with those from the first run. In the preceding example, all local and global variables are active at the marked position 1 (including the global b, although it is not visible at that point). In contrast, only the two global variables a and b live at the marked position 2.

Benefits of locality The benefits of locality can be summarized as follows:

- **Clear layout:** What belongs together appears together.

- **Secure layout:** Local variables cannot be destroyed from the outside.

- **Efficient layout:** Local variables can normally be accessed quickly.

For these reasons, declarations should ideally be made local. Global declarations should be used only for things really needed across and beyond procedure borders.

3.3.4   Functions

Functions return results Functions are used whenever expressions include computations that occur repeatedly. COBOL, too, uses such a construct, which is even invoked with the keyword FUNCTION, the so-called intrinsic functions (embedded functions), such as MIN, MAX, or MEAN. This kind of function can be implemented and can afterward be used as an operand in expressions. For example, you can encode a value assignment of the type c := 2 * Max(a, b), where Max is a function, which returns the bigger of the two values, a and b. The differences in procedures are

- The call of a function is not an instruction but an operand of an expression.

- Functions compute a value and, consequently, also have the type of this value.

Implementation of a function is characterized by the fact that the result type has to be defined in the declaration. Moreover, the function terminates by returning the result value to the caller. The following source code examples help to better illustrate this.

Delphi In Delphi, a function is introduced by the keyword function. The parameters are followed by a colon and the type of return value. Within the function itself is an implicitly declared variable result, and the result of the function has to be assigned to it. Similarly, it is also possible to assign the name of the function to the result of an implicitly declared variable. *Implicitly declared* means that the variable does not have to be explicitly declared, because it is available in general.

```
function Max (a, b: Integer): Integer;
begin
   if a > b then max := a else max := b;
   // if a > b then result := a else result := b;
   // either of the two solutions would work
end; // Max
```

Java In Java, in contrast to a procedure, a function is not introduced by void but instead by the returnTypename—that is, by int. The keyword void merely tells us that there is no result value. If the procedure name is preceded by a type name, the function will return a result with exactly this type. The result value itself has to be returned to the caller with the keyword return. The function terminates when program execution reaches this keyword.

```
static int max (int a, int b) {
   if (a > b) return a else return b
}
```

Functions vs. procedures The following summary shows when to use functions and when to use procedures.

Functions

- Exactly one return value
- When used in expressions

Procedures

- Several return values or none
- Additional actions are executed

3.3.5 Terminating a Procedure

It is possible to terminate a procedure immediately by using a certain keyword. Any instructions that follow after it will be ignored, and the program will immediately jump back to the calling instruction. This instruction reminds us a little of the GOTO instruction of COBOL: it can make a program hard to read. For this reason, it should be used carefully.

Delphi In Delphi, a procedure can be terminated immediately with the keyword exit.

Java In Java, a procedure can be terminated immediately with the keyword return.

3.3.6 Recursion

A procedure calls itself A procedure is recursive when it calls itself. We distinguish between *direct recursion* (a procedure P calls itself, that is, it calls P), and *indirect recursion* (a procedure P calls a procedure Q, which in turn calls P). In contrast to object-oriented programming, a procedure called recursively in COBOL has to be specially prepared with a LINKAGE SECTION. This preparation is not required in object-oriented programming.

The Fibonacci numbers from the last exercise are also a good recursion example Recursion is also known in mathematics; for example, the factorial calculation is defined recursively. As we know, the factorial of a number n is the product of all numbers from 1 to n: n! = 1 * 2 * 3 * . . . * (n − 1) * n. However, this can also be defined recursively so that the factorial of 1 corresponds to the value 1: 1! = 1. Then the factorial of n can also be

defined as follows: n! = (n - 1)! * n. The implementation of this function can, recursively, look as follows:

```
function Fact (n: Integer): Integer;
begin
  if n = 1
    then result := 1 // special case 1! = 1
    else result := Fact(n - 1) * n; // n! = (n - 1)! * n
end; // Fact
```

The easiest way to explain the functionality of this procedure is a desk
test. For example, if Fact is called with a value of 4, then a value of Fact(3)
* 4 is returned. Similarly, if Fact(3) is called, then Fact(2) * 3 is returned.
On the other hand, a call of Fact(2) means again that Fact(1) * 2 is
returned. When Fact(1) is being processed, the value 1 will finally be
returned. This also specifies the result of Fact(2), namely 1 * 2 = 2.

Building on this ground, we can determine Fact(3) from 2 * 3,—that
is, we obtain a value of 6. The starting point Fact(4) returns the value
6 * 4, or 24. This process can be represented in graphical form, as we
see in Figure 3.3.

Simple recursion example The following source code fragment provides an additional recursion
example. Try on your own to find the output generated from the call B(3):

```
procedure B (x: Integer);
begin
  if x > 0 then B(x - 1);
  WriteLn(x);
end; // B
```

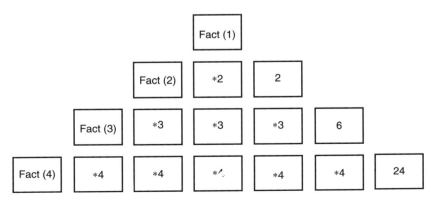

Figure 3.3 Graphical representation of the recursive call Fact(4).

The result of the call B(3) is

```
0
1
2
3
```

Why? The first call is to B(3), which will in turn call B(2). This calls B(1), which in turn calls B(0). Eventually, the if query is processed, and we obtain an output of 0. At this point, the other procedures are still active, and the outputs are executed one after the other.

Recursion pattern   Recursions always follow a pattern. Each recursion has several branches, and one of these branches is not recursive (otherwise, we would get an endless loop). Consequently, the pattern looks as follows:

```
if problem is small enough then
    non-recursive branch
else
    recursive branch
end;
```

The following comments should complete our recursion issue:

■ Every recursive problem can also be solved iteratively.

■ The iterative solution is normally more efficient but more complex and harder to understand.

■ Recursions are particularly important for recursive data structures (see also Section 4.2).

3.3.7   Exercises

Task 1 (15 minutes): Simplifications

Correct the following three Delphi code fragments, which are independent of one another and were programmed in a complicated way. These fragments are not arbitrarily constructed but were observed by the author in various programs (most of them in examination papers).

```
i := 0; (* where j >= 0 is true at this position *) // task part A
while i <> j do begin
  i := i + 1;
end;
if a = 0 then begin // task part B
  a := 2 * c;
end
else begin
  if c <> 0 then begin
    a := a * b + 2 * c;
  end
  else begin
    a := a * b;
  end;
end;
while a < b do begin // task part C
  c := a; a := b; b := c;
end;
```

Task 2 (5 minutes): Desk Test

Which values will the following procedure return, if the procedure is called
with x := 5; P(x, x); ?

```
procedure P (var x, y: Integer);
begin
  y := 2 * x;
  if x > 7 then y := y * x;
  WriteLn(x); WriteLn(y);
end;
```

Task 3 (40 minutes): Largest Common Divisor

Write a function LCD (x, y: Integer): Integer or int LCD (int x, int y)
that computes the largest common divisor of the numbers x and y. As a
basis, you can use the following Euclidean algorithm. Based on the two
input values, x and y, and assuming that x is bigger than y, this algorithm
determines the largest common divisor, lcd.

```
i := i of x / y;
while i <> 0 do begin
   x := y; y := i;
   i:= i of x / y;
end;
lcd := y;
```

Task 4 (90 minutes): Integer Fractions

Write a program that reads two integer fractions (four numbers, *a*, *b*, *c*, and *d*), and then outputs their sum and product, also as integer fractions. Simplify the result by truncation (use the LCD function from task 3 for this task). Structure your program by its subtasks into procedures.

```
Example:
   Input:
      1.numerator: 2
      1.denominator: 3
      2.numerator: 4
      2.denominator: 6
   Output:
      sum = 4 / 3, product = 4 / 9
```

3.4   Arrays, Strings, Records

Simple data types are not sufficient

So far, we have introduced simple data types that can be used, for example, to manage individual characters or numbers. These data types are important, but they are not sufficient. Think only of the simplest applications, for example from the accounting discipline—an account has not only a balance (which could easily be mapped with a floating-point number) but also a name, a unique number, and so on; and it also requires a list (table) of postings.

We can see that the simple data types are not sufficient, which means we need composite types. Simple forms of these composite types are arrays, strings, or records. These forms are also known in COBOL: Arrays correspond to the OCCURS entries of COBOL, strings are character strings, and records are used like COBOL group fields.

3.4.1 Arrays

Homogeneous data structure: all elements have the same type

An *array* is a table of elements (variable cells). All elements are of the same type, so we also speak of a homogeneous data structure. The variable, which was declared as an array, always identifies the entire array. When accessing this variable, we always access the array. If we want to access a single element of that array, access is possible by using the index. Arrays are known from COBOL; for example, an array with 100 integer elements could be defined as follows in COBOL: A OCCURS 100 TIMES PIC X(4).

Array Definition

Delphi: array of

In Delphi, such an array could be defined as follows: var a: array[1..100] of integer. This array declaration begins with the keyword array. It is followed by the index limits within square brackets. Delphi supports arbitrary index limits. After that, the keyword of and the element type (which can be any arbitrary type) are stated.

Delphi allows not only limits such as lower limit = 1, upper limit = number of array elements, but also any arbitrary integer number. An array in the form of array[-3..+6] is possible. Other examples for valid array declarations are array[1..20] of real or array[0..10*3] of integer.

These are *static declarations*: The number of array elements is known at the moment of compiling, so the index limits are constants. In connection with Delphi particularities (see Section 3.6.1), we will discuss *dynamic* arrays, for which the number of elements is known only at runtime (for example, from an input). This construct is similar to, but mightier than, COBOL's OCCURS DEPENDING ON instruction.

In Java, composite data types, such as arrays or records, are always dynamic. To avoid confusing you with too many details at this poir', we describe this issue later. For now, it is important to understand that the declaration of an array in Java is actually a creation. For that reason, we have to use the keyword new, which is discussed in Section 3.7.2.

The array from our previous example could be created in Java as follows: int a[] = new int[100]. We can see that this creation of the array begins with the element type, followed by the variable name, a pair of square brackets, the assignment operator, and the keyword new. Next is, once more, the element type and the number of elements within square brackets.

In Java, the array limits always reach from 0 to the number of elements −1—in this case from 0 to 99. Consequently, in contrast to COBOL, the first element does not have index 1 but index 0. In Java, it would also be feasible to state the elements during declaration of the array—for example, int a[] = {1, 17, 25, 6} would create an array with four elements, where the first element would have value 1, the second value 17, and so on.

Type declaration: own types will be built

The type declaration is of primary importance at this point. In object-oriented programming, all types not already included in the language can be built and an arbitrary number of variables of these types can be created. This improves the readability of the program, because we can assign proper type names and do not have to repeat the same structure. Another advantage is that two variables of the same type are always assignment-compatible.

Delphi

In Delphi, the type declaration is always at the beginning of the declaration part, even before the variable declaration. It begins with the keyword type, followed by the type name, an equal sign, and finally, the type (for example, array). In the variable declaration, we can then create a variable of that type. For example:

```
type
    IntArr = array[1..100] of Integer;
var
    a: IntArr;
```

Java

In Java, a type declaration is possible by a class declaration, which is described in Section 5.1.

Accessing Array Elements

Access as in COBOL: through index

As in COBOL, object-oriented programming lets you access individual array elements from their index. For example, while you can use A(3) in COBOL to access the element from index Three, you can do this both in Java and Delphi with a[3]. The main difference is in the use of square brackets instead of parentheses. Of course, access is permitted only within the index limits; otherwise, a runtime error will be thrown. A special data type for index access, such as the INDEX format in COBOL, is not available in object-oriented programming. Also, there is no special command to search the array similar to the SEARCH instruction in COBOL.

Examples simplify everything

We will use two examples to better explain how to work with arrays. The first example is SearchElement (Listings 3.3 and 3.4), and the second is DaysOfMonth (Listings 3.5 and 3.6). In SearchElement, we use an array, a, to search for an element, x, by starting at the first position of the array and comparing this array element with x repeatedly until we find a match. If a match is found, the index of the element found is stored in the variable pos; otherwise, the variable pos will have the value −1.

The example DaysOfMonth computes the number of days in the month specified by month, where we ignore leap years for the sake of simplicity and easier understanding.

Listing 3.3. Search for Element in Delphi

```
var
   a: array[1..100] of Integer;
   x: Integer; // element to be searched for
   pos: Integer;
   i: Integer;
begin
   . . . // -- read the array
   // -- find
   pos := -1; i := 1;
   while (i <= 100) and (pos < 0) do begin
      if a[i] = x then begin pos := i; end;
      Inc(i);
   end;
end;
```

Listing 3.4. Days of Month in Delphi

```
var
   days: array[1..12] of Integer;
   d, month: Integer;
begin
   days[1] := 31; days[2] := 28;... days[12] := 31;
   . . .
   d := days[month];
end;
```

Listing 3.5. Search for Element in Java

```
int a[] = new int[100];
int x, pos, i;
. . . // -- read the array
// -- find
pos = -1; i = 0;
```

```
while ((i < 100) && (pos < 0)) {
   if (a[i] == x) pos = i;
   i ++;
}
```

Listing 3.6. Days of Month in June

```
int days[] = {31, 28, 31, 30, 31, 30, 31, 31, 30, 31, 30, 31};
int d, month;
// . . .
d = days[month-1]; // Important note: -1, because array's lower limit is 0!
```

3.4.2 Strings

Strings are those character strings that occur frequently in programs. We could also use an array of characters instead, but strings have the advantage that many predefined functions can be operated on them.

String Definition

String is an independent type

Strings are declared just like usual variables. Once they have been declared, we can assign arbitrary string constants or other string variables to a variable. In addition, strings can be processed with many of the functions described in the next subsection.

Delphi: long strings and short strings

Accordingly, a string declaration could look like var str: String; or String str;. However, there is a large number of special cases, where the string definition (and string initialization) depends on the language.

In Delphi, we basically distinguish between long strings and short strings. The essential difference between the two is that long strings can have any given length (which means that they are dynamic), whereas short strings must have a specific length. These short strings are declared by appending the length—for example, var str: String [200]. Short strings are more efficient than long strings, and data processing is easier because of their constant lengths.

Once strings have been defined, you can assign constants to any of them. In Delphi, string constants are always written between apostrophes: str := 'MorganKaufmann'. Strings in Delphi can be used like arrays—you can access individual characters with str[i].

Java: String and StringBuffer

In Java, in addition to the type String, there is a type called StringBuffer. This latter type is used when the character string is to be modified later. For example, you cannot simply extract a character from a variable of the type String. For this purpose, a variable of the type StringBuffer is required. Although variables of this type require more storage space, they are more similar to alphanumeric fields in COBOL.

You can assign an arbitrary character string to a variable of the type string immediately after the declaration—for example, String str = "MorganKaufmann";. However, this is only an abbreviation for String str = new String("MorganKaufmann");. We can see that, in Java, string constants are written between double quotation marks.

Note a special particularity at this point: the method valueOf can be used to convert an elementary type (char, int, long, and so forth) into a string—for example, String str = String.valueOf(17);. The index and the method charAt can access the individual elements of a string, that is, the individual characters of a string. Variables of the type StringBuffer have to be created by the operator new, such as StringBuffer str = new StringBuffer("Markus");. You cannot use the index to access individual characters of this type of variable.

Direct comparison s1 == s2 is not allowed

The Java types String and StringBuffer are *dynamic data types* (see more about this in Section 3.7). For this reason, a direct comparison of two strings, s1, s2, with s1 == s2 wouldn't make sense, because it would just mean an identity comparison, not a string comparison. Instead, the following function has to be used: s1.equals(s2).

Special Functions

That character strings are important elements of a program is known from the COBOL world. In fact, COBOL offers a wide range of functions for efficient processing of character strings, such as UNSTRING or INSPECT, to name just two. In Delphi and Java, the STRING instruction can be simulated with the operator +, which is defined for strings, grouping several character strings. Other special functions for string processing are listed in Table 3.8.

Delphi string functions

- Delete (var dest: String; index, count: Integer) deletes a number consisting of count characters within the string dest, starting from position index.

- Insert (s1: String; var dest: String; index: Integer) inserts the string s1 into the string dest at the position index.

- IntToStr (i: Longint): String converts the integer value i into a string.

Table 3.8   Special functions for string processing

Function	Delphi	Java
Delete substring	Delete	Delete
Insert substring	Insert	Insert
Convert number to string	IntToStr	ValueOf
Define length	Length	Length
Define position of a substring	Pos	IndexOf
Convert string to number	StrToInt	Wrapper classes: see Section 5.4.3

- `Length (s: String): Integer` returns the length of the string s. This function determines not only the length selected during the variable declaration but also the actual length—the number of characters the string contains.

- `Pos (substr: String; s: String): Integer` searches the string s to determine whether the string substr can be found. If so, the index where it occurs (for the first time) is returned; otherwise, the value –1 is returned.

- `StrToInt (s: String): Longint` returns a string as a number if this type of conversion is permitted—for example, if s has a value of '4711'.

Java string functions As mentioned, Java distinguishes between the classes `String` and `StringBuffer`. If we want to modify a character string, we would have to use a `StringBuffer`. Functions such as `insert` or `delete` are supported only by this type.

Moreover, functions are actually methods, which are always called with `VariableName.MethodName`. For example, if there is a `StringBuffer` by the name of s, the delete method is called with `s.delete`.

The important things to remember here are that the delete operation refers to the character string s and that this string does not have to be passed on separately as a parameter. This is discussed further in Section 5.1.

- `dest.delete(start, end)` deletes all characters in the character string dest starting from position start to position end. dest has to be of type `StringBuffer`.

- dest.insert(index, s1) inserts the character string s1 into the character string dest at the position index. dest and has to be of type String-Buffer.

- s.valueOf(d) converts the integer value d into a character string.

- s.length() returns the length of the character string s. This operation determines not only the length selected during the variable declaration but also the actual length—the number of characters in the string.

- s.indexOf(substr) searches the character string s to see whether the character string substr can be found. If so, the index where this occurs (for the first time) is returned; otherwise, the value −1 is returned. This function works only with the type String.

Example

This example (Listings 3.7 and 3.8) searches for a pattern pat in a character string s. If the pattern is found, the index where the first occurrence of pat was found is stored in the parameter pos. Essentially, this corresponds to the Delphi function pos or to the Java method indexOf.

Listing 3.7.
Search String in
Delphi

```
var
   pat, s: String;
   i, j, pos: Integer;
. . .
i := 1; pos := -1;
while (i <= Length(s)) and (pos < 0) do begin
   if pat[1] = s[i] then begin
      j := 2;
      while (j <= Length(pat)) and (pat[j] = s[i + j - 1]) do begin
        Inc (j);
      end;
      if j > Length (pat) then begin pos := i; end;
   end;
   Inc(i);
end;
```

Listing 3.8.
Search String in
Java

```
String pat, s;
int i, j, pos;
. . .
```

```
i = 0; pos = -1;
while ((i < s.length()) && (pos < 0)) {
   if (pat.charAt(0) == s.charAt(i)) {
      j = 1;
      while ((j < pat.length()) &&
                (pat.charAt(j) == s.charAt(i + j))) {
       j++;
      }
      if (j >= pat.length()) {pos = i;}
   }
   i++;
}
```

3.4.3 Records

Heterogeneous data structures: various elements Records group various data structures under a single name. Think only of the data types discussed so far, which can represent arbitrary numbers, character strings, letters, or tables. However, if we want to map a date in the form *day month year*, such as 6 December 2003 to a variable, we will not be able to if we use only one variable. We would have to use three variables: two integers for day and year and a string for the month.

Accessing an element through three different variables is not particularly elegant. This is where records come in. We can use a record to group different element types into one heterogeneous data structure. This is also the fundamental difference between a record and an array. The latter consists of equal element types, which means it has a homogeneous data structure. We are familiar with this kind of data structure from COBOL, so the group fields discussed here are actually attributes of a record.

Record Definitions

The following section describes briefly how a record can define the date of our previous example.

Delphi In Delphi, records begin with the keyword `record`, followed by the individual attributes, which are declared as variables in the usual way and which should appear in a separate line to ensure good readability. The keyword `end` terminates a record, as we can see from the following short source code fragment:

```
type
  Date = record
    day: Integer;
    month: String[10];
    year: Integer;
  end;
```

Java: classes instead of records

Java has no record type. To use a record, we have to use classes. We already know a similar phenomenon from Section 3.3, where we saw that Java does not offer procedures but instead methods of a class. However, classes are a good replacement for records. We will see later that they are even more powerful. Attributes can be embedded in classes just like normal variable declarations:

```
class Date {
  int day;
  String month;
  int year;
}
```

Record Access

Access through dot notation

Naturally, an important issue is how to access a record's attributes. Although we could work with the record itself, we are interested only in how to pass the parameters of a procedure or the value assignment (for example, can a variable of type `Date` be assigned to another one of the same type?). A record's attributes can be used like any normal variables, where access is over one point, that is, over `VariableName.AttributName`. For example, we could access the attribute day of the record d over `d.day`.

In contrast to COBOL, the field name alone is not a valid value, because the attributes (fields) outside the record are visible only in connection with the record name. However, the record itself can be used like any normal variable, too—the aforementioned assignment is possible.

Delphi

```
var d: Date;
d.day := 6;
d.month := 'December';
d.year := 2003
```

Java

In Java, we first have to create an instance of the class, as in Section 3.4.1, so that the class can be processed.

```
Date d = new Date();
d.day = 6;
d.month = "December";
d.year = 2003
```

To further explain how the declaration of records works, we give additional examples in Listings 3.9 and 3.10, which describe how to map an account or a person.

Listing 3.9. Examples for Record Declarations in Delphi

```
Account = record
   name: String[64];
   number: Integer;
   balance: Real;
end;
Person = record
   name: String[32];
   birth: Date;
   adr: record // An own type address would even be better here.
      street, city: String[32];
      nr: Integer;
      end;
end;
```

Listing 3.10. Examples for Class Declarations in Java

```
class Account {
   String name;
   int number;
   double balance;
}
class Address {
   String street, city;
   int nr;
}
class Person {
   String name;
   Date birth;
   Address adr;
}
```

Of course, records and arrays can be mixed—an array can be used as an attribute of a record. Similarly, we could use an array of records. To better understand this, we will use an array of persons in the following example.

Delphi
```
var
    p: Person;
    i: Integer;
    list: array[1..100] of Person;
. . .
p.name := . . . // Access the name of person p
p.name[i] := . . . // Access the ith character of the name of p
list[i].name := . . . // Access the ith person in the list
p.adr.street := . . . // Access the street name in the address of p
```

─────────────

Java
```
Person p = new Person();
int i;
Person list[] = new Person[100];
// Create the individual persons - necessary because of the class notation
for (int i = 0; i < 100; i ++) list[i] = new Person();
p.name = . . . // Access the name of person p
p.name[i] = . . . // Access the ith character of the name of p
list[i].name = . . . // Access the ith person in the list
p.adr.street = . . . // Access the street name in the address of p
```

Examples

To deepen our understanding of records, we present a final example (Listings 3.11 and 3.12), which searches a telephone directory for a person. The array book (100 persons) is searched until the name we are looking for is found. If the name is found, the person's phone number is stored in the variable phone; otherwise, the variable is assigned a value of 0.

**Listing 3.11.
Phone Directory
Example in
Delphi**
```
type
    Person = record
        name: String;
        phone: Integer;
    end;
```

```
    PhoneBook = array[0..99] of Person;
var
   name: String;
   phone, i: Integer;
   book: PhoneBook;
. . .
i := 0;
while ((i < 100) and (book[i].name <> name)) do Inc(i);
if (i < 100) then phone := book[i].phone else phone := 0;
```

**Listing 3.12.
Phone Directory
Example in Java**

```
class Person {
   String name;
   int phone;
}
. . .
String name;
int phone, i;
Person book[] = new Person[100];
for (i = 0; i < 100; i ++) book[i] = new Person();
. . .
i = 0;
while ((i < 100) && !(book[i].name.equals(name))) i++;
if (i < 100) phone = book[i].phone; else phone = 0;
```

**Conditional
evaluation should
always be used**

In this example, the conditional evaluation of the while condition, which is often called shortcut evaluation, is important. First, the program tests within the condition of the while loop to see whether i is smaller than 100. Only then does it test the book entry at position i. If the first condition is not met, it is not necessary to test for the second, because the entire expression must be correct. The situation is similar with an or condition: If the first condition is met, the second does not have to be tested, because the entire expression must be correct.

This statement is important and raises the question, What could happen in this example if the entry did not exist? With the opposite sequence of the while condition, or if both expressions were evaluated, we would also have to test book[100]. However, given the fact that the upper index limit is 99, we would get a runtime error.

In Delphi, the conditional evaluation is always applied, while Java applies it only when the dual operator (that is, && for and or || for or) is used.

If the usual operator (that is, & or |) is used, both expressions are tested, regardless of whether this is necessary. We recommend generally using the conditional evaluation, because the other approach would not be useful, especially with regard to runtime behavior.

3.4.4 Summary

An example in COBOL, Delphi, and Java will summarize what we have learned. The following simple program computes a car's average gasoline consumption. We enter the mileage, gallons consumed, and price per gallon in cents. Next, one computation part computes and outputs the average consumption per 100 miles, the total cost, and the average cost per 100 miles in dollars. Listing 3.13 shows the COBOL program (with all lines numbered for reference in the following discussion).

Listing 3.13.
Computing
Average Gasoline
Consumption in
COBOL

```
00010 identification division.
00020*************************************
00030* program calculating the average *
00040* gasoline consumption of a car *
00050*************************************
00060 environment division.
00070 configuration section.
00080 special-names.
00090 decimal-point is comma.
00100*************************************
00110 data division.
00120 working-storage section
00130
00140 01 input.
00150 05 i-miles pic 9(4).
00160 05 i-gallons pic 9(3).
00170 05 i-price pic 9(3).
00180
00190 01 calculation-fields.
00200 05 c-average pic 9999v99 binary.
00210 05 c-costs pic 99999v99 binary.
00220 05 c-average-costs pic 99v99 ` binary.
00230
```

```
00240 01 output.
00250 05 o-average pic z9,99.
00260 05 o-costs pic zz9,99.
00270 05 o-average-costs pic z9,99.
00280***********************************
00290 procedure division.
00300 main.
00310 display "Welcome"
00320 display "miles: "
00330 accept i-miles
00340 display "gallons: "
00350 accept i-gallons
00360 display "price"
00370 accept i-price
00380******calculations*******************
00390 compute c-average = 100 * i-gallons / i-miles
00400 compute c-costs = i-gallons * i-price / 100
00410 compute c-average-costs = c-average * i-price / 100
00420******move calc-fields to output******
00430 move c-average to o-average
00440 move c-costs to o-costs
00450 move c-average-costs to o-average-costs
00460******output**********************
00470 display "average consumption for 100 miles: "
00480 display o-average
00490 display "total costs: "
00500 display o-costs
00510 display "average costs for 100 miles: "
00520 display o-average-costs
00530***********************************
00540 stop run.
```

This program is actually easy to understand, and we will gradually port it to Delphi and Java in the next two sections.

Delphi *Computing Average Gasoline Consumption in Delphi*

Delphi doesn't need the first two sections—the Identification Division and Environment Division—because showing the decimal point as a comma can be achieved only by special output functions.

Data Division   The Data Division (lines 110–270) essentially includes three records. Although not mandatory, it is useful to agree on types here, especially because the record used for computation and the output are identical. With regard to the record fields, in contrast to COBOL, Delphi doesn't let you specify how many decimal places before and after the comma should be used in the computation. This is why we have to use a default type, such as integer or real. Consequently, the type definitions in Delphi look like this:

```
type
  Input = record
    miles: Integer;
    gallons: Integer;
    price: Integer;
  end;
  Calculation = record
    average: Real;
    costs: Real;
    averageCosts: Real;
  end;
```

Program Division   However, unlike in COBOL, the field names are not linked by dashes. Then the variables i, c, and o have to be declared of these types.

This takes us to the core of the program: the Program Division. Initially, lines 310–370 handle the inputs. This is similar to Delphi, but the variable name and a dot have to be added to the beginning of the field name: i.miles. However, the input should always be easy to understand:

```
// input
WriteLn('Welcome');
Write('miles: '); ReadLn(i.miles);
Write('gallons: '); ReadLn(i.gallons);
Write('price: '); ReadLn(i.price);
```

The next step involves the computations, which are similar to the COBOL example, although they use the := assignment instead of the COMPUTE command. Because we use types, we can easily assign c to o:

```
// calculation
c.average := 100 * i.gallons / i.miles;
c.costs := i.gallons * i.price / 100;
c.averageCosts := c.average * i.price / 100;
o := c;
```

Output Finally, we get to the output. This is easy in COBOL, because the Data Division already specified the output format. Unfortunately, this is not possible in Delphi, where we would have to do a special preparation, such as splitting into parts before and after the comma. For the sake of simplicity, we do without formatted output in this example, so assignment to the output variable is not really necessary. In fact, we could output c right away. Listing 3.14 shows the complete example in Delphi.

Listing 3.14. Computing Average Gasoline Consumption in Delphi

```
// Sample for a Program in the first unit
// Name, date, and short description
program Gasoline;
type // types
  Input = record
    miles: Integer;
    gallons: Integer;
    price: Integer;
  end;
  Calculation = record
    average: Real;
    costs: Real;
    averageCosts: Real;
  end;
var // variables
  i: Input; c, o: Calculation;
  dummy: Char;
begin
  // input
  WriteLn('Welcome');
  Write('miles: '); ReadLn(i.miles);
  Write('gallons: '); ReadLn(i.gallons);
  Write('price: '); ReadLn(i.price);
  // calculation
```

```
        c.average := 100 * i.gallons / i.miles;
        c.costs := i.gallons * i.price / 100;
        c.averageCosts := c.average * i.price / 100;
        o := c;
        // output
        Write('average consumption for 100 miles: ');
        WriteLn(o.average);
        Write('display total costs: ');
        WriteLn(o.costs);
        Write('average costs for 100 miles: ');
        WriteLn(o.averageCosts);
        Read(dummy);
end.
```

Java   *Computing Average Gasoline Consumption in Java*

The first two sections—Identification Division and Environment Division—are not really needed in Java. We could show the decimal point as a comma by special output functions. However, it is important to state the auxiliary procedure readInt, because Java does not offer predefined functions for input.

Data Division   The Data Division (lines 110–270) essentially include three records. Although they are not mandatory, it is useful here to agree on types, especially because the record for computation and the output are identical. With regard to the record fields, unlike COBOL, Java does not let you specify how many decimal places before and after the comma should be used in the computation. This is why we can use only a default type, such as int or float. Consequently, the type definitions in Java look like this:

```
class Input {
   int miles;
   int gallons;
   int price;
}
class Calculation {
   float average;
   float costs;
   float averageCosts;
}
```

In contrast to COBOL, the field names are not linked by dashes. Then we have to declare the variables i, c, and o of these types and create records or classes in Java. Accordingly, a new also has to follow—unless the variables have already been created, similarly to the o case, and are merely assigned now.

Program Division This takes us to the core of the program—the Program Division. Initially, lines 310–370 handle the inputs. This is similar to Java, but the variable name and a dot have to be added to the beginning of the field name: i.miles. However, the input should always be easy to understand:

```
// input
System.out.print("Welcome");
System.out.print("miles: "); i.miles = readInt();
System.out.print("gallons: "); i.gallons = readInt();
System.out.print("price: "); i.price = readInt();
```

The next step involves the computations, which are similar to the COBOL example, although they use the = assignment instead of the COMPUTE command. Because we use types, we can easily assign c to o:

```
c.average = 100 * i.gallons / i.miles;
c.costs = i.gallons * i.price / 100;
c.averageCosts = c.average * i.price / 100;
o = c;
```

Output Finally, we get to the output. This is easy in COBOL, because the Data Division already specified the output format. Unfortunately, this is not possible in Java, where we would have to do a special preparation, such as splitting into parts before and after the comma. For the sake of simplicity, we do without formatted output in this example, so assignment to the output variable is not really necessary. In fact, we could output c right away. Listing 3.15 shows the complete example in Java.

Listing 3.15.
Computing the
Average Gasoline
Consumption
in Java

```
// Sample for a Program in the first unit
// Name, date, and short description
class Gasoline {
    public static int readInt () { // auxiliary procedure
        String s = "";
```

```
      try {
        s = new java.io.DataInputStream(System.in).readLine();
      }
      catch (java.io.IOException e) {}
      return java.lang.Integer.parseInt(s);
    }
  public static void main (String args[]) {
    class Input {
      int miles;
      int gallons;
      int price;
    }
    class Calculation {
      float average;
      float costs;
      float averageCosts;
    }
    Calculation o;
    Input i = new Input();
    Calculation c = new Calculation();
    // input
    System.out.println("Welcome");
    System.out.print("miles: "); i.miles = readInt();
    System.out.print("gallons: "); i.gallons = readInt();
    System.out.print("price: "); i.price = readInt();
    // calculation
    c.average = 100 * i.gallons / i.miles;
    c.costs = i.gallons * i.price / 100;
    c.averageCosts = c.average * i.price / 100;
    o = c;
    // output
    System.out.print("average consumption for 100 miles: ");
    System.out.println(o.average);
    System.out.print("display total costs: ");
    System.out.println(o.costs);
    System.out.print("average costs for 100 miles: ");
    System.out.println(o.averageCosts);
  }
}
```

3.4.5 Exercises

Task 1 (40 minutes): Sorting

Assume we want to input a list of n numbers ($n \leq 1000$). Write a program that reads these numbers into an array a and outputs them in sorted form. Use iterated execution of the following process for all $i = 1, 2, \dots, n-1$ for your sorting operation:

1. Find the smallest value in a[i + 1]..a[n].

2. Replace this entry by a[i] if necessary.

Your program should also read the sort order (ascending or descending, that is, "up" or "down"). Example for an input: up 3 5 17 2 27 16 9 –1 (each separated by a return, where the negative value –1 terminates the input).

Task 2 (40 minutes): Formatting

Write a program that takes a name, consisting of first name, middle name, and last name (each separated by a blank), and then converts the input into another format and outputs the result.
Examples:

Markus Hermann Knasmüller → Knasmüller, Markus H.

John Fitzgerald Kennedy → Kennedy, John F.

Task 3 (100 minutes): Calculating a Date

Assume that a date is defined by the following type:

```
type
  Date = record
    day, mon, year: Integer;
  end;
```

First, represent this type as a Java class. Next, write a program that reads two date inputs and outputs their difference in days. Take leap years into account (leap years can be divided by 4. A year that can be divided by 100 but not by 400 is not a leap year.) You can assume that the date inputs are correct. Try to split your program into several procedures (and functions).

Language Particularities

Focus on the programming language of your choice

This section focuses on the programming languages of interest in our study. In particular, it describes special functionalities, such as procedure variables, overloaded methods, or nontypified parameters. All these functionalities are normally specific to a language: each language has its own particularities. Accordingly, we have divided this tutorial into two parts. The first discusses the particularities of Delphi, and the second those of Java. Readers who are interested only in one of these languages can skip the other.

3.5.1 Delphi Particularities

Open-Array Parameter

In Delphi, fixed sizes are assigned to arrays during the declaration. This is not necessarily an advantage, as we can easily see in the following example. For instance, if we have a given array[1..30] of Integer, a procedure for the output of this array would look as follows:

```
procedure Print (a: array[1..30] of Integer);
   var i: Integer;
begin
   for i := 1 to 30 do WriteLn(a[i]);
end;
```

Array without limits

This procedure has a fixed parameter list. For example, if a second array[1..32] of Integer were given and also had to be output, the procedures would have to be written a second time—certainly a useless additional cost. The solution is an *open-array parameter,* which means that the array is declared without limits. When limits of the array are required within the procedure, they will always reach from 0 to High. Accordingly, the procedure could look as follows:

```
procedure Print (a: array of Integer);
   var i: Integer;
begin
   for i := 0 to High(a) do WriteLn(a[i]);
end;
```

This procedure can now be called by an arbitrary array of Integer—for example, even by Print([3, 5, 7]). However, open arrays may be used as parameters only.

Memory consumption: be careful about it!

Another important issue in Delphi and arrays used as parameters is memory consumption. As explained in Section 3.3.2, the procedure creates copies of the parameters with normal input parameters, and the program actually works with these copies. Of course, this leads to a problem when passing on an array, as in our previous example. If this array is large, the local copy would occupy an unnecessarily large amount of memory unless it is modified. An array[1..1000] of String[255] may well mean a storage space of 250*T*KB wasted.

If the array is not to be modified within the procedure, which is normally the case, it would be useful to save storage space by declaring this input parameter as an output parameter, using var. An alternative is a declaration with const, which means that it concerns an input parameter that does not require a local copy, because no change will be made to the array within the procedure.

Dynamic Arrays

Dynamic arrays: size is determined only at runtime

Dynamic arrays have no fixed size. A decision as to how many elements the array should accommodate is made only at runtime. Such arrays are defined without index borders.

Before we can use the array, we have to specify the number of elements, which we achieve by calling SetLength(a, n). This means that array a is created with n elements. The index of this array will then reach from 0 to $n - 1$, because it always begins with 0 for dynamic arrays. The following source code fragment shows an example for a dynamic array:

```
var myArr: array of Integer; n: Integer;
. . .
// read n
SetLength(myArr, n);
// work with myArr
```

Nontypified Parameters

Nontypified parameters offer an option to write an open procedure in Delphi. When declaring the parameter, we just do not specify any type; the parameter can then also be of an arbitrary type. To be able to access the parameter within the procedure, we first have to convert between types.

This kind of procedure is inefficient and should, therefore, be used sparingly. A known example is the procedure WriteLn (. . .), although this was specially optimized by the compiler vendor.

Forward Declaration

The basic rule says that a procedure can be used only if it has been previously defined. This causes problems, for example with an indirect recursion, that is, if a procedure P calls a procedure Q and Q calls P in turn. In this case, P would have to be defined before Q, but Q would also have to be defined before P, which is not possible. To solve this problem, we can use a forward declaration, which requires only the procedure head followed by the keyword forward. The implementation follows later; of course, the procedure heads have to match. Listing 3.16 shows an example.

Listing 3.16.
Forward
Declaration in
Delphi

```
program ExampleForward;

procedure Q (x: Integer); forward;

procedure P (x: Integer);
begin
  if x <> 0 then begin
    WriteLn(x);
    Q(x - 1);
  end;
end;

procedure Q (x: Integer);
begin
  if x <> 0 then begin
    WriteLn(x);
    P(x - 1);
  end;
end;
. . .
end.
```

Procedure Variables

Procedure
variables: a
mighty construct

Delphi lets us store procedures in variables. A program could look as follows:

```
procedure P
. . .
end; // P
. . .
var v: procedure;
. . .
v := p;
```

Procedure variables are used mainly when we parameterize algorithms. For example, we could use procedure variables to write a general procedure (see Listing 3.17) and draw arbitrary functions. The desired function is then passed on when the call is made (see Listing 3.18).

```
type Func = function (x: Integer): Integer;
procedure Plot (f: Func);
   var x: Integer;
begin
   for x := 0 to 100 do DrawDot(x, f(x));
end; // Plot
```

```
function F1 (x: Integer): Integer;
begin result := 2 *x;
end; // F1

function F2 (x: Integer): Integer;
begin result := x * x - 9 * x;
end; // F2
```

To be able to draw the function y = 2 * x, all we need to do is call Plot(F1). To draw the function y = x2 - 9 * x, we call Plot(F2).

Procedures can
also be defined
as types
 As we already showed at the beginning of this section, it is also possible to define procedure types of the kind type BinaryOperation = function (x, y: Integer): Integer;. Just as with any type declaration, this declaration specifies the "form" of the container. It is important that no procedure name be specified. After such a type declaration, we can also declare variables of this type, and because these variables contain procedures, we could also call these procedure variables. Listing 3.19 summarizes these points.

Listing 3.19.
Summary of
Procedure
Variables

```
type
    BinaryOperation = function (x, y: Integer): Integer;
var
    v: BinaryOperation; a: Integer;
    . . .
function Sum (x, y: Integer): Integer;
    . . .
end;
. . .
v := sum;
a := v(7, 12);
```

In this example, the assignment v := sum is without parameter specification and v contains the procedure constant sum. Such an assignment is allowed when both procedures have the same number of parameters and the parameters are of the same type and the same kind (input or output). Whether the parameter names are identical is irrelevant.

3.5.2   Java Particularities

Java Virtual Machine (VM)

The Java Virtual Machine ensures that programs are platform-independent

Java programs are platform-independent. For example, a program written for a CISC machine (that is, Intel Pentium), can also be used on a RISC machine. This platform independence is provided by the Java Virtual Machine (VM), which introduces a platform-independent layer, representing an interface between the hardware and the Java program. This VM has to be installed on each computer that runs Java programs. The programs are then compiled into a kind of interpretable code, the *Java bytecode*. The VM can interpret this code, regardless of and independently of the underlying processor.

Constant Parameters

final   As mentioned in Section 3.3.2, Java does not distinguish between input parameters and output parameters on the basis of a keyword but on the basis of the parameter type. In addition, it has an option to declare a parameter with the keyword final, which specifies that we are dealing with a "call by value." This prevents the parameter from ending up on the left side of an assignment. More specifically, instead of creating a security copy, undesired changes to a parameter are prevented solely by the compiler.

Conditional Expression

Compact notation A conditional expression can formulate compact value assignments that depend on a logical condition, such as condition ? then-branch : else-branch. The following if instruction could then be represented by means of a conditional expression.

```
if (x > y) {return x;} else {return y;}
```

The corresponding conditional expression is simply:

```
return (x > y) ? x : y;
```

3.5.3 Exercises

Task 1 (180 minutes): Marriage Brokerage

Who seeks shall find! A marriage brokerage agency's core business is marrying its customers off. For this business, the agency uses a program to enter all customer information and output the three best pair matches. The customer information is structured as follows:

Delphi
```
const
    BLACK = 0; BROWN = 1; RED = 2; GREEN = 3; BLOND = 4; WHITE = 5;
    BLUE = 6; GRAY = 7; OTHER = 8;
type
Candidate = record
  firstname, secondname: String[32];
  male: Boolean;
  income: Integer;
  hair: Integer;
  eyes: Integer;
  prefIncome: Integer;
  prefHair: array[1..2] of Integer;
  prefEyes: array[1..2] of Integer;
end;
```

We use constants here for simplicity, but in a real application, an enumeration type would be preferable.

Java
```
class Candidate {
    static final int BLACK = 0;
    static final int BROWN = 1;
    static final int RED = 2;
    static final int GREEN = 3;
    static final int BLOND = 4,
    static final int WHITE = 5;
    static final int BLUE = 6;
    static final int GRAY = 7;
    static final int OTHER = 8;
    String firstName, secondName;
    boolean male;
    int income;
    int hair, eyes;
    int prefIncome;
    int[] prefHair;
    int[] prefEyes;
}
```

The number of candidates to be checked by the program is always less than 50. The following information is read in for each candidate: first name, last name, sex, salary, hair color, color of eyes, preferred salary, two "preferred hair styles" (which may be identical), and two "preferred eyes" (which may also be identical).

A match is admissible only provided that the candidates are of different sex and that at least one "preferred" value is met for each candidate. Each candidate may appear in more than one dream match. The sequence of matches results from the sum of correspondences.

Try to split the program into procedures by applying the stepwise refinement technique.

3.6   Modules

Modules are similar to external subprograms

This tutorial discusses modules. Modules are similar to external subprograms of COBOL, and even copies in COBOL are not unlike the modules discussed here. In COBOL, you can use the command COPY to embed program parts so that subprograms, particularly data definitions, can be managed in separate text files. However, when a copy changes, all programs that import this copy have to be recompiled. This is not the case with modules.

This section discusses the motivation for modules. Subsequently, it explains in detail what such modules look like and how they can be used. Finally, it describes rules to implement modularization.

3.6.1 Motivation

Splitting things into manageable parts

Modules split a program into manageable parts. This is a familiar technique: Section 2.4 presented the stepwise refinement technique, which is aimed at splitting complex things into smaller, more manageable parts. Another benefit of modules is their abstraction capabilities. Details can be hidden. Such an abstraction forms the basis for dynamic data structures, which are described in Section 3.7.

Collecting declarations

Modules consist of a collection of declarations. This means that constants, types, variables, and procedures are defined within modules. Each module can be compiled by itself, thereby serving as a building block others can use.

The essential features of a module are its interfaces, which define what is defined in the module and what will be made available for others. The declarations contained in these interfaces are called *public,* because this is a keyword used in most languages to identify interfaces. All clients can then import and use these declarations. For example, a constant PI can be defined in a module, and programs can then import and use it.

One of the numerous benefits modules offer is obvious: Any change to the constant (for example, taking the more detailed value 3.141592 instead of 3.14) must be effected in one place only, and not in several places. Whoever imports these declarations does not have to know or even be aware of the implementation. For example, all the listings given so far use an imported procedure for output, without knowing the respective implementation. A module could be thought of as a fence that can be surmounted only by an import or export.

3.6.2 Export

Making things "public"

To ensure that others can use the declarations of a module, we have to make them "public," which means that we have to provide them for

general use. This specification is independent of the programming
language.

Delphi   In Delphi, a module is called a *unit.* With a unit, we first define the interface and then proceed to the implementation. A module begins with an
introduction, which is opened by the keyword `interface`. All declarations
that follow are "public."

The implementation, introduced by the keyword `implementation`,
follows those public declarations. This part contains the implementation
of the public procedures and additional *private* declarations. Private declarations are those that will not be exported. Listing 3.20 shows an example
of such a module, with the exported names in bold.

Listing 3.20.
Delphi Example
for the
Implementation
of an Export
Interface

```
unit ExampleUnit;
interface
  type
    R = record
      f: Integer;
    end;
  var
    y: R;
  procedure P (a: Integer);
implementation
  procedure Q (b: Char);
  begin
    // . . .
  end; // end - Q
  procedure P (a: Integer);
    var x: Integer;
  begin
    // . . .
  end; // end - P
initialization
  y.f := 3;
end.
```

Initialization   The code after the keyword `initialization` initializes global variables.
This code piece is executed when the module is accessed for the first time.

Java: package   In Java, exported declarations are specified by the modifier `public`. This
keyword is simply written before the declaration. Java offers other modi-

fiers, which is described later in the relevant sections. Basically, we should note here that Java does not know the term *module*. Instead, it introduces the term *package,* which has a similar meaning. Each file begins with the keyword package, followed by the name of the package. It is possible and customary to group several files into one package. All you have to do in this case is use the same name after the keyword package. Listing 3.21 shows an example for a package in Java, with the exported names in bold.

Listing 3.21. Java Example for the Implementation of an Export Interface

```java
package ExampleUnit;
public class R {
    public int f;
    public static R y;

    static void q (char b) {
        //. . .
    }
    public static void p (int a) {
        int x;
        // . . .
    }
    static {
        y = new R();
        y.f = 3;
    }
}
```

Initialization
The code in the last block after the keyword static (that is, y = new R(); y.f = 3;) initializes the global variable y. This piece of code will be executed during the first access to the module. Such an initialization may be implemented only for variables declared with static.

Only global names can be exported
The two listings export different names. In general, we can say that constants, types, variables, and procedures can be exported, but they all have to be global. Our examples export the type R, the record component R.f, the global variable y, and the procedure p. Things like the local variable x or the procedure q are not visible and are therefore not exported.

Modules encourage teamwork
A highly recommended approach for creating modules is to first define the interfaces, then compile these modules. This means that clients can import the declarations before their implementations have been completed. The module can then be completed stepwise. Therefore, this approach is particularly useful and encouraging for programming teams.

3.6.3 Import

All exported names can be imported by programs or other modules. For this purpose, they must have their own import instruction to define the modules to be imported.

Delphi   In Delphi, a unit has to be imported by the instruction uses Unitname. If more than one unit is to be imported, the names of these units must be separated by commas. The individual names can then be used as if they were defined in that program. Similarly, we could use the notation Unit-Name.VariableName, which would be mandatory in case of conflicting names. An import in Delphi could look like this:

```
program Client;
uses ExampleUnit;
var x: R; // var x : ExampleUnit.x;
// . . .
x := y; // x := ExampleUnit.y;
P(3); // ExampleUnit.P(3);
```

Java   In Java, we could do an import with import PackageName.ClassName. If all classes of a package are to be imported, this could also be done by using import Package.Name.*. The individual names could then be used as if they were defined in that program. Similarly, we could use the notation PackageName.ClassName instead of the name. This is mandatory in the event of conflicting names. An import in Java could look like this:

```
import ExampleUnit.R;
class Client {
  public static void main (String args[]) {
    R x;
    x = ExampleUnit.y;
    ExampleUnit.p(3);
  }
}
```

Sequence: beware of circular imports!   An important question with regard to an import is the sequence, because circular imports are forbidden. For example, if module A imports module B and module B imports module C, module C is forbidden to import module A. The same applies to direct circular references; if module A imports module B, module B must not import module A.

3.6.4 Modularization

Modules serve for data abstraction or procedure collection

Modules are used mainly for data abstraction (see also Section 4.1) and procedure collection (for example, grouping all procedures for input and output). A module must meet the following guidelines:

Rules for modularization

- **Completeness:** All data and procedures belonging to a specific task should always be contained in *one* module.

- **Streamlined interfaces:** The interface of a module should be clear (rule of thumb: less than one page). It should contain few and simple procedures, which should have a limited number of parameters (rule of thumb: maximum of four).

- **Manageability:** The module should not be too big (rule of thumb: 1000 lines maximum—approximately 15 printed pages). However, also avoid producing too many small modules.

We will often have to make compromises between these rules. Nevertheless, they help derive various features that characterize good interfaces:

- Simplicity
- Consistency
- No redundancy (the same operations are not provided in two ways)
- Elementariness (operations required individually should not be grouped)
- Generality (do not tailor operations for specific cases)
- Robustness

3.6.5 Exercises

Queues: important example to be continued

Task 1 (180 minutes): Priority Queue

Assume that several people are waiting in line in front of a teller. Each person should get his or her turn, depending on how long she or he has been waiting. Unfortunately, the teller does not treat everybody waiting in line equally. He distinguishes the waiting customers as unpleasant, normal, or pleasant. Normal customers get priority over unpleasant ones. Pleasant customers get priority over normal and unpleasant ones. But among several persons of the same type, the one who has been waiting longest gets priority. There are never more than 100 people in the queue.

Write a module that simulates this situation. It should have the following interface:

Delphi

```
interface
    const UNPLEASANT = 1; NORMAL = 2; PLEASANT = 3;
    procedure Add (name: String; k: Integer);
    (* adds a new person - type k - to the queue *)
    procedure GetNext (var name: String);
    (* supplies the name of the next person and removes that person *)
    function Count (): Integer;
    (* supplies the number of persons *)
```

Java

```
class PriorityQueue {
    public final int UNPLEASANT = 1;
    public final int NORMAL = 2;
    public final int PLEASANT = 3;
    public static void add (String name, int k) {
        // adds a new person - type k - to the queue
    }
    public static String getNext () {
        // supplies the name of the next person and removes that person
    }
    public static int count () {
        // supplies the number of persons
    }
}
```

Write an additional test program that calls these operations.

3.7

Pointers: Introduction

This tutorial is just an introduction; Chapter 4 discusses the issue in more detail

To conclude our first major part of this OOP course, we provide a short overview about *pointers*. Pointers form a core feature in object-oriented programming, because objects are always realized by use of pointers. COBOL offers a few similar approaches, in particular the extension USING BY REFERENCE in OO-COBOL. However, traditional COBOL programmers typically do not know this issue well, although the concept is powerful. For this reason, this topic is introduced here and deepens our discussion in the second part of our OOP course.

3.7.1 Explanation of Terms

Pointers

In general, a pointer is a dynamic data structure. *Dynamic* means that the storage space is not available in advance; instead, it is created upon demand. Moreover, a pointer has an unlimited size and shape—for example, in contrast to an array, which is always limited.

Lists

In general, the simplest use of pointers are lists. For example, a list of names can be represented in an array but also in the form of a linked list. One name always points to the next. The last name points to an end identifier—a *NIL pointer*. Figure 3.4 shows these two options. The line originating from D, limited by a vertical line, is the graphical representation of a NIL pointer.

A dynamic list can have any length

The difference between an array and such a linked list is mainly that the list can de facto have an arbitrary length. In contrast, all arrays have an upper limit, where the number of elements is fixed. A linked list can begin with few elements, and more elements can be added at any time. Another

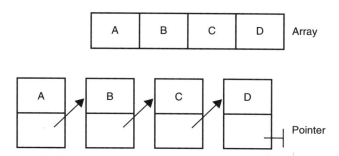

Figure 3.4 Possible representation form for a list.

advantage of the list form is that insert and delete operations are relatively easy and quick (also depending on runtime behavior). We can see in Figure 3.5 that pointers help build arbitrary data structures.

Inserting in and deleting from a linked list: easier than expected

As mentioned, insert and delete operations on a linked list are relatively easy. To get a first intuitive feeling of how to work with pointers, we discuss these algorithms before concentrating on the data types. Figure 3.6

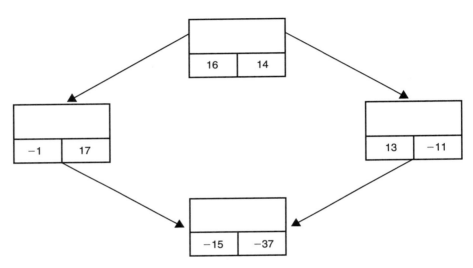

Figure 3.5 Example for complex pointer data structures.

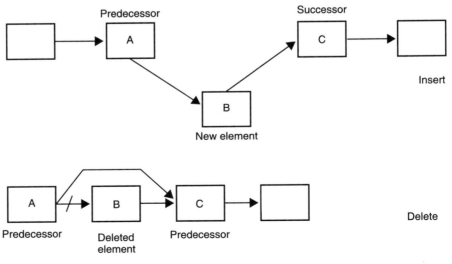

Figure 3.6 Inserting in and deleting from a linked list.

helps explain this issue. When a new element (labeled B in the figure) is inserted into a list, it simply has to point to its successor (element C). The predecessor (element A) has to point to the new element B instead of pointing to C. Deleting is just as easy: To delete element B from the list, we ensure that element A no longer points to B but instead to the new successor, C.

Insert and delete operations on an array are much more complex. Although not more than three elements are involved in a list linked by pointers, all elements may be involved in an array—for example, when deleting the first element of the array. Then the index for all array elements reduces by a value of 1.

3.7.2   Pointers

Pointers are independent data types
Pointers can be thought of as data types. Accordingly, variables of this type also have to be declared. Normally, we define a type that is a pointer to a record. Variables of this type can then be interpreted as pointer variables, which point to a memory block in the heap (Figure 3.7). This memory block is the object referred to by the pointer (variable).

Naturally, the actual declaration depends a lot on the language you use. The following example shows a declaration for a linked linear list, composed of character strings.

Delphi
In Delphi, the record is declared as a usual type, preceded by a special type to serve as pointer. The syntax is as follows:

```
type
  Node = ^NodeDesc;
  NodeDesc = record
    data: String[16];
    next: Node;
  end;
```

Java
Java does not know a pointer data type; that is, we cannot explicitly use a pointer type. However, the rule is simple: All arrays and records (classes)

Pointer variable

Memory block in the heap

Figure 3.7 Graphical representation of a pointer variable.

are pointers, and the type is always implicit. Consequently, a linked list can be represented as a "normal" class:

```
class Node {
    String data;
    Node next;
}
```

Recursive definition   We can see from the two preceding examples that these definitions are recursive. This is absolutely logical, because each node in the list points to another node. Considering that we are dealing with a special case in a special way, the respective compiler will not have any problem and no syntax error will be thrown. A variable p of the type node is represented in the memory exactly as shown in Figure 3.8.

New creates a block in memory   A variable of the type pointer (whether declared implicitly or explicitly) must be created before it can be used. It is created with the New function, which creates a memory block (heap block) of the required size. The declaration of a pointer variable alone does not yet claim the object's storage space. This storage space will be used only when the object is created by new. Another special case here is the uncreated pointer that points to no object—the NIL pointer.

We can then access the variable or the components of the record that the pointer refers to by using a normal record; that is, we access the component data in the previous example by using p.data. We could also work with the pointer variable itself. We could use a variable q of the type node and simply assign the variable p to it.

The value assignment does not create new storage requirements, and no new node is created: After the assignment, both p and q point to the same node (Figure 3.9). Any change to the component p.data will also cause a change to the component q.data. We saw this effect before, in connection with the var parameters (see example "Dirty" in Section 3.3.2), which is intuitive, because a var parameter is basically a pointer (albeit one that is implicitly declared).

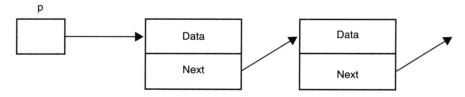

Figure 3.8 Graphical representation of the node data type.

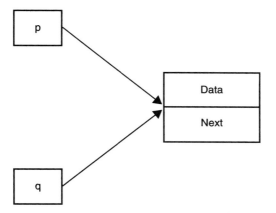

Figure 3.9 Pointer assignment: both pointers refer to the same object.

This behavior is known as *reference semantics* and is a difference between C++ or similar languages and Delphi or Java. C++ uses *copy semantics*—that is, q := p would create a new object, a copy of p. The reference semantics used in Delphi and Java leads to the fact that p and q reference the same object after a q := p. As already mentioned, a change of p.data would lead to a change of q.data.

3.7.3 Standard Algorithms

A list has heads and tails

This section uses a few short operations to show how a simple list works. The given case has two important pointers: head and tail. Head is the pointer to the head of the list (the first list element), and tail is the pointer to the tail of the list (the last list element). At the beginning, when the list is empty, both pointers refer to NIL. This could look as follows:

Delphi

```
var head, tail: Node;
. . .
initialization head := nil; tail := nil;
```

Java

```
static Node head, tail;
. . .
static {
    head = null; tail = null;
}
```

Nodes have to be entered first
For the sake of simplicity, all nodes in this example are always added to this list. Adding nodes to a list is easy. First, the node has to be (dynamically!) created, then the new value is written to this node, and the pointer tail has to point to this new object (which is now the new last element in the list).

Well, this was pretty easy, but we still have to consider two points. First, we have to test for the special case when the list is empty, because then the head pointer will have to refer to this new element. If an element is added to an empty list, this new element is not only the first element in the list but also the last.

Second, we naturally have to test for the case when the list is not empty. The predecessor of the new element—the current last element—has to point to it. This is also easy to implement, because all we have to do is set tail.next to the new element, as follows:

Delphi
```
procedure AddNode (data: String);
   var p: Node;
begin
  New(p); p.data := data; p.next := nil;
  if head = nil then head := p else tail.next := p;
  tail := p;
end; // AddNode
```

Java
```
public static void addNode (String data) {
  Node p = new Node();
  p.data = data; p.next = null;
  if (head == null) head = p; else tail.next = p;
  tail = p;
} // addNode
```

The memory block survives the procedure
The memory block created for p survives the end of the procedure, although the procedure limits the lifetime of the variable itself.

Walking through a list
When working with lists, stepwise execution—beginning with the first element—is important. For example, we output the first element, then continue with the second element, and so on, until the last element in the list has been processed. We can achieve this easily with a variable, p, that points to the first element, calls a procedure with p.data (for example, the output

procedure), and finally uses the assignment p := p.next to point to the next element.

Delphi
```
procedure PrintList;
   var p: Node;
begin
  p := head;
  while p <> nil do begin
     WriteLn(p.data);
     p := p.next;
  end;
end; // PrintList
```

Java
```
public void printList () {
   Node p;
   p = head;
   while (p != null) {
      System.out.println(p.data);
      p = p.next;
   }
} // printList
```

These are the most important functions when working with pointers. Once we have understood these principles, we can work with the examples in the next chapters, which provide deeper insight. However, we will first study how to delete previously created dynamic data structures.

3.7.4 Delete

Dynamic data structures must be explicitly created, which makes us wonder whether they also have to be explicitly released. The general answer is yes, but there are language-specific differences.

Delphi   In Delphi, New (p) can be used to create a new memory block. This block will then be used until it is released by the instruction Dispose (p). If we forget to release a block, that storage space will be used until the program ends, which can indeed lead to memory space problems. These delete operations can be difficult, which is often overlooked. Of course, they can be executed only provided that the objects are all still accessible.

For example, if we run a Dispose(head), the list head is deleted, but the other list elements remain intact. Unfortunately, although they are still there, they can no longer be accessed, because it is no longer possible to access head.next and no additional pointers are available to refer to these list elements. This situation means that the memory space required by the list is still occupied and cannot be released. The following code fragment shows how to properly delete a list:

```
procedure DeleteList;
   var p, q: Node;
begin
  p := head;
  while p <> nil do begin
     q := p.next;
     Dispose(p);
     p := q;
  end;
end;
```

Dangling pointer
Another problem that can arise is a *dangling pointer*. This is a pointer that points to an unspecified target. For example, if variables p and q are two pointers referring to the same object (for example, after a p := q assignment) and if a Dispose(p) is executed, p automatically takes the value NIL. However, because q pointed to the same object, this object was also deleted. Consequently, the value of q is now undefined, and an attempt to access q.data would lead to an error.

Java: Garbage Collector
Java uses a Garbage Collector, which automatically removes memory blocks that are no longer used. If a block can no longer be reached by a pointer, it is automatically released. In the case of our list, the head and tail have to be set to null to ensure that the Garbage Collector will release all list elements that can no longer be reached.

3.7.5 Other Examples for Dynamic Lists

There are other forms of dynamic lists. Depending on the specific application, it could be useful to use one or the other. This section briefly introduces various forms of lists. Section 4.2 describes these forms in more detail.

Doubly Linked List

An element has a successor and a predecessor

With this list form, the list element points not only to its successor but also to its predecessor. Although this makes the list somewhat more complicated, it allows easier execution in descending sort order (from the last element to the first).

Stack

Stack: push and pop

A stack is a pushdown automaton that uses two operations: *push* and *pop*. Push puts an element on top of the stack, whereas pop takes the top element from the stack and returns it. Such a stack works by the LIFO (last in, first out) principle, because pop always returns the object that has been inserted last.

Sorted List

Sorted list: elements are sorted in ascending order

With a sorted list, elements are not simply added to the beginning or the end but rather in the correct position. For example, the value 5 would be added after the value 3 but before the value 7. Consequently, it is easy to create a sorted printout of a list. If the list happens to be a doubly linked list, it could also be printed easily in ascending or descending order.

Let's draw some conclusions: The advantages of lists and similar linked structures with respect to arrays have been mentioned in several instances. So let's not forget to mention their drawbacks for the sake of completeness: In addition to the space taken by the pointers, accessing the nth element is slow, and the creation and deletion of many small dynamic objects may be costly.

3.7.6 Exercises

Task 1 (170 minutes): Priority Queue

Priority queue— now with pointers

Assume that several people are waiting in a line in front of a teller. Each person should get his or her turn, depending on how long she or he has been waiting. Unfortunately, the teller does not treat everybody waiting in line equally. He distinguishes the waiting customers as unpleasant, normal, or pleasant. Normal customers get priority over unpleasant ones. Pleasant customers get priority over normal and unpleasant ones. But among several persons of the same type, the one who has been waiting longest gets priority.

This problem is analogous to the last exercise, but this time the number of persons is not limited. For this reason, we have to use pointers. To complete this exercise, use an interface from task 1 in Section 3.6.5 and write an appropriate module.

Write an additional test program that calls these operations. You can use the test program you created in the last exercise. It requires only minimal modifications, because we are using a different module here.

Task 2 (10 minutes): Troubleshooting

Find the error in the following source code fragment:

```
New(p); p := nil;
```

4

Data Structures and Algorithms

Intensive dealing
with pointers Now that we have introduced static data structures as well as dynamic data structures (also called *pointers;* see Section 3.7), this chapter deals more intensively with that subject. Dynamic data structures are important, because the only way to create objects in object-oriented programming is to create them dynamically.

   This chapter begins with a discussion of data abstraction, which will help you understand the concept of an object-oriented class easily, then discusses algorithms that use dynamic data structures. Although such algorithms can also be used in COBOL, experience has shown that they rarely are, especially by programmers who made their way into the COBOL world through a crash course from a different discipline, where they did not get a chance to work with any programming language intensively. This chapter is particularly important for those who feel addressed by this statement.

4.1   Abstract Data Types

The tutorial shows a few preparatory steps for how programmers can create their own data types. Our discussion concentrates less on syntactic details (which have been dealt with in Section 3.4.1) than on how this operation works efficiently from the contents point of view. We know that data types are normally made available to various other programs. Therefore, the client needs to know only the essential things about the data type. In most cases, no detailed knowledge is required. Behind this concept is the term *abstraction*. The *abstract data structure* and *abstract data type* build on this abstraction.

4.1.1   Term: Abstraction

The term *abstraction* is interpreted as a generalization that allows us to better handle the complexity of a program. We can neglect unnecessary details and concentrate more on the essentials. The following two examples explain this concept.

CD player: power on, play, fast forward

Our first example uses a CD player, which all of us are familiar with. A CD player could well be thought of as a data type, offering operations such as power on, play, fast forward, and so on. The most important things behind the CD player remain hidden from the user (the client). Details such as printed circuits, sensor systems, and power supply do not directly concern the user. This is what makes the use of a CD player so simple: Users can concentrate on what is relevant to them.

String: join, substring, search

Another example is the data type string, which is normally predefined in many languages, offering operations such as join, substring, and search. Again, details such as memory representation or number of bits are hidden from the user. This facilitates the use of data types.

The aim is here to hide the implementation of data from the client, which is exactly what a data type should achieve. Data are accessed over a clearly defined interface. However, the important point is not that the clients of a module should not see those data but rather that it is not necessary that they see them. Returning to our example with the CD player, users indeed have the possibility (albeit not the most intuitive) to gain detailed knowledge of this CD player, but they don't need to know these details to be able to use the device!

Information hiding

This concept of abstraction is often called *information hiding* [Par72]. The abstract data structures (ADS) and abstract data type (ADT) discussed in the next two sections are based on this concept.

4.1.2   Abstract Data Structures

ADS: abstract data structure, an item

A data structure that any client can use by accessing clearly defined procedures, but with an open implementation, is called an *abstract data structure* (ADS). One good example is the Priority Queue, from the tasks in

Sections 3.6.5 and 3.7.6. Another example is a telephone directory (PhoneBook) with two procedures: Enter (to enter a data record) and Lookup (to search for a data record), as shown in Listings 4.1 and 4.2. For better readability, the exported names in the listings are printed in bold, as in the previous listings.

Listing 4.1. Delphi Implementation of PhoneBook

```
unit PhoneBook;

interface
   procedure Enter (name: String; phone: Integer);
   procedure Lookup (name: String; var phone: Integer);

implementation
   type
      Person = record
         name: String;
         phone: Integer;
      end;
   var
      book: array[1..1000] of Person;
      n: Integer;

   procedure Enter (name: String; phone: Integer);
   begin
      if n <= 1000 then begin
         book[n].name := name;
         book[n].phone := phone;
         Inc(n);
      end;
   end;

   procedure Lookup (name: String; var phone: Integer);
      var i: Integer;
   begin
      i := 1; phone := -1;
      while (i < n) and (phone = -1) do begin
         if book[i].name = name then begin phone := book[i].phone end;
         Inc(i);
      end;
   end;

initialization
   n := 1;
end.
```

Listing 4.2. Java Implementation of PhoneBook

```
class Person {
   String name;
   int phone;
};

public class Phonebook {
   static Person [] book;
   static int n;

   public static void enter (String name, int phone) {
      if (n <= 1000) {
         book[n].name = name;
         book[n].phone = phone;
         n++;
      }
   }

   public static int lookup (String name) {
      int i = 0;
      int phone = -1;
      while ((i < n) && (phone == -1)) {
         if (book[i].name.equals(name)) {phone = book[i].phone;};
         i++;
      }
      return phone;
   }

   static {
      book = new Person[1000];
      for (int i = 0; i < 1000; i++) {
         book[i] = new Person();
      }
      n = 0;
   }
}
```

These examples show that the implementation is open due to the interface.
These examples were implemented by using an array, but we could just as
well implement them with pointers. The telephone book could easily be
used through the two procedures Enter and Lookup. In addition, the implementation of the abstract data structure can be modified any time, without
having to change the programs that use it.

4.1.3 Abstract Data Types

ADT: abstract data type, arbitrary number of copies

The preceding abstract data structure has a major drawback: It works only for one telephone directory. If several are required, such as one for each state or one for private (home) and another one for work (office) purposes, we cannot use this structure.

The *abstract data type* (ADT) offers a solution for cases in which we need several structures of the same kind. This solution not only exports access procedures for a structure but also exports a type. Clients can create an arbitrary number of variables with this type. The difference between an ADS and an ADT is simple: The abstract data type packs the global variables that would be used in an ADS into one type and exports this type. Listings 4.3 and 4.4 show how such an abstract data type can be implemented.

Listing 4.3. Delphi Implementation of the Abstract Data Type PhoneBook

```delphi
unit PhoneBooks;

interface
   type
      Person = record
         name: String;
         phone: Integer;
      end;
      PhoneBook = record
         book: array[1..1000] of Person;
         n: Integer;
      end;
   procedure Enter (var pb: PhoneBook; name: String; phone: Integer);
   procedure Lookup (var pb: PhoneBook; n: String; var p: Integer);
   procedure Init (var pb: PhoneBook);

implementation

   procedure Enter (var pb: PhoneBook; name: String; phone: Integer);
   begin
      pb.book[pb.n].name := name;
      pb.book[pb.n].phone := phone;
      Inc(pb.n);
   end;

   procedure Lookup (var pb: PhoneBook; n: String; var p: Integer);
      var i: Integer;
   begin
```

```
      i := 1; p := -1;
      while (i < pb.n) and (p = -1) do begin
         if pb.book[i].name = n then begin p := pb.book[i].phone end;
         Inc(i);
      end;
   end;
   procedure Init (var pb: PhoneBook);
   begin
      pb.n := 1;
   end;
end.
```

This solution is not really an abstract data type in the true sense of the word, because the individual components of the record are exported. Although the clients do not need it, they could access it. The possibility with Delphi to implement complete abstract data types is provided by the language construct class (see also Section 5.1).

The parameter pb in the procedure Lookup is actually only an input parameter. For storage savings, the parameter is nevertheless defined by var (see also Section 3.5.1), but a declaration with const would also be appropriate.

Listing 4.4. Java Implementation of the Abstract Data Type PhoneBook

```
package PhoneBooks;

class Person {
   String name;
   int phone;
};

public class PhoneBook {
   Person [] book;
   int n;

   public static void init (PhoneBook pb) {
      pb.book = new Person[1000];
      for (int i = 0; i < 1000; i++) {
         pb.book[i] = new Person();
      }
      pb.n = 0;
   }

   public static void enter (PhoneBook pb, String name, int phone) {
      pb.book[pb.n].name = name;
```

```
      pb.book[pb.n].phone = phone;
      pb.n++;
  }

  public static int lookup (PhoneBook pb, String name) {
      int i = 0;
      int phone = -1;
      while ((i < n) && (phone == -1)) {
          if (pb.book[i].name.equals(name))
              {phone = pb.book[i].phone;};
          i++;
      }
      return phone;
  }
}
```

We should mention, for the sake of completeness, that the declaration of such procedures with static in Java is not customary. The methods (declared without static) described in Section 5.1 are much more common.

Additional parameter required   We can see clearly from the previous listings that each operation has a parameter of the type PhoneBook, which is then addressed in the procedure. Moreover, a procedure Init substitutes the initialization part of the abstract data structure. When using this ADS, we have to declare one (or several) variables of the type PhoneBook and subsequently initialize it with Init. The respective calls will then pass these variables as parameters. The following two short code fragments demonstrate a possible use.

Delphi
```
var home: PhoneBooks.PhoneBook;
...
PhoneBooks.Init(home);
PhoneBooks.Enter(home, 'Markus', 437242);
```

Java
```
PhoneBook home = new PhoneBook();
PhoneBook.init(home);
PhoneBook.enter(home, "Markus", 437242);
```

Abstract data types would have prevented the Y2K problem   The major advantage of abstract data types emerges from the fact that the Y2K problem (see Chapter 1) could have been solved easily if the date had been made available as an abstract data type. Considering that the components of clients remain hidden, it doesn't matter whether the number representing the year is composed of two or four digits. Consequently, the year could change without the other programs taking notice and without the need to change any of these programs.

An abstract data type *Date* could have attributes *day* and *mon*. Functions could compute the difference between two dates, to check the day of a *Date*, and so on. When the Y2K problem became obvious, an attribute *year* had to be added and all the functions had to be changed. However, application programs would not have needed to be changed.

4.1.4 Exercises

Task 1 (170 minutes): Relations

This task is based on a concrete example. When implementing object-oriented databases, it is necessary to store each data structure (object) in the main memory and a second time on the disk. For this reason, each object has two addresses. One is an OID (Object Identifier)—the address of the copy on the disk—and the second is the usual (transient) storage address.

Naturally, a pointer that refers to an object can include only one address. To obtain the second address, we have to maintain allocation tables (the transient address adr corresponds to the disk address oid). *B-trees* or *hash lists* (see also Sections 4.3 and 4.4) normally implement such lists.

Implement a module PersRel that implements an allocation (OID transient address). To keep things simple, you could use a sorted linear list. As a unique OID—that is, for the disk address—use a character list (32 characters maximum) to allow for simpler test cases. If an attempt is made to insert an OID a second time, it should not be executed and, instead, the global error variable err should be set to TRUE.

In addition to the transient memory address, a property (quality) is stated during the insert operation, which can also be queried. The creation and initialization of a relation should be done by calling the procedure Init.

The interface of the module should look as follows:

Delphi
```
type
    Relation = ^RelationDesc;
    RelationDesc = record
```

```
      ...
    end;

function Adr (r: Relation; oid: String): Integer;
procedure Delete (r: Relation; oid: String);
function Entries (r: Relation): Integer;
procedure Insert (r: Relation; oid: String; adr: Integer; q: Boolean);
function Quality (r: Relation; oid: String): Boolean;
procedure Init (var r: Relation);

var err: Boolean;
```

Java

```
package Relations;
public class Relation {

  ...
  public static boolean err;
  public static int adr (String oid) {...}
  public static void delete (String oid) {...}
  public static int entries () {...}
  public static void insert (String oid, int adr, boolean q) {...}
  public static boolean quality (String oid) {...}
  public static void init() {...}
}
```

Test your solution for PersRel carefully in a separate test program.

Task 2 (10 minutes): Abstract Data Type

Converting from ADS to ADT

Assume the following abstract data structure List:

```
unit List;

interface
  type
    ListItem = record
       x: Integer;
    end;
  procedure Enter (item: ListItem);
  procedure Print;

implementation
  var
```

```
      l: array [0..30] of ListItem;
      n: Integer;

  procedure Enter (item: ListItem);
  begin
    l[n].x := item;
    Inc(n);
  end;

  procedure Print;
    var i: Integer;
  begin
    for i := 0 to n - 1 do begin
      WriteLn(l[i].x);
    end;
  end;

initialization
  n := 0;
end.
```

Building on this basis, implement an abstract data type Lists.List. This exercise is identical for Java users, because it is not concerned with language details but the basic concept of abstract data types.

4.2 Dynamic Data Structures in Detail

Dynamic data structures and the data type list, as well as stacks and sorted lists, were briefly introduced in Chapter 3. The following section discusses these structures in detail.

4.2.1 Linear Lists

A linear list is the dynamic data structure most frequently used. In contrast to an array, it offers the advantage that it can grow or shrink so that it always occupies only the storage space required. Another advantage is that it greatly facilitates insert and delete operations.

Sorted list!   We have described unsorted linear lists in Section 3.7. This section discusses sorted lists in detail. With these lists, insert operations are always

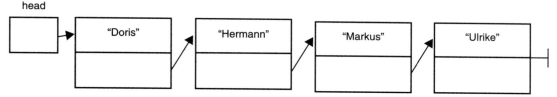

Figure 4.1 Example for a sorted list of character strings.

effected in the correct position, according to the sort order. This is similar to insertion sort, which is introduced in Section 4.4.4. Figure 4.1 shows an example for a sorted list of character strings.

Inserting in a sorted list is a little more complex

The implementation of insert operations for a sorted list is a little more complex, whereas search and delete operations do not differ much from unsorted lists. This is an advantage, but only in the special case when the element we search for (or the element to be deleted) does not exist in the list. If this occurs, we can abort the search process when an element bigger than the one we are looking for is found in the list. For example, if we were to look for the value "Gertraud" in Figure 4.1, we would not have to search the entire list to find out that the element does not exist; instead, we could stop searching at the element "Hermann."

"Dummy" element

The following source code examples for sorted lists introduce another novelty, the so-called dummy element at the beginning of a list. This means that an "empty" list—a list without any elements—has a head node (such an empty list is shown in Figure 4.2). The next pointer of the last list element points to the head node, resulting in a *ring list*. In an empty list, the head node points to itself.

Although this trick will always cost us at least minor additional storage space, the special case of inserting things into an empty list, which we know from Section 3.7.3, does not have to be fully tested in all cases. The insertion concentrates now only on finding the correct position in the list—the

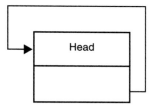

Figure 4.2 Empty list with dummy element.

predecessor node of the new element. In the case of an empty list, this is always the dummy element, and the new element is inserted after it. This situation is shown in the following source code fragments:

Delphi

```
procedure Insert (val: Integer);
   var cur, prev, x: Node;
begin
   cur := head.next; prev := head; // head is dummy element
   while (cur <> head) and (cur.val < val) do begin // find element
      prev := cur; cur := cur.next;
   end;
   if (cur <> head) and (cur.val = val) then exit; // not new
   New(x); x.val := val; x.next := cur; // create as new
   prev.next := x;
end;
```

Java

```
public static void insert (int val) {
   SortedList cur, prev, x;
   cur = head.next; prev = head; // head is dummy element
   while ((cur != head) && (cur.val < val)) { // find element
      prev = cur; cur = cur.next;
   }
   if ((cur != head) && (cur.val == val))
      {return;} // already included
   x = new SortedList(); x.val = val; x.next = cur; // create as new
   prev.next = x;
}
```

Special case: doubly linked list

Another special case of a list is a doubly linked list. In such a list, each list element points not only to its successor but also to its predecessor. Figure 4.3 shows an example of a doubly linked list.

This approach has the advantage that we do not always have to maintain the predecessor of an element (for example, when deleting), because the predecessor can always be determined by a single pointer access. Moreover, when working with a sorted doubly linked list, we can execute the list easily in reverse order.

Which is more efficient?

Finally, we need to ask whether sorted lists are more efficient than unsorted lists. Intuitively, we would answer this question with a clear yes,

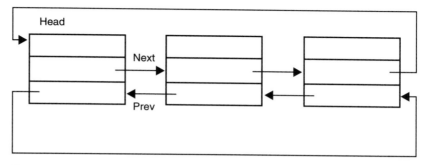

Figure 4.3 A doubly linked list.

because we do not have to execute the entire list if the respective element is not present during a search or delete operation. The truth is that this does not justify the increased cost of insert operations. For such cases, the trees described in Section 4.3 would be much better.

4.2.2 Stacks

Stack: LIFO A stack is a special data structure that manages elements in a *pushdown memory*, which is based on the "last in, first out" (LIFO) principle, similar to a stack of books. The book placed on top of the stack is the first one removed. Figure 4.4 shows a stack with elements of the integer type, where the following actions are taken consecutively: Insert value 1, remove a value, insert value 5, insert value 9, remove a value, insert value 3.

Java implementation on the book CD A stack like this has two main operations: Push and Pop. Push is applied to put a new element onto the stack. Pop supplies the element last placed on the stack and removes it from the stack. Listing 4.5 shows a possible Delphi implementation of this data structure. For space-saving reasons, the Java implementation is available on the book CD.

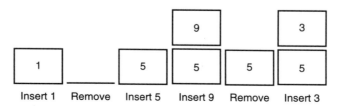

Figure 4.4 Example for a stack.

Listing 4.5. Delphi Implementation of a Stack

```
unit Stack;

interface
   procedure Push (val: Integer);
   procedure Pop (var val: Integer);
implementation
   type
      Node = ^NodeDesc;
      NodeDesc = record
         val: Integer;
         next: Node;
      end;
   var
      top: Node; // pointer refers to top (first) element
   procedure Push (val: Integer);
      var x: Node;
   begin
      New(x);
      x.val := val;
      x.next := top; // points to formerly first element
      top := x; // new first element
   end;
   procedure Pop (var val: Integer);
      var h: Node;
   begin
      if top = nil then begin val := -1; exit; end;
      h := top; // formerly first element for memory release
      val := top.val;
      top := top.next; // second element becomes first
      Dispose(h);
   end;
initialization
   top := nil;
end.
```

4.2.3 Queues

Queue: FIFO In contrast to a stack, a queue works by the (fairer) "first in, first out" (FIFO) principle and can therefore be compared with a regular queue. Whoever

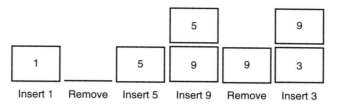

Insert 1   Remove   Insert 5   Insert 9   Remove   Insert 3

Figure 4.5 Example for a queue (see also Figure 3.4).

comes first will be served first (for example, a checkout line in a supermarket). Figure 4.5 shows a queue with elements of the integer type, running the following actions consecutively: Insert value 1, remove a value, insert value 5, insert value 9, remove a value, insert value 3.

Delphi implementation on book CD

Such a data structure has two main operations: Enqueue and Dequeue. Enqueue is used to add a new element to the queue. Dequeue supplies the element that has been sitting in the queue longest and removes it. Listing 4.6 shows a possible Java implementation of this data structure. For space saving reasons, the Delphi implementation is available on the book CD.

Listing 4.6. Java Implementation of a Queue

```java
public class Queue {
    Queue next;
    int val;
    static Queue top;

    public static void enqueue (int val) {
        Queue x, cur;
        x = new Queue(); x.val = val; x.next = null; // create element
        if (top == null) {top = x;}
        else {
            cur = top;
            while (cur.next != null) {cur = cur.next;}
            cur.next = x;
        }
    }

    public static int dequeue () {
        int val;
        if (top == null) {return -1;}
        val = top.val;
            top = top.next; // second element becomes first
```

```
        return val;
    }
    public static int elements () {
        Queue x;
        int result = 0;
        x = top;
        while (x != null) {
            result ++;
            x = x.next;
        }
        return result;
    }
    static {
        top = null;
    }
}
```

4.2.4 Exercises

Task 1 (200 minutes): Queue

Implement a dynamic data structure Queue. The module should be based on a definition that looks as follows:

Delphi

```
type
    Queue = ...; // should be found by itself
    Proc = procedure (x: Integer);

procedure EnQueue (var q: Queue; elem: Integer);
(* appends the element elem to the queue q *)

procedure DeQueue (var q: Queue; var elem: Integer);
(* returns the first element (elem) of the queue q and deletes this element
from the queue. If the queue is empty, then the value of elem is undefined *)

procedure NewQueue (var q: Queue);
(* creates a new (empty) queue *)

function NrOfElems (q: Queue): Integer;
(* returns the number of elements in the queue *)

function Full (q: Queue): Boolean;
(* returns TRUE if the queue is full; otherwise FALSE *)
```

```
function Empty (q: Queue): Boolean;
(* returns TRUE if the queue is empty; otherwise FALSE *)

procedure Iterate (q: Queue; p: Proc);
(* iterates over all elements of q *)
```

_____

Java

```java
public class Queue {
   // ...

   public static void enQueue (int elem) {
      // appends the element elem to the queue
   }

   public static void deQueue (int elem) {
      // returns the first element (elem) from the queue and deletes
      // this element from the queue. If the queue is empty, then
      // the value of elem is undefined
   }

   public static in nrOfElems () {
      // returns the number of elements in the queue
   }

   public static bool full () {
      // returns TRUE if the queue is full; otherwise FALSE
   }

   public static bool empty () {
      // returns TRUE if the queue is empty; otherwise FALSE
   }

   public static void print () {
      // prints all elements of q
   }
}
```

Test your module carefully in an independent test program.

Task 2 (20 minutes): Discussion

Comparing dynamic and static data structures

Compare dynamic and static data structures and list the respective benefits and drawbacks. Take into consideration how you would have solved task 1 with a static data structure.

Trees

Trees: particularly efficient data structures

As mentioned in Section 4.2.1, sorted lists are not really the best data structures to implement fast search and insert operations. *Trees* are a better option. A tree is a data structure that allows you to insert various elements, just as you would insert elements in a list. However, the structure of such a tree is not linear (that is, one element after the other), but treelike (with several branches).

Although both trees and lists are normally available in class libraries, the tutorial in this section presents the underlying concept of trees. It will be helpful to get a rough idea of the concept, and it is a good example for the use of pointers.

The following sections first explain the term *tree* and then describe the special data structure of a binary tree. Finally, a balanced tree is briefly described as a special case.

4.3.1 Definition of Terms

A tree is a finite set of nodes and edges

A tree is (by a somewhat scientific formulation) a finite set of nodes and edges, where each node has exactly one father node. The only exception to this rule is the root of the tree—the node from which everything originates. Figure 4.6 shows an example of a tree.

The following terms, based on Figure 4.6, are important in connection with trees:

- **Root:** This is the head node, comparable to the head of a list. The root is labeled R in the figure.

- **Father node:** Each node under which there is at least one other node is a father node. The father node can also be thought of as the root of a subtree. All nodes labeled I or R in the figure are father nodes.

- **Son:** A node underneath the father node.

- **Leaf:** Each node that is not a father node. These nodes are labeled L in the figure.

- **Inner node:** Each node that is neither a root nor a leaf. These nodes are labeled I in the figure.

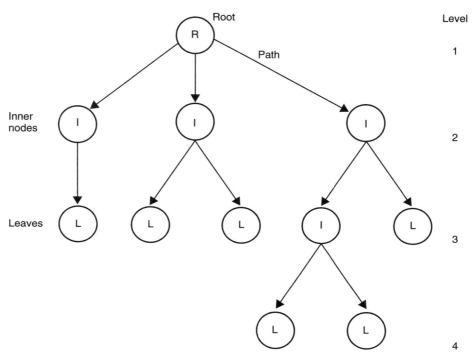

Figure 4.6 Example of a tree.

- **Degree of a node:** Number of sons.

- **Height of a tree:** The maximum levels of all nodes. The tree of our example in Figure 4.6 has a height of 4.

- **Path:** The sequence of edges between two nodes.

- **Ordered tree:** A tree in which the sequence of sons is fixed for each node. One example for such a tree is the binary lookup tree discussed in the next section.

4.3.2 Binary Trees

Binary tree: each node has at most two sons

A binary tree is an ordered tree, where each node has a maximum of two sons (= maximum degree two). Such a tree can be defined by the following type (if the element is of type integer):

Delphi
```
Tree = ^TreeDesc;
TreeDesc = record
   val: Integer;
   left, right: Tree;
end;
```

Java
```
class Tree {
   int val;
   Tree left, right;
}
```

The declaration of this type becomes clear when taking another close look at the definition of the term *father node:* each node under which there is at least one other node. A father node can also be thought of as the root of a subtree. Both the left and right sons are then father nodes and, in turn, the roots of the trees (or subtrees) underneath them. In the case of a leaf, the `left` and the `right` pointers have a value of NIL.

Binary search tree　　The most important case of a binary tree is the binary search tree. This tree is always based on the rule that each right son includes a value greater than or equal to the value of the father node and each left son includes a value smaller than the value of the father node. Figure 4.7 shows an example. The binary search tree is extremely popular, so when speaking of a binary tree, most actually mean this special case.

Binary search: an efficient method　　The special arrangement of the nodes in a binary search tree allows simple searches. Initially, the value we look for is compared with the root.

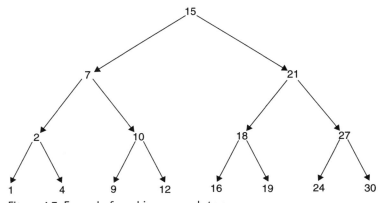

Figure 4.7 Example for a binary search tree.

If the value is not equal (which means that it was found), a decision has to be made as to whether the lookup value is greater or smaller than the value of the root. Accordingly, we have to continue our search in the right or left subtree in the same way. This search is continued until either the value is found or a leaf has been reached. In the latter case, the value is not included in the binary tree. The following source code fragments show a way to implement such a binary search.

Delphi
```
function Search (val: Integer): Boolean;
   var p: Tree;
begin
  p := root;
  while (p <> nil) and (p.val <> val) do begin
    if val < p.val then p := p.left else p := p.right;
  end;
  result := p <> nil
end;
```

Java
```
public static boolean search (int val) {
   BinTree p;
   p = root;
   while ((p != null) && (p.val != val))
     if (val < p.val) p = p.left; else p = p.right;
   return (p != null);
}
```

Desk test: hands-on experiment   To better understand these algorithms, we recommend running a desk test—for example, to search for the values 9, 21, and 13, in this order, in Figure 4.7.

As opposed to a sorted list, a binary search tree is characterized by this efficient search method. Although a list will always be walked through consecutively so that no element can be skipped, this approach always skips one of the two trees, making the search operation (and consequently the insert operation and so forth) much more efficient. This becomes clear when we investigate the number of search steps required, depending on the number of nodes. For example, if we need five search steps with 63 nodes, we require six steps for 127 nodes and seven steps for 255 nodes. Therefore, the search time is proportional to the logarithm of the tree size.

Inserting

Inserting into a binary tree
The central problem of an insert operation is that each value has to be inserted in the correct position. A simple binary search tree is based on the rule that the new value is always inserted as a leaf. This reduces the big problem to the smaller one of finding the corresponding father node. This node must be either a leaf itself or have not more than one son. Once the corresponding position is found, a new node has to be created to store the value to be inserted, and this node must become a son of the father node found. This approach becomes clearer in the following source code examples:

Delphi

```
procedure Insert (val: Integer);
    var p, f, n: Tree;
begin
  p := root;
  while p <> nil do begin
    f := p;
    if val < p.val then p := p.left else p := p.right;
  end;
  New(n); n.val := val; n.left := nil; n.right := nil;
  if root = nil then begin
    root := n
  end
  else begin
    if val < f.val then f.left := n else f.right := n;
  end;
end;
```

Java

```
public static void insert (int val) {
BinTree p, father, n;
p = root; father = p;
while (p != null) {
  father = p;
  if (val < p.val) {p = p.left;} else {p = p.right;}
}
n = new BinTree();
n.val = val; n.left = null; n.right = null;
```

```
    if (root == null) {root = n;}
    else {
      if (val < father.val) {father.left = n;}
      else {father.right = n;}
    }
}
```

Why not solve the insert problem recursively?   We said in Section 3.3.6 that recursive procedures are particularly useful for recursive data structures. Considering that each tree consists of two (sub)trees, a binary tree is an excellent example for such a recursive data structure. In other words, we could also solve the insert problem recursively:

Delphi

```
procedure InsertRec (var t: Tree; val: Integer);
begin
  if t = nil then begin
    New(t); t.val := val; t.left := nil; t.right := nil;
  end
  else begin
    if val < t.val then begin
      InsertRec(t.left, val);
    end
    else begin
      InsertRec(t.right, val);
    end;
  end;
end;
```

In this connection, the var parameter is of particular importance. For example, with a recursive call such as InsertRec(t.left, val), we could create a new node and return it as t.left.

Java

```
public static BinTree insertRec (BinTree t, int val) {
  if (t == null) {
    t = new BinTree();
    t.val = val; t.left = null; t.right = null;
    return t;
  }
  else {
```

```
        if (val < t.val) {
            t.left = insertRec(t.left, val); return t;
        }
        else {
            t.right = insertRec(t.right, val); return t;
        }
    }
}
```

To better understand these algorithms, Figure 4.8 shows a tree built gradually as the values 7, 2, 10, 1, 4, 9, and 12 are inserted.

Deleting

Deleting a node from the tree is relatively complicated

Deleting an element from a tree is relatively complicated and represents the only drawback of trees versus linked lists, apart from a slightly larger storage consumption. It is easy to understand where this complexity comes from if we consider what happens when an inner node is deleted. When a node is deleted, another node has to move up, so, for example, a leaf could become an inner node. Figure 4.9 shows this situation. In this example, the value 2 was deleted from the tree of Figure 4.8.

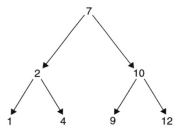

Figure 4.8 Example of the creation of a tree.

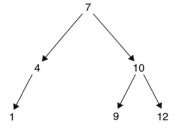

Figure 4.9 The binary tree of Figure 4.8 after deletion of the value 2.

Logical delete: known from COBOL

One easy way to implement a delete operation for a tree is to delete the element only logically. This is not really a memory-saving approach, because it merely marks the node to be deleted as deleted but leaves the node in the tree. Each node requires an attribute deleted, which is set to TRUE if the element is to be deleted. All algorithms, such as search, insert, and so on, must ignore a node marked as deleted. This is similar to deleting data records from index-sequential files in COBOL, because it also merely does a logical deletion.

The book CD contains an algorithm you can use to delete an element from a binary tree.

Traversing

Traversing a tree: pre-order, post-order and in-order

An important operation that can be executed on trees is the *traversing* (= stepping through the elements) of a tree. The tree is traversed in a certain sequence, and a certain operation (such as print) is executed on each element. For example, this would be a way to print all elements of a tree. Due to the traversing sequence, we distinguish between pre-order, post-order, and in-order traversing.

- **Pre-order:** First, the operation is executed on the root; then the left and right subtrees are traversed in pre-order sequence.

- **Post-order:** First the left and then the right subtrees are traversed in post-order; then the operation is applied to the root.

- **In-order:** First, the left subtree is traversed in in-order sequence; then the operation is applied to the root, and finally the right subtree is traversed in-order. This sequence means that the tree is traversed in ascending sort order.

Figure 4.10 shows all these traversing types.

Recursive procedures can be used to traverse a tree easily. This could look as follows in algorithm notation:

Pre-order

```
procedure Preorder (t: Tree);
begin
  if t <> NIL then begin
    ... process t.val ...
    Preorder(t.left);
```

```
      Preorder(t.right);
   end;
end;
```

Post-order
```
procedure Postorder (t: Tree);
begin
   if t <> NIL then begin
      Postorder(t.left);
      Postorder(t.right);
      ... process t.val ...
   end;
end;
```

In-order
```
procedure Inorder (t: Tree);
begin
   if t <> NIL then begin
      Inorder(t.left);
      ... process t.val ...
      Inorder(t.right);
   end;
end;
```

4.3.3 Balanced Trees

A binary search tree carries the risk of degenerating, because each new value is inserted merely as a leaf. This risk can be better explained by an

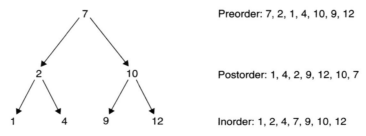

Preorder: 7, 2, 1, 4, 10, 9, 12

Postorder: 1, 4, 2, 9, 12, 10, 7

Inorder: 1, 2, 4, 7, 9, 10, 12

Figure 4.10 Pre-order, post-order, and in-order.

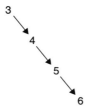

Figure 4.11 Example of a degenerated tree.

example. If the values 3, 4, 5, and 6 are consecutively inserted in a tree, we obtain the tree shown in Figure 4.11.

A tree can degenerate to a list

The tree shown in Figure 4.11 is not different from a normal sorted list. Therefore, in the worst case (and only then), algorithms, such as search or insert, are not more efficient than with a list. This also means that a tree would no longer offer any advantage when inserting elements in sorted sequence. For this reason, elements should be inserted in a randomly mixed way, although this is not always easy.

B-tree: basis for IS files in COBOL

To neutralize this drawback, special types of trees allow us to rearrange the nodes such that all leaves are (ideally) on the same level. Examples of such balanced trees are *Red-Black trees* or *B-trees* [Sed88]. These trees are based on a similar principle, but they are much more efficient and should preferably be used if available in a class library. B-trees are particularly important in this respect and are often used for sorted file management. Such trees support several keys for each node to reduce the number of time-consuming disk access processes. For example, the index-sequential files of COBOL are based on this tree type.

We do not discuss this type of tree here, because its implementation is rather complicated.

4.3.4 Exercises

Task 1 (180 minutes): BinTree Queue

Implement the following dynamic data structure Queue by means of a binary search tree. The module should be based on a definition that looks as follows:

Delphi

```
const
    PRE = 0; INO = 1; POST = 2;
```

```
type
   Queue = ...;
   Proc = procedure (x: Integer);

procedure EnQueue (var q: Queue; elem: Integer);
(* appends the element elem to the queue q *)

procedure NewQueue (var q: Queue);
(* creates a new (empty) queue *)

function NrOfElems (q: Queue): Integer;
(* returns the number of elements in the queue *)

function Full (q: Queue): Boolean;
(* returns TRUE if the queue is full; otherwise FALSE *)

function Empty (q: Queue): Boolean;
(* returns TRUE if the queue is empty; otherwise FALSE *)

procedure Iterate (q: Queue; p: Proc; s: Integer);
(* iterates over all elements of q in sequence s *)
```

Java

```java
public class Queue {
public final static int PRE = 0;
public final static int IN = 1;
public final static int POST = 2;
// ...

public static void enQueue (int elem) {
   // appends the element elem to the queue
}

public static int nrOfElems () {
   // returns the number of elements in the queue
}

public static bool full () {
   // returns TRUE if the queue is full; otherwise FALSE
}

public static bool empty () {
   // returns TRUE if the queue is empty; otherwise FALSE
}
```

```
public static void print (int s) {
    // prints all elements in sequence s
}
}
```

Deletion is omitted

For the sake of simplicity, the preceding examples ignore delete operations. You should test your module in your own test program. Of course, this test program could be a slightly adapted version of the one you used for task 1 in Section 4.2.4.

Furthermore, a queue is normally not implemented with the help of a binary tree. We just used this element to save you the time needed to implement a test driver.

4.4 Algorithms

This section provides a brief introduction to various standard algorithms. Normally, these algorithms are provided by class libraries or procedure collections, so all we have to do is to call the respective procedure. For this reason, it is not absolutely necessary to know all the details of the implementation. However, a rough insight into some important basics, as described in this section, is useful. The following books are recommended for those interested in learning more about standard algorithms:

- Sedgewick, *Algorithms* [Sed88]. This is one of the best textbooks on the subject. It is considered the standard reference, recommended for all interested readers. It introduces all algorithms in the Pascal programming language.

- Wirth, *Algorithms + Data Structures = Programs* [Wir85]. This concise book discusses the B-tree in detail. The author uses the Modula-2 programming language, which is similar to Pascal or Delphi.

- Cormen, Leiserson, and Rivest, *Introduction to Algorithms* [CLR01]. Throughout this book, the authors anchor their discussion of algorithms with current examples drawn from molecular biology, business, and engineering. Each section ends with short discussions of related historical material, often discussing original research in each area of algorithms. Regardless of the chosen language, this text deserves a close look for extending the range and performance of real-world software.

4.4.1 Heaps

Heap: a data structure for sort operations
The previous sections presented several data structures, where elements are inserted by using an insert operation and removed by using a delete operation. During such operations—for example, a sort operation—the following special case occurs relatively often:

- `Insert (x)` should insert x into the data structure.

- `Remove (x)` should remove the largest element from the data structure and return it in x.

Inserting and removing is fast
For example, this data structure could be solved with an unsorted or even a sorted list. Unfortunately, neither solution is satisfactory, because the former allows fast insertion but removing is slow, whereas the latter allows fast removal but insertion is slow. A data structure called heap could be used for such a special case, because it allows both fast insertion and fast removal.

Binary tree as an array: a heap is implemented as a binary tree and stored as an array
A heap is implemented as a binary tree (not as a binary search tree!), where the tree is stored in an array. This array maintains a special heap order, by which the father must always be greater than both his sons (naturally, this applies to each subtree in turn) and the father and son of an element a[i] can both be determined by one array access. The father of a[i] is defined by a[i div 2], and the sons are defined by a[2 * i] and a[2 * i + 1].

Figure 4.12 shows this data structure as a heap in the well-known binary tree representation with pointers (left) and in array form (right). Contrary to binary search trees, there is no ordering between the two children of a node. The value of the left child could be smaller than, equal to, or greater than the value of the right child. However, the value of the parent is always less than or equal to the value of the children, which means that the root has the smallest value of the entire structure.

We now introduce the insert and delete operations. Both operations are based on the rule that first, an element is either inserted or deleted, and next, the heap order is restored by a suitable procedure:

- **Insert:** The new element is added as a leaf to the back of the heap; subsequently, the heap order is restored, and this will always require only a few swaps.

| 16 | 14 | 12 | 10 | 8 | 6 | 4 |

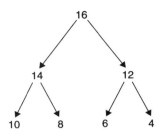

Figure 4.12 Comparing the binary tree and the array representations of a heap.

- **Remove the largest element:** The first element of the array is removed, because it is always the biggest element by the heap order. Subsequently, the last element is moved to the first position, and the heap order is restored.

Listings 4.7 and 4.8 show these algorithms in pseudocode.

Listing 4.7. Inserting an Element in a Heap

```
procedure Insert (x: Integer);
   n := n + 1; a[n] := x;
   UpHeap(n);
end Insert;

procedure UpHeap (pos: Integer);
   x := a[pos];
   while (pos > 1) & (x > a[pos DIV 2]) do
      a[pos] := a[pos DIV 2]; pos := pos DIV 2
   end;
   (* (pos = 1) or (x <= a[pos DIV 2]) *)
   a[pos] := x ;
end UpHeap;
```

Listing 4.8. Deleting an Element from a Heap

```
procedure Delete (var x: Integer);
   x := a[1];
   a[1] := a[n]; n := n - 1;
```

```
    DownHeap(1);
end Insert;

procedure DownHeap (pos: Integer);
  x := a[pos];
  loop
    if pos > n div 2 then exit end; (* no more sons *)
    i := 2 * pos;
    if (i < n) and (a[i] < a[i + 1]) then i := i + 1 end;
    if x > a[i] then exit end; (* both sons smaller than x *)
    a[pos] := a[i]; pos := i;
  end;
  (* (pos > n DIV 2) or (x > a[i]) *)
  a[pos] := x ;
end DownHeap;
```

A heap is used in situations that require elements to be removed from a set in ascending order of value, beginning with the smallest. A typical example is a set of processes to be ordered according to time or priority.

4.4.2 Graphs

Example for graphs: a road network

Graphs are a generalization of trees used to represent different situations, such as a road network between two locations or a network plan, by means of a data structure. Various standard algorithms from graph theory can be used to produce important results, such as the shortest path between two points or the critical path in a network plan. Figure 4.13 shows an example for a graph, where the nodes could represent railroad stations.

A graph could be declared as follows:

Delphi
```
Node = ^NodeDesc;
NodeDesc = record
  marked: BOOLEAN; // serves as an identifier for various algorithms
  data: ...; // values to be stored
  sons: array[1..MAX_SONS] of Node;
end;
```

Java
```
class Node {
  bool marked; // serves as an identifier for various algorithms
```

```
    ... data; // values to be stored
    Node sons[];
}
```

Standard algorithms for graphs

The attribute marked used here serves as an identifier to tell us whether the node has already been visited during an iteration, because there is no predefined sequence, as opposed to a list or tree. Building on this data type, we could implement various algorithms, which are mentioned here only briefly, because they are normally supplied by procedure collections:

DFS and BFS
- **Iterating all nodes:** Depth-First-Search (DFS: visits faraway nodes first) and Breadth-First-Search (BFS: visits the neighborhood first).

- **Smallest spanning tree:** The graph is transformed into a tree by deleting individual edges (so that each node, except the root, will have only one predecessor). The edges are deleted in such a way that the sum of the weights of all remaining edges is a minimum. Application: Road network between two given locations so that each location can be reached but where the road mileage to be constructed is a minimum.

- **Shortest path:** Calculates the path with the lowest weight between two nodes—for example, to calculate the least cost for a trip between two locations.

- **Graph input and output:** These algorithms serve to save graphs to a file.

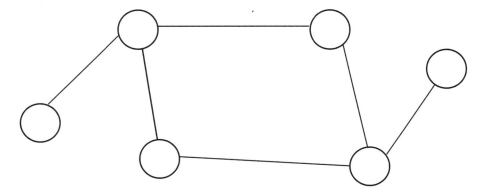

Figure 4.13 Example for a graph.

4.4.3 Hashing

A hash algorithm
has order O(1)

Hashing is a fast search method of order O(1); it is much faster than the linear search (in a list) with an order of only O(n). Moreover, hashing is also faster than a binary search in a binary search tree (see Section 4.3.2) with order O(log n).

O-notation

Orders can be assigned to algorithms based on the algorithms' speed. We first find out how an algorithm's speed changes in relation to the number of elements to be processed. The simplest case is order O(n) (read "O of n"), which means that duration depends linearly on the number of elements. For example, if an algorithm takes 1 second for three elements, then it needs 10 seconds for thirty elements (that is, exactly the tenfold duration). A good example for such behavior is searching a linear list. Because the entire list has to be processed, the duration of the search process depends linearly on the number of elements.

However, an algorithm's duration does not always depend linearly on the number of elements. An extreme example for this situation is the *bubble sort algorithm*, where each element is compared with each other element and where any two elements may be swapped. We actually have a situation with two nested loops, where almost all elements are normally visited, so the order is $O(n^2)$.

For example, if it takes 1 second for one element, then 100 seconds (10^2) are required for ten elements. Another extreme example for this situation is O(1), which means that the duration of the algorithm is constant and does not depend on the number of elements. If it takes 1 second for one element, it will also take only 1 second for a hundred elements. A good example is the hash algorithm discussed in this section.

How could a
listing of all
employees of a
country be
stored?

The idea behind the hash algorithm is taken from real life. Assume, for example, that we want to store a listing of all employees of a country (admittedly an ambitious goal). How could we achieve this goal? An unsorted list or a binary tree (sorted by names) is unsuitable,

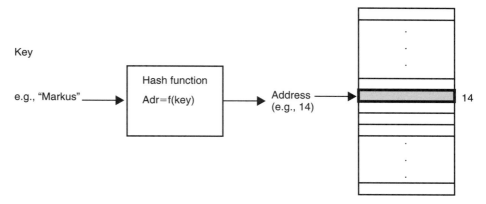

Figure 4.14 Functionality of a hash function.

for logical reasons. Instead, we will use the social security number as our key.

For example, if we stored all employee listings in an array—although hard to imagine—we could determine the index by which an employee is stored directly from the social security number. This task, here assumed by the social security number, also offers a hash function. Our goal is to use a key (which does not even have to be unique) to find an address at which the element we are looking for is stored. Figure 4.14 shows how a hash function works.

Large value ranges can be mapped onto smaller ones

A hash function also allows mapping of large value ranges (for example, all employees of a location) onto small ones. If we use the huge array mentioned earlier, we would obtain a result with many large gaps. Therefore, a smaller array is sufficient, where the index can be determined by a hash function.

A detailed description of all kinds of hash functions would go beyond the scope and purpose of this book, and it is also not necessary to understand and apply these principles. Rather, it is important to understand that these functions should be simple and fast, and they should also avoid collisions. However, such collisions—such as when a hash function calculates the same result for two different values—are not forbidden. Various techniques (including overflow lists) are available to solve these problems.

Sort algorithms: bubble sort, insertion sort, quick sort, heap sort, merge sort

4.4.4 Sort Algorithms

Almost every program needs to sort a wide range of values, for example, to sort customers by sales volume or just to print an alphabetical list of all service buyers. For this reason, sorting is a common programming task. The best-known, but also—unfortunately—the most overused sort algorithm (at least in smaller programs) is the bubble sort, where each element is compared with each other one. Naturally, this is a very inefficient method and should be avoided. For this reason, this section shows alternative methods, which are normally implemented in various class libraries.

The SORT instruction

- **Insertion sort:** This is a fairly efficient method, provided, however, that the data are rebuilt. The individual records are inserted directly in the correct places. This corresponds roughly to the SORT instruction of COBOL, which can be used to create a sorted SORT file from an existing unsorted file, as we know.

- **Quick sort:** This algorithm is based on the "divide and conquer" principle. The file is divided into two parts, and each part is subsequently sorted independently from one another. Listing 4.9 shows the basic principle of this algorithm in algorithmic notation, where the parameters used—d and u—specify the partial file within the original file to be sorted. The call Quicksort(1, n) sorts the entire file if n is the index of the last element. Proper reordering of the elements is then done in the procedure Partition.

- **Heap sort:** This algorithm is based on the operations introduced in Section 4.4.1. The idea is simple: building a heap that contains the elements to be sorted. Subsequently, all these elements are removed in the correct sequence.

- **Merge sort:** This algorithm corresponds to a sort algorithm defined by standard in COBOL. MERGE can merge previously sorted files to an output file. Merge sort works such that a given (unsorted) file is divided into two halves, and the two halves are then sorted (recursively) and finally joined (merged) again. Merge sort is the preferred method to sort a linked list.

Listing 4.9. Basic Structure of Quick Sort

```
procedure Quicksort (d, u: Integer);
    var i: Integer;
begin
    if u > d then begin
        i := Partition(u, d);
```

```
        Quicksort(d, i - 1);
        Quicksort(i + 1, u);
    end;
end;
```

We can see from the preceding discussion that there are also two different types of sorting: file sorting and memory sorting. Merge sort is appropriate for the previous task and most others for the latter.

4.4.5 Exercises

Task 1 (10 minutes): Heap

Heap: yes or no? Consider the array in Figure 4.15. Determine whether this array represents a heap, as discussed in Section 4.4.1. If so, draw the heap in graph form. If not, explain your answer.

Task 2 (170 minutes): Hash Table

Write a program that checks the spelling of words by searching a dictionary for each word and reporting an error if it is not found in that dictionary.

Instead of storing all correct words in a dictionary (which would take huge storage space), use the following approach, based on a hash table. The dictionary is stored as a bit list with length n, where n should be selected to be very large in this case (say, 100,000). Each correct word is mapped onto a range of $0..n-1$ by means of a hash function, and the corresponding bit is set in the dictionary.

To check a word from the text for correctness, that word is also mapped onto this range. If this bit is set in the dictionary, it is assumed that the word is spelled correctly; otherwise, an error is reported. Of course, faulty diagnostics could occur as a result of collisions, but the probability that they occur should be small when n is big enough.

17	15	13	14	11	9	10	7	6	4	5	8

Figure 4.15 Heap in array representation.

For simplicity, you can select an array with Boolean values to serve as a bit list. A meaningful hash function would, for example, be the sum of ASCII values of all letters, multiplied by their position within the character string. The result must then be n calculated. We use this hash function because of simplicity; there are, of course, much better methods. So be careful when using the hash function; only a negative result is certain.

Delphi The function ORD(ch) can be used to calculate the ASCII value of the character ch.

Java In Java, you can also use the predefined method hashCode instead of the ASCII value. The following program code lines calculate the value of the character ch:

```
Character ch1 = new Character(ch);
int h = ch1.hashCode();
```

5

True Object–Oriented Programming

We have learned important basics and fundamental differences between object-oriented programming languages and COBOL in the previous chapters. This chapter discusses the nuts and bolts of object-oriented programming.

The first sections explain important terms, including *classes* and *inheritance*, then discuss possible applications of object-oriented programming in detail. Class libraries, basic to object-oriented programming, are also described.

Although the examples are shown in Java and Delphi, it would also be possible to implement them in OO-COBOL. However, OO-COBOL was explained in Section 1.5; therefore, this chapter includes only the short Section 5.2.4, which covers the new COBOL variant.

5.1 Classes

Classes: the fundamental concept of OOP

This first tutorial section presents the fundamental concept of object-oriented programming: the *class*, with its *attributes* and *methods*. It also discusses the main ideas and characteristics behind object-oriented programming.

5.1.1 Class Definition

Classes are similar to records A class is similar to the record we know from a previous chapter. For example, in connection with the Java definition, we said Java has no real records, but instead classes. A better comparison is to compare a class with an abstract data type (see Section 4.1). Like an abstract data type, a class offers attributes and operations (procedures). In object-oriented programming, these operations are also called *methods*. The short source code fragments we use in this chapter show how the abstract data type previously discussed can be represented as a class.

Delphi In contrast to a record, a class definition in Delphi begins with the keyword class (TObject). The term between parentheses is explained in connection with inheritance in Section 5.2. All we need to know at this point is that it is part of a class definition. As in a record, the keyword is followed by the attributes and (before the keyword end, which terminates the class definition) the methods.

A method definition is similar to a procedure definition, except that the addressed abstract data type—PhoneBook in the following example—does not have to be passed as a parameter. The latter is already implicitly included. Moreover, we have to define whether our attributes and methods will be exported, because a class enables us, for example, to export certain attributes but not others. This is defined by preceding the attribute or method to be exported with the keyword public or private, respectively. Accordingly, a class definition could look as follows:

```
PhoneBook = class (TObject)
  private
    book: array[1..1000] of Person;
    n: Integer;
  public
    procedure Enter (name: String; phone: Integer);
    procedure Lookup (name: String; var phone: Integer);
    procedure Init;
end;
```

Java As mentioned in Section 3.4.3, the record type of Java is mapped by the type class, so it changes only slightly. The major difference is that the methods are not declared with static, as we briefly mentioned in Section 4.1.3:

```
public class PhoneBook {
  Person [] book;
  int n;
  public void init () {...}
  public void enter (String name, int phone) {...}
  public int lookup (String name) {...}
}
```

Difference between an object and a class

Before discussing the implementation of these methods, it is useful to make a clear distinction between classes and objects. An object is an item in our world—for example, a chair or a table is an object. In relation to object-oriented programming, an *object* can be defined as data (attributes) and a set of behaviors (methods). A class is then a group of objects that share common attributes and common methods.

For example, a set of chairs can be seen as a class of chairs. They can have different sizes, colors, and so on (attributes), but they all belong to the same class. The class can therefore be seen as the type of an object, and the object can be seen as a single instance of a class.

Difference between an object and a record

Another interesting point is the similarities between an object and a record. The record, which is well known in the COBOL world, could be seen as an item in our world, too. It can be defined as data (attributes). There are two differences between a record and an object:

■ An object has a set of methods, in addition to its attributes.

■ An object is a dynamic data structure and has to be allocated at runtime, whereas a record (at least in Delphi and COBOL) is a static data structure.

Other than these differences, we can work with an object as with a record.

Method implementations use the implicitly declared parameter

Next is the implementation of methods. As mentioned, the telephone directory in the example—the element of the class itself—exists in the procedures only as an implicitly declared parameter. Before discussing the details of such an implementation, we briefly discuss how methods are invoked.

As with an abstract data type, a class lets you declare an arbitrary number of variables, which are also called objects. Classes are always dynamic data structures, which means that such objects have to be created first (see Section 3.7).

For example, we could declare and create a variable home of the type PhoneBook. This object will then have the attributes and also the methods listed in the class declaration. This means that all methods can operate on this object. The call itself could be realized with home.Init—the name, separated by a dot, is simply appended to both methods and attributes. The object home is then passed implicitly as a parameter.

Delphi
```
var home: PhoneBook;
...
home := PhoneBook.Create; // corresponds to New (home)
home.Init;
home.Enter('Knasmueller', 664);
```

Java
```
Phonebook home = new PhoneBook();
...
home.init();
home.enter("Knasmueller", 664);
```

Naturally, we can also access this implicitly passed parameter in the method implementation. Considering that the object itself is the elementary center of each method, all we need to do is access the attribute n, and it will always be clear that we mean the attribute n of the implicitly passed telephone directory. The two following source code fragments show how the method Enter could be implemented.

Delphi
```
procedure PhoneBook.Enter (name: String; phone: Integer);
begin
   Inc(n);
   book[n].name := name;
   book[n].phone := phone;
end;
```

The notation PhoneBook.Enter results from ClassName.MethodName and is required for uniqueness in Delphi, because it allows several classes within one unit.

Java
```
public void enter (String name, int phone) {
   book[n].name = name;
```

```
    book[n].phone = phone;
    n++;
}
```

In many cases, however, it is not that simple to access an attribute (say, n)—for example, because of a naming conflict with another parameter. To solve this problem, most programming languages support the implicit declaration of variables—the implicitly passed receiver parameter.

In Delphi, this implicitly declared variable is called self. Consequently, the preceding source code fragment could also look as follows:

Delphi: self

```
procedure PhoneBook.Enter (name: String; phone: Integer);
begin
    Inc(self.n);
    self.book[self.n].name := name;
    self.book[self.n].phone := phone;
end;
```

In Java, this implicitly declared variable is this, so the preceding source code fragment could look as follows:

Java: this

```
public void enter (String name, int phone) {
    this.book[this.n].name = name;
    this.book[this.n].phone = phone;
    this.n++;
}
```

This class notation and the way methods are implemented form the basis of object-oriented programming, but there are more advantages, which the following sections describe. For now, it is sufficient to understand that class notation offers one great advantage: We can see immediately what belongs together.

5.1.2 Creating and Releasing Objects

Instance

Considering that objects are dynamic data types, it is easy to understand that they have to be created before they can be used, just like pointer variables. Such a created object is also referred to as the *instance* of a class.

Delphi   A Delphi object is created by calling the implicitly existing method Create, for example, home := PhoneBook.Create. This corresponds roughly to creating something by use of New.

Java   A Java object can be created like a pointer variable—with new—for example, PhoneBook home = new PhoneBook().

Constructors   However, objects are complex things, so simply creating them won't do the trick. We also have to initialize them. Such an Init method was introduced in connection with abstract data types in Section 4.1.3, where it was called immediately after the data type was created or declared.

Object-oriented programming offers a way to unify creation and initialization by implementing a *constructor*. A constructor is a special method to be implemented; it contains all instructions required for initialization and is invoked automatically while it is created.

Programmers who use such objects do not have to deal with initialization any more. Our PhoneBook example simply writes a construction instead of using the procedure Init, which initializes the component n. The syntax used to implement such a constructor differs slightly in each of the programming languages of interest here.

Delphi   In Delphi, a constructor is a special method that begins with the keyword constructor instead of the keyword procedure.

```
PhoneBook = class (TObject)
   private
      book: array[1..1000] of Person;
      n: Integer;
   public
      procedure Enter (name: String; phone: Integer);
      procedure Lookup (name: String; var phone: Integer);
      constructor Create;
end;


constructor PhoneBook.Create;
begin
   n := 0;
end;
```

Java   The method is normally called Create, but it could also have a different name. The selected name has to be taken into account when creating the object.

In Java, a constructor is implemented like a normal method named after the class. This method must not have any return types:

```
public Phonebook () {
   book = new Person[1000];
   n = 0;
}
```

Because constructors are basically normal methods, it is also possible to use additional parameters for the initialization. For example, to implement a class, Person, that provides the attributes name and phone, our code could look like this:

Delphi
```
Person = class (TObject)
   private
      name: String;
      phone: Integer;
   public
      constructor Create (n: String; p: Integer);
end;

constructor Person.Create (n: String; p: Integer);
begin
   name := n; phone := p;
end;
```

The creation could then be realized by p := Person.Create('Knasmueller', 664).

Java
```
public class Person {
   String name;
   int phone;

   public Person (String n, int p) {
      name = n;
      phone = p;
   }
}
```

The creation could then be realized by Person p = new Person ("Knasmueller", 664).

Destructors
Just like pointer variables, once they are no longer required, objects have to be released (see Section 3.7.4). Also, just as creation can be supported by a constructor, it is possible to free an object by using a *destructor.* In many situations, although an object is no longer required, there may still be certain instructions to be executed. Considering the differences in the way the languages discussed in this book release dynamic data structures, it may not come as a surprise that they also differ significantly when it comes to releasing objects.

Delphi: Free and Destroy
In Delphi, objects are released by calling the method Destroy. This can be implemented in its own right, initiated with the keyword destructor instead of the keyword procedure. Particularly when an object points to other dynamic objects that are no longer required, these objects have to be released in a destructor implemented especially for this purpose. Otherwise, a standard destructor will do the job.

The method Free is often called instead of the method Destroy. This method is provided implicitly (by inheritance), and it then calls Destroy, unless the object was already released, so it actually prevents an error.

Java
Thanks to the Garbage Collector of Java, it is not necessary to release objects by a specific instruction. This is taken care of automatically as soon as the object can no longer be reached. If some jobs remain before an object is released, it is possible to write a finalize method that the Garbage Collector calls automatically.

5.1.3 Frequent Errors

OOP beginners often make these errors
Given the fact that objects are dynamic, our knowledge about pointers also applies to them. For this reason, great emphasis is placed on a thorough understanding of this issue. Nevertheless, there are errors that are typically made. The most important ones are discussed in this section; they should absolutely be avoided.

- **Equality of objects:** To check two objects for equality, we cannot simply use the simple comparative operator, because it will detect only whether two objects are the same (identity comparison). Note the subtle difference between the same two objects (that is, two pointers or references point to the same object) and two identical objects (that is, two pointers or references point to different objects that have the same attribute values)! To test for equality, we have to compare all individual attributes, which usually works fine with an `Equal` method: `if o1.Equal(o2) then . . .`

- **Copying of objects:** Accordingly, the mere copying of an object cannot work with a simple instruction. In this case, all that is produced is a *shallow copy*, which means that only the pointer is copied. If a new object were to be created and all attribute values were to be copied, we would have to do a *deep copy*. For this purpose, the classes should provide their own copy methods.

- **Creation of objects:** Another problematic issue is the method call of an object. Before we can call a method, we have to create that object; otherwise, the program will exit due to an illegal memory access.

- **Modification of the calling object:** An absolutely fatal effect would result if we were to modify or—worse—release the current object (`self` or `this`) within the method. This implicitly passed parameter itself (the pointer) must not be modified. Of course, attributes of objects can be modified.

5.1.4 The Main Ideas of Object-Oriented Programming

A system is a set of independent data and operations

Object-oriented programming allows us to represent a system as a set of independent objects with private data (not in the sense of private to an object but to a whole class) and operations. Private data serves to map the state of an object, and operations can be used to work with objects. The object-oriented idea reflects in the actual environment: Each object manages its own range of tasks, like the departments of a corporate organization. Data can be implemented in the sense of abstracting details—that is, hiding those details—like the sales department of a company that does not necessarily need to know all the details of production or engineering.

Important characteristics of object-oriented programming

We can identify three important characteristics of object-oriented programming:

- Data abstraction

- Inheritance (type extension)

- Dynamic binding

The term *data abstraction* was discussed extensively in Section 4.1, and the two other terms are explained in Section 5.2. An important advantage of object-oriented programming is reusability, which the following tutorial sections discuss in detail.

5.1.5   Terminology

Terms used in object-oriented programming

- **Class:** A class corresponds roughly to an abstract data type—one for which variables can be declared that will then dispose of attributes and operations.

- **Object:** An object is an instance of a class. Considering that this always concerns dynamic data structures, an object not only has to be declared but also created.

- **Attribute:** This is a data component of an object and is often called an *instance variable* or *member*.

- **Method:** A method is an operation (procedure) provided by a class.

- **Message:** A message is a dynamically bound procedure call.

- **Inheritance:** This type of extension can be used to specialize a class (see Section 5.2).

5.1.6   Exercises

Task 1 (180 minutes): Queue

Use the information from task 1 in Section 4.2.4. Then modify this task so that a class Queue is defined instead of a simple dynamic data structure Queue.

5.2   Inheritance and Dynamic Binding

Inheritance is one of the major advantages of object-oriented programming. Inheritance uses the fact that we often have to code similar but not entirely identical classes. When starting to work on the solution of a new task, we often find that a similar task has already been solved.

For example, we may find a class that can process the name, address, employee number, and salary of an employee of a company. It may well be that another class was implemented that merely manages a normal person, without employee number or salary. In this case, we could apply inheritance to yield the new class from the existing one. Such an inheritance and the closely related issues—type compatibility, dynamic binding, and abstract classes—are the main focus of this section.

5.2.1 Introduction

The previous example can be specified in more detail. Assume that a class, Person, with the attributes name and address and the methods Init to initialize and Print to output all attributes, already exists. Listings 5.1 and 5.2 show possible implementations of this class.

Listing 5.1. Delphi Implementation of Person

```
interface
  type
    Person = class (TObject)
      private
        name: String;
        address: String;
      public
        procedure Init (name, address: String); virtual;
        procedure Print; virtual;
    end;

implementation

  procedure Person.Init (name, address: String);
  begin
    self.name := name; self.address := address;
  end;
  procedure Person.Print;
  begin
    WriteLn(self.name);
    WriteLn(self.address);
  end;
```

The keyword virtual used in Listing 5.1 is explained further later.

Listing 5.2. Java Implementation of Person

```java
public class Person {
    private String name;
    private String address;

    public void init (String name, String address) {
        this.name = name;
        this.address = address;
    }

    public void print () {
        System.out.println(name);
        System.out.println(address);
    }
}
```

Similar component wanted? Consider inheritance

Now we require a component, Employee, that should offer exactly these functionalities and also new attributes and a function, Salary. This function returns the salary of the employee based on his or her salary category (for the sake of simplicity, we multiply the salary category by 1500 to calculate the salary). To achieve this goal, we could write the class Employee from scratch or copy the existing source code and modify it. Neither of the two solutions is particularly useful; it would be preferable to use inheritance in this case.

Employee inherits everything from Person

Inheritance means that the class Employee inherits everything from Person: the attributes name and address as well as the methods Init and Print. We can add more attributes and methods, in this case the attributes number and salaryCat, and a method, Salary.

Of course, for the class definition, we have to state that the class Employee inherits the attributes and methods of Person, which means that Employee is derived from Person. Person is then called a *superclass*, or *base class*, of Employee. Similarly, we could speak of an extension of the class Person by Employee, because more attributes and methods are added. Accordingly, the class Employee is then called a *subclass* or *derived class*.

Delphi

In Delphi, the keyword class is followed by the superclass within parentheses—the class from which we derived this class.

```
Employee = class (Person)
  public
    salaryCat: Integer;
```

```
      procedure Init (name, address: String); override;
      procedure Print; override;
      function Salary: Real;
end;
```

This also helps us better understand the preceding notation, class (TObject), because it means that the defined class is derived from the base class TObject. In Delphi, this class is the base class of all objects.

Java   In Java, the class name is followed by the keyword extends and the name of the superclass——the class being extended.

```
public class Employee extends Person {
   public int salaryCat;
   . . .
   public float salary () {
      return salaryCat * 1500;
   }
}
```

A child of its parents . . .   Just as a child inherits its properties from his or her parents, our Employee inherits the properties from Person. This human analogy is appropriate, because inherited properties may change often. Taking a closer look, we can see that our Employee must modify the properties to some extent, because we are currently not doing anything with the new attributes. Also, the method Print should output these attributes, and the method Init should initialize them.

This is possible by properly implementing the methods within the class Employee and then extending it by this functionality. Programming experts use the term *override* to describe this case. The method interface has to be maintained, which means that no further parameters can be added. Override does not mean that the method has to be a totally new implementation; it could also be used to call the inherited method.

Delphi   The overwritten method can be reached by calling it with the preceding keyword inherited. To be able to override a method, it has to be declared by the keyword virtual in the base class. This ensures that nothing stands in the way of future extensions, so it is surely useful to declare all methods in this way. Also, the overwritten method has to be declared by the keyword override. Listing 5.3 shows a complete implementation of the class Employee.

Listing 5.3. Delphi
Implementation
of Employee

```delphi
interface
  type
    Employee = class (Person)
      public
        salaryCat: Integer;
        procedure Init (name, address: String); override;
        procedure Print; override;
        function Salary (): Real;
    end;

implementation
  function Employee.Salary (): Real;
  begin
    result := salaryCat * 1500;
  end;

  procedure Employee.Init (name, address: String);
  begin
    inherited Init(name, address);
    salaryCat := 0;
  end;

  procedure Employee.Print;
  begin
    inherited Print;
    WriteLn(Salary());
  end;
```

Java

In Java, the overwritten method can be reached by calling the method with the preceding keyword super. Listing 5.4 shows the complete implementation of the class Employee.

Listing 5.4. Java
Implementation
of Employee

```java
public class Employee extends Person {
  public int salaryCat;
  public void init (String name, String address) {
    super.init(name, address);
    salaryCat = 0;
  }

  public float salary () {
    return salaryCat * 1500;
  }
```

```
  public void print () {
    super.print();
    System.out.println(salary());
  }
}
```

A few pieces of additional information about inheritance seem to be meaningful at this point:

- **Inheritance can be optionally continued as needed.** We could derive further classes from Employee, which would then also inherit the attributes and methods. Moreover, other classes can be derived from a class; for example, we could derive another class, Workers, from Person, where this additional class may provide other methods. Figure 5.1 shows such an inheritance hierarchy.

- **Inheritance means is-a relationship.** In the context of inheritance, we often speak of an *is-a* relationship: Each Employee is also a Person.

- **Inheritance means specialization.** An Employee is also a special Person.

5.2.2 Type Compatibility

Inheritance also means type compatibility

Some of the benefits of inheritance versus copying and modifying source code have become obvious from the preceding example. A lot of implementation cost can be saved, especially with long method implementa-

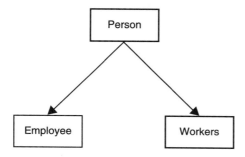

Figure 5.1 Inheritance hierarchy.

tions, because many do not have to be modified at all or only slightly. Another benefit of inheritance is type compatibility. Each subclass is compatible with its superclass. If we apply this statement to our previous example, each program that can work with a variable of the type Person will accept a variable of the type Employee. However, this compatibility does not work in the opposite direction.

Building on type compatibility, we should attempt to understand the difference between static and dynamic types. Each variable has a static and a dynamic type. These two types can be equal but do not have to be. The static type is always defined by the declaration. The dynamic type is defined at runtime and must be type-compatible with the static type. The following short source code pieces help explain this concept.

Delphi
```
var p: Person // the static type of p is Person
. . .
p := Employee.Create; // Case 1: the dynamic type of p is Employee
p := Person.Create; // Case 2: the dynamic type of p is Person
```

Java
```
Person p // the static type of p is Person
. . .
p = new Employee(); // Case 1: the dynamic type of p is Employee
p = new Person(); // Case 2: the dynamic type of p is Person
```

Dynamic and static types of a variable

The dynamic type of a variable cannot simply be specified by creating an object. For example, with a variable p of the type Person, and another variable q of the type Employee, we could easily use a p := q kind of assignment so that the dynamic type of p would then be Employee. The opposite assignment, q := p, is not allowed, which is fairly logical: The allowed assignment (p := q) may have attributes and methods that cannot be addressed (directly). The forbidden case (q := p) carries the risk of accessing nonexistent features.

Because the static and dynamic types may differ, it is useful to test for the dynamic type at runtime. The programming languages of interest here offer different options:

Delphi
In Delphi, the query is-a can be used to determine whether a variable has a certain dynamic type. If so, its static type can be converted to this type by use of the operator as:

```
if p is Employee then begin
  with p as Employee do begin s := Salary() end;
end;
```

Java   In Java, the query `instanceof` can be used to determine whether a variable has a certain dynamic type. If so, its static type can be converted to this type by preceding the type name within parentheses:

```
if (p instanceof Employee)
  {
     Employee e;
     Float s;
     e = (Employee) p;
     s = e.salary();
  }
```

Note that both queries concern a control to see whether the dynamic type of the variable, or a subtype of the stated type, is equal. Neither query checks whether we are dealing with exactly that specific type. For this reason, queries such as `p is Person` or `p instanceof Person` would result in a value of TRUE.

Runtime error   If we want a type conversion to take place that is not possible due to the dynamic type, we would get a runtime error. For this reason, we should always do a type check before such a conversion, as shown in our example.

5.2.3 Dynamic Binding

Always calling the "right" method   We mentioned in the previous section that a variable can accept different dynamic types. For example, a variable p with static type Person can have the dynamic type Person or the dynamic type Employee. When the method Print is called, it is important to distinguish which one is to be called—the one of Person or Employee. Fortunately, the runtime system relieves the programmer from having to make this decision, because it always calls the correct method. So, if p is of the dynamic type Employee, the method of Employee is called. The message—the method call—is bound dynamically to a specific method at runtime.

5.2.4 Object–Oriented COBOL

Class definition in OO-COBOL

Section 1.5 described some important aspects of object-oriented COBOL. The basic structure of classes in OO-COBOL is similar to the approaches shown here, but there are big differences in the syntax. A class is preceded by the keyword CLASS-ID. All classes are derived from the base class BASE, and they dispose of their own Factory Data Division, which serves as a constructor. We discuss the term *factory* more thoroughly in Section 6.2.1 in connection with a design pattern by the same name.

These explanations should suffice to be able to read the definition of the class COUNTER in Listing 5.5, a simple class that manages a pointer.

Listing 5.5. OO-COBOL Implementation of COUNTER

```
CLASS-ID. COUNTER
   DATA IS PRIVATE
   INHERITS FROM BASE.
CLASS-CONTROL.
   BASE IS CLASS "BASE"
   COUNTER IS CLASS "COUNTER".
FACTORY.
WORKING-STORAGE SECTION.
METHODE-ID. "NEW".
WORKING-STORAGE SECTION.
LINKAGE SECTION.
01 IS-COUNTERHANDLEOBJECT REFERENCE.
PROCEDURE DIVISION RETURNING IS-COUNTERHANDLE.
   INVOKE SUPER "NEW" RETURNING IS-COUNTERHANDLE.
   INVOKE IS-COUNTERHANDLE "INITIALIZE".
END METHOD "NEW".
END FACTORY.
OBJECT.
WORKING-STORAGE SECTION.
01 COUNTER-INFORMATION.
   05 COUNTER-N  PIC 9(3).
METHOD-ID. "INITIALIZE".
PROCEDURE DIVISION.
   MOVE 0 TO COUNTER-N.
END METHOD "INITIALIZE".
METHOD-ID. "ADD".
LINKAGE SECTION.
```

```
01   X              PIC 9(3).
PROCEDURE DIVISION USING X.
   COMPUTE COUNTER-N = COUNTER-N + X.
END METHOD "ADD".
END OBJECT.
END CLASS COUNTER.
```

5.2.5 Abstract Classes

In practice, situations often arise where two classes are very much alike. Examples include an account from financial accounting and an account from payroll accounting. The behavior of the two accounts is similar: Both manage postings, both should be printed and summed, and so on. Depending on the application, it would be useful to apply the benefits offered by inheritance to this example. However, a quick look at the previous definitions is sufficient to understand that neither account is a superclass of the other. An abstract class could provide a solution in such a case.

Abstract classes serve as artificial superclasses

Such an abstract class merely serves as an artificial superclass and is itself not normally used as an object type. This example introduces an abstract class, Account, from which two concrete classes, SalaryAccount and FinancialAccount, are derived. In the abstract class, the methods implemented in the two derived classes are defined only abstractly, without implementation. Implementation will occur later in the concrete classes. Because this implementation is not there, we cannot create any instances for the abstract class.

The syntax of the definition of an abstract class depends on the programming language we select.

Delphi

In Delphi, the methods defined to be abstract have to be identified by the directive abstract in the interface part but do not exist in the implementation part:

```
Account = class (TObject)
   private
      balance: Integer;
   public
      name: String;
      procedure Print; virtual; abstract;
```

```
      function GetBalance (): Integer; virtual;
        . . .
end;
```

Java   In Java, both the class in its entirety and the abstract methods are identified by the keyword abstract. The methods consist merely of the method
head followed by a semicolon:

```
public abstract class Account {
   int balance;
   public String name;
   public abstract void print ();
   public int getBalance () {
      return balance;
   }
   . . .
}
```

It is necessary to implement or override the abstract procedure Print in
the concrete classes, SalaryAccount and FinancialAccount. In contrast, the
method GetBalance can be overwritten but does not have to be.

5.2.6   Options to Access Attributes and Methods

**The most
important access
types are public,
private, and
protected**
In addition to public access (an option to make an attribute or a method
publicly available), there are more access types. The best known are private
and protected. The underlying concept is the same in the programming
languages of interest here, but a few differences are worth noting.

Delphi
In Delphi, the access type private is almost exactly the opposite of
public. All fields declared in this way are visible only in that module and
cannot be accessed from any other module. In contrast, all methods of a
class derived from the class with the element declaration can access an
element declared with protected, regardless of the module in which they
exist.

Java
In Java, too, the access type private is more or less the exact opposite of
public. All fields declared in this way are available only in the class where
they are defined. Such components are not inherited, so they are not
defined in the subclasses. If a method is defined in a subclass that was

already defined in a superclass by use of `private`, it will be considered a new definition and will not be overwritten.

All methods of a class derived from the class with the element declaration can access an element declared with `protected`. It can even be accessed if access is made from within the package in which the class is defined. In this case, whether it is a subclass is irrelevant.

A further access method in Java is `package`. No explicit specifier is used, and by using this method, classes can access the attributes of the other classes in a package.

5.2.7 Overloading Methods

Method overloading and overriding are not quite the same

Under certain circumstances, it is useful to overload existing methods. Overloading differs slightly from overriding. When a method is overwritten, the parameters of the method remain unchanged. Overloading gives the methods other parameters, which means that a new variant can be created. Furthermore, overloading is always resolved at compilation time and never by dynamic binding, in contrast to overriding.

Method overloading is not supported by all object-oriented programming languages, and there are big differences between Java and Delphi.

Delphi

In Delphi, it is possible to redeclare a method by using the instruction `overload`. When the parameter information differs from that of its predecessor, the inherited method is overloaded, but without hiding it. For example, if a write method in a class, `MyFile2`, is declared with parameters that differ from those in the base class, `MyFile`, this method is overloaded. In this case, `reintroduce` has to be used to identify a second method.

```
MyFile = class (TObject)
  . . .
  procedure Write (s: String); overload; virtual;
end;

MyFile2 = class (MyFile)
  . . .
  procedure Write (i: Integer); reintroduce; overload;
end;
```

Furthermore, an object o of the type `MyFile2` could call the method `Write` by using `o.Write('string')` or `o.Write(123)`. The first case calls

MyFile.Write (s: String), and the second calls MyFile2.Write (i: Integer). The important point is that, within one class, you cannot declare more than one overloaded method by the same name.

Java   In Java, we can have several variants of a method within one class that differ only in their parameters. We can be sure the correct variant will be used, because it depends on the parameters used during the method call. For example, one class, MyFile, could have two different write operations—one for strings and the other for integers.

```
public class MyFile {
  . . .
  public void write (String s) {
    . . .
  }
  public void write (int i) {
    . . .
  }
}
```

An object o of the type MyFile could call the method write by using o.write("string") or o.write(123). The first case calls MyFile.write (String s), and the second calls MyFile.write (int i). However, if write is called by a parameter of another type, the compiler will report an error.

5.2.8   Exercises

Task 1 (210 minutes): Inheritance

The last three exercises dealt with queues. In one task, you were asked to implement a queue as a list, then as a binary tree, and finally as a class. In this exercise, implement an abstract class, Queue. From that class, you then derive ListQueue, to be implemented as a list, and BinTreeQueue, which is a binary tree.

In principle, the interfaces should be similar to those of the last exercise. With regard to the definition of the abstract class, think about the methods the two queues should have. Use an appropriate test program to thoroughly test your new classes.

Task 2 (30 minutes): Inheritance: Application

Find a few examples for application cases where inheritance could be used.

<table>
<tr><td>5.3</td></tr>
</table>

5.3 Typical Applications of Object–Oriented Programming

Now that we have learned the basics and advantages of object-oriented programming, this section introduces several typical applications. In addition to the known data abstraction, these examples include heterogeneous data structures or extensible components [Mös99, p. 89 ff.].

5.3.1 Data Abstraction

Section 4.1 discussed abstract data types in detail

Using classes as an abstraction tool to structure programs provides a way to also use them without inheritance or dynamic binding. The benefit for those who use classes, that is, for clients, is that the classes can easily be used and reused as often as needed. This behavior is also useful for the implementer of these classes: First, the implementation can always be replaced; for example, a binary search tree could be used instead of a less efficient array. All clients could continue working as usual, only much more efficiently, as long as the interface of the class does not change. On the other hand, data abstraction also offers protection against inadvertent destruction.

5.3.2 Generic Components

List with optional elements

Generic components are a useful extension of the abstract data structures with which we are already familiar. With these data structures (list, tree, and so forth), we can insert, search, or delete elements, but these elements must be of the same type. Therefore, it is not possible to store strings and numbers in a single list.

This problem can be solved by using generic components, which can accept arbitrary objects. This is possible by using inheritance, because generic components are implemented in such a way that they can accept objects from a base class. In addition, the type compatibility between a base class and its derived classes ensures that derived objects can be accepted.

Delphi   Generic components can be implemented elegantly in Delphi, where all objects are derived from the abstract base class TObject. When you are implementing a list that can handle elements of the type TObject, this actually includes all objects. The Delphi class library, which Section 5.4.2 describes in detail, includes several generic components of this type.

Java   Java also supports generic components, which can accept elements compatible with the type Object. This class is an implicit superclass of all Java classes, so it allows you to use objects from all classes in these components. Moreover, standard types such as int or float can be converted into objects of the type Object.

5.3.3   Replaceable Behavior

Replaceable behavior is one of the features most frequently used in object-oriented programming. The following example shows what this means.

Payroll accounting is normally based on the same general principles: The main task is to acquire master data, such as employees, contracts, or salary types. Salaries are calculated based on work hours and can be used for different kinds of statistical reports (such as cost accounting or salary summary reports). Depending on the organization, additional information, such as sick leave lists, may be required.

For example, many divisions of a global corporation may be identical in different countries, whereas salaries and wages may be calculated on a country-specific basis. If the corporation were to adapt its payroll accounting system designed for the United States to, say, Canada, it could reuse a large part of the system.

However, the behavior of the payroll accounting system is to be replaced by overwriting the methods involved. If extensions in the original payroll accounting system are made available, such as for salary increases, they will naturally also be available in the Canadian version. Only a specific behavior was replaced while all other functions of both payroll accounting systems remained the same. This example is greatly simplified, but it is sufficient to explain the approach and its benefits.

What methods are to be replaced?   In general, when a replaceable behavior is required, we first have to investigate which behavior or methods are to be replaced. Subsequently, an abstract class that includes the relevant method interfaces should be designed. At the same time, additional methods could be implemented. The methods to be replaced will be implemented later in the derived specific classes. The application to be developed will then work with the variables of the abstract class.

This process makes sense only if, in our example, a version for the United States already exists and should now be extended for Canada. Starting from scratch, we should have abstract, country-independent classes and then different subclasses for the United States and Canada.

5.3.4   Extensible Components

Object-oriented programming creates a way to make extensible components available. An example would be to implement a simple account, which has posting and output functions, and offer it to potential clients. If it then appears that this simple account is not sufficient for the intended application, a new account type could be derived from it, offering additional functions, such as for bonus analysis.

The current clients of the simple account could be maintained, without new compilation, and could also work with the specialized account type, thanks to the type compatibility. However, to use a new function—bonus analysis in this example—the application would have to be adapted accordingly.

When designing simple classes, it is advisable to take future extensions into consideration.

5.3.5   Heterogeneous Data Structures

The OLE elements of Windows are a good example of heterogeneous data structures

Heterogeneous data structures are characterized by the fact that an object can exist in different variants, and the same operations can be executed on all variants. New variants can be added as needed. A typical example for such a heterogeneous data structure is the OLE elements of Microsoft Windows. They support the integration of text with objects. In Microsoft Word, for example, variants of objects, such as equations, images, or even audio clips, can be integrated. All objects support certain operations, such as insert and save, draw, or respond, by simply clicking them.

The same is possible in object-oriented programming by deriving individual elements from an abstract class and inheriting their methods. Some of these methods have to be overwritten, whereas others may have to be added. Figure 5.2 shows the object-oriented implementation of heterogeneous data structures (the UML representation used in this figure is discussed in Section 6.1.4).

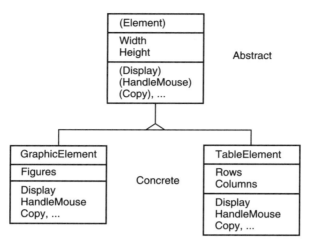

Figure 5.2 UML representation of heterogeneous data structures.

Building on this basis, we can add more elements as needed. Other programmers can write new variants by deriving them from this abstract base class. For example, new elements could be integrated in Microsoft Word and viewed, loaded, or saved, without the need for Word to know these elements.

The design of heterogeneous data structures requires a targeted approach. First, we have to think about the data and operations that should be common to all variants. Based on these common features, we can design an abstract class. The application (for example, Word) is then implemented by means of the interface of this abstract class. Each single element (such as images or equation elements) can then be derived from the abstract class and implemented in an independent class.

5.3.6 Example

Object-oriented programming is complex!

Let's look at a larger example for object-oriented programming. Object-oriented programming *is* indeed complex!

This example deals with writing code for a simple payroll accounting program that should handle a maximum of 100 employees. It should distinguish between workers and clerks, where the pay for the two groups should be calculated differently. Workers are paid an hourly wage, so the system should multiply the number of hours worked by an hourly rate. Clerks are paid a fixed salary and an additional overtime amount if they work more than 160 hours in a month. For each overtime hour, 1/160 of the salary plus 50% is added.

Following are two solutions written in Delphi and Java. A class, `Employ-eesList`, is implemented, which has an array of employees. From the abstract class `Employee`, two specific classes, `Worker` and `Clerk`, are derived; both implement the function `Salary`. Besides the methods used to insert workers and clerks, the class `EmployeesList` includes the method `PrintSalary`, which outputs the name and `Salary` of each employee stored in the system.

Delphi In Delphi, an additional destructor has to be implemented for `Employ-eesList` to free all employees later on. Listing 5.6 shows the calling program, and Listing 5.7 shows the classes `EmployeesList`, `Workers`, and `Clerks`.

Listing 5.6. Calling Program of PayrollAccounting in Delphi

```delphi
program ExampleSalary;

uses
    payroll accounting in 'PayrollAccounting.pas';

var
    x: Integer;
    el: EmployeesList;
    ch: Char;

begin
    el := EmployeesList.Create;
    ReadLn(x); // 1: worker, 2: clerk, 3: end
    while x <> 3 do begin
        if x = 1 then el.InsertWorker
        else el.InsertClerk;
        ReadLn(x);
    end;
    el.PrintSalary;
    el.Free; // required in Delphi
    ReadLn(ch); // in order not to delete the screen
end.
```

Listing 5.7. The Classes EmployeesList, Worker, and Clerk in Delphi

```delphi
unit PayrollAccounting;
interface
    type
        Employee = class (TObject)
            public
                name: String;
                hours: Integer;
```

```
                     rate: Integer;
                     procedure Read; virtual;
                     function Salary (): Real; virtual; abstract;
                end;

            Clerk = class (Employee)
               public
                     function Salary (): Real; override;
            end;

            Worker = class (Employee)
               public
                     function Salary (): Real; override;
            end;

            EmployeesList = class (TObject)
               public
                     procedure PrintSalary; virtual;
                     procedure InsertWorker; virtual;
                     procedure InsertClerk; virtual;
                     constructor Create; virtual;
                     destructor Destroy; override;
                 private
                     list: array[1..100] of Employees;
                     n: Integer;
            end;
    implementation

       procedure Employee.Read;
       // gets the employees, regardless of whether worker
       // or clerk
       // worker: enter number of hours + hourly rate
       // clerk: number of hours + fixed salary
       begin
          ReadLn(name);
          ReadLn(hours);
          ReadLn(rate);
       end;

       function Clerk.Salary (): Real;
       begin
          result := rate + (rate/160) * 1.5 * (hours - 160);
```

```
end;
function Worker.Salary (): Real;
begin
   result := rate * hours;
end;


constructor EmployeesList.Create;
begin
   n := 1;
end;


destructor EmployeesList.Destroy;
// free all employees
   var i: Integer;
begin
   for i := 1 to n - 1 do begin
      list[i].Free;
   end;
end;
procedure EmployeesList.InsertClerk;
   var e: Employee;
begin
   e := Employee.Create;
   e.Read;
   list[n] := e;
   Inc(n);
end;
procedure EmployeesList.InsertWorker;
   var w: worker;
begin
   w := Worker.Create;
   w.Read;
   list[n] := w;
   Inc(n);
end;
procedure EmployeesList.PrintSalary;
// iterate over all employees
// output name and salary
   var i: Integer;
```

```
      begin
        for i := 1 to n - 1 do begin
          Write(list[i].name);
          WriteLn(list[i].Salary());
        end;
      end;
    end.
```

Java   Java implements a separate class, IO, to supply methods used to read a string and a number. We do not describe this part here, because it is covered in Appendix A. Otherwise, the required classes are embedded in the package PayrollAccounting. It is not necessary to release objects no longer needed, because this job is done automatically by Java's Garbage Collector. Listing 5.8 shows the main program, and Listings 5.9 through 5.12 show the package.

Listing 5.8. Calling Program of PayrollAccounting in Java

```
import PayrollAccounting.*;

class ExampleSalary {
  public static void main (String args[]) {
    int x;
    EmployeesList el = new EmployeesList ();
    x = IO.readInt(); // 1: worker, 2: clerk, 3: end
    while (x != 3) {
      if (x == 1) {el.insertWorker();}
      else {el.insertClerk();}
      x = IO.readInt();
    }
    el.printSalary();
  }
}
```

Listing 5.9. The Class Employee in Java

```
package PayrollAccounting;
public abstract class Employee {
  public String name;
  public int hours;
  public int rate;
  public abstract float salary ();
  public void read () {
  // gets the employee, regardless of whether worker
```

```
// or clerk
// worker: enter number of hours + hourly rate
// clerk: hourly rate + fixed salary
   name = IO.readName();
   hours = IO.readInt();
   rate = IO.readInt();
}
}
```

Listing 5.10. The Class Worker in Java

```
package Payroll Accounting;
public class Worker extends Employee {
   public float salary () {
      return rate * hours;
   }
}
```

Listing 5.11. The Class Clerk in Java

```
package Payroll Accounting;
public class Clerk extends Employee {
   public float salary () {
      float x, x1, dif;
      x = (float) rate; // Attention: type of intermediate results!
      dif = hours - 160;
      x1 = (float) x/160;
      x1 = x1 * (float) 1.5;
      return (x + x1 * dif);
   }
}
```

Listing 5.12. The Class EmployeesList in Java

```
package PayrollAccounting;
public class EmployeesList {
   employees list[];
   int n;
   public EmployeesList () {
      list = new Employees[100];
      n = 0;
   }
```

```
public void insertClerk () {
   clerk c = new Clerk ();
   c.read();
   list[n] = c;
   n ++;
}

public void insertWorker () {
   worker w = new Worker ();
   w.read();
   list[n] = w;
   n ++;
}

public void printSalary () {
// iterate over all employees
// output name and salary
   int i;
   for (i = 0; i < n; i ++) {
      System.out.print(list[i].name);
      System.out.println(list[i].salary());
   }
}
}
```

With regard to the array list, in Java the array begins with index 0.

5.3.7 Drawbacks of Object–Oriented Programming

Nothing has only advantages

So far in this chapter, we have discussed the applications and advantages of object-oriented programming (see also Section 1.2). Like most things, object-oriented programming has not only benefits but a few drawbacks:

- Designers must familiarize themselves with object-oriented programming and get used to an object-oriented programming language, which can be a rather time-consuming process, particularly for those with extensive experience in procedural programming—probably the majority of the readers of this book.

- Although this familiarization with the programming language is time-consuming in itself, just as important is acquiring knowledge of the class library. Only those who know what classes exist and what interfaces they provide will be able to use them.

- Care must be taken when changing a class, because reusability can mean that the change affects a number of programs. Often, these are programs the developer of a class is not even aware of.

- Under certain circumstances, it is also important to note the drawbacks of dynamic data structures. They normally use more storage space than necessary (for pointers) and could (although minimally) extend the program runtime due to dynamic binding. In addition, objects have to be released when they are no longer needed.

5.3.8 Exercises

Task 1 (180 minutes): Implementing the Account Class

Basically, we distinguish between two types of accounts: personnel and inventory. Personnel accounts are characterized by being *OI-leading* (a leading account for open items) and subject to turnover.

Both account types have a unique number, a name, and several postings. A posting consists of a posting date, an offset account, debit and credit identifiers, and a posting amount. The sum of these postings results in the account balance. It should be possible to add a posting entry to the account and to print a list of all postings of an account. Implement this class in Delphi and Java; assume that each account has to handle at most 100 postings.

5.4   Class Libraries

A class library is a collection of classes intended for reuse

Class libraries are a typical feature of object-oriented programming. Considering that we repeatedly use base classes on many occasions, it appears obvious to collect as many classes as possible and make them available in a sort of library. Many programming languages or development environments come with such a class library, and large programming projects often begin with development of their own libraries. This section gives a general introduction to class libraries and then discusses the class libraries of Delphi and Java, including real-world examples.

5.4.1 Introduction

Class libraries improve productivity and ensure a uniform look

A class library lets you use ready-made components, thus increasing productivity. In fact, many class libraries can be used to write smaller programs that create only few objects and call a limited number of methods. Another advantage is that class libraries ensure a uniform look.

For example, if a class library offers a file search dialog, it would be efficient not only to avoid having to code it all over again for each program but also to ensure that the programs have a uniform look and feel. This means both a useful effect and increased productivity, particularly for large projects. Popular Windows programs have a highly uniform look and feel, thanks to the similarity of all class libraries as far as user interface classes are concerned.

However, class libraries also have some problems—for example, a high learning curve—because the designer has to learn a "virtual" language. The main difference is that this language does not consist of keywords and syntactic rules but of class names, method names, and parameter names. This can often mean that the designer must handle hundreds of classes with thousands of method calls. This situation is often complicated by poor documentation, meaning that designers frequently must look at the source code to decide what exactly a method does.

A class library consists of many different class categories, and some classes may fall into more than one category. Table 5.1 shows a few class categories, including examples.

Table 5.1 Categories of classes

Category	*Examples*
Data structures	List, Array, Stack, Queue, . . .
Graphical classes	Point, Rectangle, Circle, . . .
User interface classes	Dialog, RadioButton, CheckBox, . . .
Application-specific classes	Postings, Account, . . .
Operating system classes	Process, Stream, File, Server, . . .
Frameworks	See following text

Component classes and frameworks

Let's briefly describe the differences between component classes and frameworks. Component classes, such as a list or hash table, can be used independently. Such classes support reusability to a small extent. By contrast, frameworks are true bodies for a program. A framework consists of a set of classes that can be used jointly, such as dialog screen management or file system classes. Frameworks allow reusability to a larger extent.

In general, we can see that individual classes depend largely on each other, as Figure 5.3 shows (taken from [PoBl96, p. 260]). Therefore, in many cases, it is possible to just use a specific part. For this reason, it is difficult to produce an application that is a combination of different class libraries. The only way is often to extend an existing library.

Class libraries are an important decision criterion when selecting a development environment. It is almost more important to ask what a class library can do than which programming language could be used. In fact, the major strengths in object-oriented programming are not found in the language, unlike in COBOL (600 keywords), but in class libraries.

The following section provides an introduction to the class libraries of Delphi and Java. Moreover, it describes how developers can design their own class libraries (for example, for a large project).

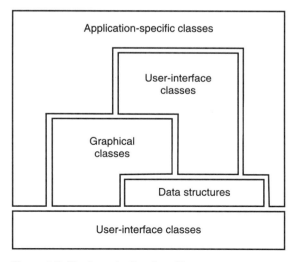

Figure 5.3 The layout of a class library.

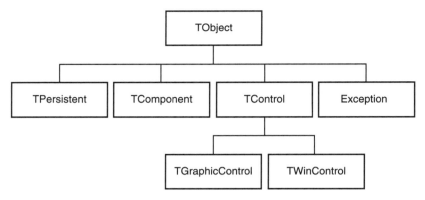

Figure 5.4 Structure of the Delphi class library.

5.4.2 Delphi

Delphi offers an extensive class library, with several hundred classes. For this reason, this section cannot provide more than a rough overview (Figure 5.4) of the mighty options this library offers. Interested readers will find all details in the Delphi documentation.

TObject

Starting point of the Delphi class hierarchy: TObject TObject is the starting point of the Delphi class hierarchy. This abstract class is the superclass of all classes. It encapsulates the fundamental behavior is common to all Delphi objects. With the methods introduced by TObject, we can create, manage, and dissolve object instances, and we can access object-specific information, such as class type, at runtime. TObject supplies a number of methods, such as ClassName, DefaultHandler, Free, or InheritsFrom, which means that all objects can use them. A number of classes, such as exceptions (see also Section 5.5.1), Internet objects, table objects, lists, or XML objects, can be directly derived from TObject.

TPersistent

Persistent classes can be stored TPersistent forms the superclass for all persistent classes. These are all classes with objects that should not only be available at runtime but that also need to be stored. Of special importance is the method DefineProperties, which defines the attributes of the class with regard to the storage medium (for example, a file). If a class derived from TPersistent introduces additional attributes that should also be stored, this method has to be over-written accordingly. Important classes derived from this superclass are, for example, string objects (string lists), collections (generic components), graphical objects, or HTML objects.

TComponent

The TComponent class is a predecessor common to all component objects in Delphi. These are objects that are part of the user interface of a Windows application, such as menus, database components, Web components, or the application itself. These components are covered in Chapter 8.

TControl

Abstract base class for visual components TControl is used as an abstract base class for all visual components. This includes, for instance, the position of a control element, the cursor linked to this control element, or methods to draw or move control elements, and events that can respond to mouse actions. We can distinguish between two kinds of controls:

- TGraphicControl: This type includes all user-defined control elements that are not window-oriented. The important point to remember is that control elements derived from TGraphicControl cannot be focused, nor can they include other control elements, which is why they require only few system resources. Examples are labels or the speed button.

- TwinControl: This type of control element concerns window-oriented control classes that can be focused. Examples include buttons, check-boxes, groupboxes, or editors, which are all known from popular Windows programs.

Chapter 8 describes all these controls in detail.

Exceptions

An exception in object-oriented programming is a special construct to handle exceptional events, such as division by zero. Exceptions are dis-cussed in detail in Section 5.5.1.

5.4.3 Java

Java is another language that offers an extensive class library. For this reason, we limit ourselves to a brief introduction of the most important classes. Interested readers will find all details in JDK 1.2 *(http://java.sun.com/products/jdk)*, which defines the Java class library. It is customary in Java for classes to be grouped into packages. Table 5.2 lists the most important packages.

The following sections describe the language package, the utilities, and the AWT package to some extent. The SQL package is covered in Section 7.4.

Language Package

java.lang Java's language package (java.lang) contains the most important support classes and is de facto required in each Java program. Among other classes, it includes Object, which serves as base class for all classes, even if none of those classes is listed in the class definition. This class offers various methods, such as for copy or convert operations.

The method equals can be used to compare two objects for equality. If the values of all attributes of the two objects are the same, the value TRUE is returned. Other important classes are Math (offers various mathematical functions, such as sin, cos, or random—counterparts to the intrinsic COBOL functions), the previously discussed class String (see Section 3.4.2), or the class System, which allows you to access platform-independent

Table 5.2   Introduction of important Java packages

Package	Description
Language package	Main component of the Java language
Utilities	Various useful data structures
IO	Input/output support
Network support	TCP/IP support
AWT	User interface programming
Text	Support for globalization
Security	Support for security (encoding)
RMI	Support for distributed programming
Reflexion	Runtime class information
SQL	Support for database query language

resources. This package also defines most exceptions (see Section 5.5.1) and errors.

Utilities

java.util java.util offers various data structures, including Stack (see Section 4.2.2), HashTable (see Section 4.4.3), or the class Vector (dynamic object array). In addition, it includes classes for calendar functions (Calendar and Date) and time management (SimpleTimeZone).

AWT

java.awt java.awt (abstract Windows toolkit) offers platform-independent components for graphical user interfaces, including the classes Button, CheckBox, Scrollbar, and TextField. In addition to constructors and event processing (method processEvent), this package includes many other methods (such as setLabel and setActionCommand) for these classes. The package also includes the events themselves (class Event), Cursor, and ready-to-use dialogs, such as FileDialog (to select a file). Chapter 8 covers graphical user interfaces.

A special subpackage of java.awt is java.awt.datatransfer, which implements the Clipboard, enabling users to copy and paste data between applications.

IO Package

java.io java.io defines input and output streams for various purposes. For example, it can implement the sequential files well known from COBOL.

Wrapper Classes

Wrapper classes convert simple data types into objects *Wrapper classes* included in the class library convert variables from simple data types into objects. These classes, available for every simple data type, have names similar to the relevant types but beginning with an uppercase letter: Integer for the type int, Character for char, or Float for float.

Converting simple data types into objects is important because, for example, generic data structures can accept arbitrary objects (but objects only). A good example is the class java.util.Vector, which can store a list of objects.

The following source code fragment shows how an integer value can be inserted into this list:

```
int i = 4711;
Integer j = new Integer(i);
myVector.addElement(j);
```

Wrapper classes also offer a few important methods, including `toString` (), to convert something into a character string, or `valueOf` (), to convert something into a floating-point number.

5.4.4 Creating Your Own Class Library

How can I create my own class library?

Developing a class library is a highly complex task. Normally, it is not sufficient to simply collect classes over the course of time and let others use them, although this may surely be a first step. It is more useful to plan and develop a class library tuned to specific requirements—and, naturally, not to forget to eventually use it.

Many large corporations have several programmers who work exclusively for the class library and ensure that it is actually used. This group of programmers normally serves as central point of coordination, ensuring that other programmers work with current material as far as the class library is concerned. As mentioned in an early section of this chapter, it is necessary to learn this class library to be able to use it.

Some effort may be required at the psychological or motivating level to ensure that the classes offered in a tailored class library are used. This improves teamwork, because each programmer can work better within the team and see other programmers' work. This issue may require some organizational policies, such as bonuses for writing and/or applying reusable classes.

As far as the structure of a class library is concerned, all classes written by programmers (that is, not included in standard packages) should be specially marked, and this marking should be started in an early phase, when selecting a name for your class. Class names such as `TBMDObject` or `TBMD-Button` are undoubtedly useful.

It may also be helpful to group all your classes in a separate class library. For example, although Delphi provides a `TButton`, a `TBMDButton` could indeed be useful, because it should be able to do more later (or right away), or because a future change to the Delphi class library would then have no impact on the entire program package. The Delphi type `TButton` would then be embedded in `TBMDButton`. If a change really occurs, it merely has to be updated in `TBMDButton` to reflect that change.

5.4.5 Exercises

Task 1 (30 minutes): Online Help

Whoever seeks shall find! Take a look at the online help of your development environment and try to gain an overview of the class library underlying that online help system.

Task 2 (100 minutes): Using Ready-Made Class Libraries

Modify task 1 from Section 5.1.6 so that it builds on existing classes from the respective class library. This should make the solution considerably shorter and simpler. You should not change the test program, but take the definition of the interface into account.

5.5 Particularities of the Selected Programming Languages

In closing our discussion of object-oriented programming, we will cover a few language particularities, such as exceptions and interfaces. Although these terms are known both in Delphi and Java, they do not exist in many other object-oriented programming languages. Subsequently, we will describe language-specific constructs, such as properties or compiler directives of Delphi, and final classes or methods of Java.

5.5.1 Exceptions and Error Handling

Exceptions facilitate troubleshooting In COBOL, the *Declaratives Section* of a COBOL program also traps runtime errors, especially runtime IO errors. In object-oriented programming, the counterpart is exceptions, which offer a way to handle errors. Until recently, an error in object-oriented programming, such as division by zero, caused a program to abort. Of course, this is not what we want to happen.

Exceptions provide a solution to the problem, because when an error occurs, they can make sure the program will not exit. Instead, it merely exits the current code piece and jumps to an exception-handling routine. Subsequently, the program recovers and continues as usual. Such exceptions are objects derived from the base class Exception of the class library.

An exception basically is implemented such that the program code, which could potentially throw an exception, is placed into a *try block*, which is initiated by the keyword try. This block is followed by another independent block, stating all kinds of exceptions and offering appropriate instructions, which are executed sequentially for the relevant case. The most important—mostly self-explanatory—exceptions are as follows:

Delphi
```
EAbstractError
EDatabaseError
EHeapException
EInOutError
EoutOfMemory
```

Java
```
java.lang.ClassNotFoundException
java.lang.CloneNotSupportedException
java.lang.IllegalAccessException
java.lang.InstantiationException
java.lang.InterruptedException
java.lang.NoSuchMethodException
java.sql.SQLException
```

A large number of other exceptions are available in the respective class libraries, and some can be derived from them. Although they are by far mightier, exceptions can be compared to some extent with the COMPUTE addition ON SIZE ERROR instruction in COBOL.

Let's use a simple example to better understand exceptions. A functional procedure to calculate a mean value must always test for the special case of division by zero. This can be done by throwing an exception when this error occurs and setting the result accordingly.

Delphi
```
try
    result := sum div number;
except
  on EDivByZero do result := 0;
end;
```

Java
```
try {
    result = sum / number;
}
catch (ArithmeticException e) {
    result = 0;
}
```

The finally part will be executed in any event Another alternative is to initiate the exception block with the keyword finally. Both in Delphi and Java, this has the advantage that the finally part will be executed in any event. For instance, the finally block can release objects, and it is always executed, even when no exception was thrown and even when the block was terminated by exit, break, continue, or a similar way.

The program itself can also initiate an exception—for example, by using individual exception definitions. Such exceptions are derived from the basic type Exception.

Delphi In Delphi, an exception can be thrown by the keyword raise—for example, raise EInvalidOp.Create(s). The parameter s can pass an arbitrary string.

Java In Java, an exception can be thrown by the keyword throw—for example, throw new MyException(). For this purpose, the method that triggers this exception has to be specially identified by executing throws MyException after the parameter list. A method identified in such a way can be called only within a try block, which means that the exception must be caught in any event.

To further explain this issue, we inserted our own exception, ETooManyEntries, in the example of Section 5.3.6, to provide for an attempt to add another employee when the array is full. For this purpose, we define this exception (Listings 5.13 and 5.15), then raise it (Listings 5.13 and 5.16), and finally catch it in the calling program (Listings 5.14 and 5.17).

Listing 5.13. ETooManyEntries in Delphi: define and raise

```
unit PayrollAccounting;

interface
   uses SysUtils;
   const EMC = 100;
   type
      ETooManyEntries = class (Exception)
      end;
      . . .
      EmployeesList = class (TObject)
         public
            procedure InsertWorker; virtual;
            procedure InsertClerk; virtual;
            . . .
         private
```

```
                      list: array[1..EMC] of Employees;
                      n: Integer;
            end;

implementation

    procedure EmployeesList.InsertClerk;
        var c: Clerk;
    begin
        if n > EMC then begin
            raise ETooManyEntries.Create('too many entries');
            exit;
        end;
        c := Clerk.Create;
        c.Read;
        list[n] := c;
        Inc(n);
    end;

    procedure EmployeesList.InsertWorker;
        var w: Worker;
    begin
        if n > EMC then begin
            raise ETooManyEntries.Create('too many entries');
            exit;
        end;
        w := Worker.Create;
        w.Read;
        list[n] := w;
        Inc(n);
    end;
    . . .
end.
```

Listing 5.14.
ETooManyEntries
in Delphi: try
Block

```
program ExampleSalary;
uses
    PayrollAccounting in 'PayrollAccounting.pas';
var
```

```
    x: Integer;
    el: EmployeesList;
    ch: Char;
begin
    el := EmployeesList.Create;
    ReadLn(x); // 1: worker, 2: clerk, 3: end
    while x <> 3 do begin
      try
        if x = 1 then el.InsertWorker
        else el.InsertClerk;
      except
        on ETooManyEntries do WriteLn(Too many entries!');
      end;
      ReadLn(x);
    end;
    el.PrintSalary;
    el.Free;
    ReadLn(ch); // in order not to delete the screen
end.
```

―――――――――

**Listing 5.15.
ETooManyEntries
in Java: define**

```
package PayrollAccounting;
public class ETooManyEntries extends Exception {
}
```

―――――――――

**Listing 5.16.
ETooManyEntries
in Java: throw**

```
package Payroll Accounting;
public class EmployeesList {
    Employees list[];
    int n;
    final static int EMC = 100;
    public EmployeesList () {
      list = new employee[EMC];
      n = 0;
    }

    public void insertClerk () throws ETooManyEntries {
      if (n >= EMC) {
        throw new ETooManyEntries();
```

```
        }
        else {
          Clerk c = new clerk();
          c.read();
          list[n] = c;
          n ++;
        }
      }

      public void insertWorker () throws ETooManyEntries {
        if (n >= EMC) {
          throw new ETooManyEntries();
        }
        else {
          Worker w = new worker();
          w.read();
          list[n] = w;
          n ++;
        }
      }
    . . .
}
```

Listing 5.17.
ETooManyEntries
in Java: try Block

```
import PayrollAccounting.*;
import java.io.*;
class ExampleSalary {
  public static void main (String args[]) {
    int x;
    EmployeesList el = new EmployeesList();
    x = IO.readInt(); // 1: worker, 2: clerk, 3: end
    while (x != 3) {
      try {
        if (x == 1) {el.insertWorker();}
        else {el.insertClerk();}
      }
      catch (ETooManyEntries e) {
        System.out.println("Too many entries!");
      }
      x = IO.readInt();
```

```
      }
      el.printSalary();
   }
}
```

5.5.2 Interfaces

Multiple inheritance
Interfaces offer a way to implement *multiple inheritance*. With this type of inheritance, a class can have several superclasses rather than one (as in Delphi or Java). A simple example can be an analogy from the real world: A houseboat could inherit the properties of a superclass—house (walls and windows)—and of a second superclass—boat (anchor and mooring). In some programming languages, such as C++, this is possible, but not in all programming languages. Multiple inheritance is normally inefficient, and only few good application examples can be found for it. Delphi and Java support multiple inheritance by means of interfaces.

Interfaces differ from classes in that they contain no implementations at all—they can include only abstract methods and constant data elements. These methods themselves have to be implemented in a class. One single class can implement several interfaces, so multiple inheritance can be simulated.

Similarly, various classes can implement the same interface, so they respond to the same method calls, but the things they execute during each call can be different.

Interface Definition

Like classes, interfaces have to be defined before they can be used. This interface definition is similar to a class definition, but it begins with the keyword `interface` and not with the keyword `class`. Just like classes, interfaces can be derived (in this case from base interfaces).

Delphi
In Delphi, all interfaces are derived from the base interface `IUnknown`. Accordingly, an interface definition could look as follows:

```
type
   MyInterface = interface (IUnknown)
      public
         procedure P1;
         procedure P2;
   end;
```

Java   In Java, interfaces can be defined as public, which means that the interface will also be available outside the package in which it is defined. In contrast to the class definition, public applies then automatically to all methods.

```java
public interface MyInterface {
   void p1 ();
   void p2 ();
}
```

Implementing an Interface

As mentioned before, interfaces themselves contain only the method definitions. The implementation is then realized directly in classes.

Delphi   When an interface is implemented in Delphi, the interface name has to be stated next to the name of the base class (separated by a comma).

```delphi
type
   MyClass = class (TObject, MyInterface)
      public
         procedure P1;
         procedure P2;
   end;

procedure MyClass.P1;
begin
   WriteLn('method P1');
end;

procedure MyClass.P2;
begin
   WriteLn('method P2');
end;
```

If a class implements several interfaces, these interfaces are separated by commas: MyClass = class (TObject, MyInterface, MyInterface2).

Java   In Java, the keyword implements is used to implement an interface.

```java
public class MyClass implements MyInterface {

   public void p1 () {
      System.out.println("method P1");
   }
```

```java
    public void p2 () {
       System.out.println("method P2");
    }
 }
```

A class can also implement several interfaces. In this case, the interfaces have to be written after the keyword implements, separated by commas: public class MyClass implements MyInterface, MyInterface2 {. . .}.

If other classes are derived from the class MyClass, these classes also implement the interface MyInterface, regardless of whether an implement clause is present.

Using Interfaces

Classes that define interfaces can normally be used like any other class. We can also create objects of that type. The situation becomes more complicated if objects are to be created that should have the type of the interface. The problem is that this cannot be done directly. Instead, a reference to an object of the class that defines the interface has to be assigned to the variable. If a class defines several interfaces, an object of this class can be assigned to references pointing to all interfaces implemented by this class.

Delphi
```pascal
var
    c1: MyClass;
    i1: MyInterface;
begin
    c1 := MyClass.Create;
    i1 := c2;
    i1.P;
end;
```

_____

Java
```java
MyInterface i1 = new MyClass();
i1.P;
```

Inheritance and Interfaces

Similarly, interfaces can be inherited and extended like classes. This inheritance is done by syntax, as with classes; the main difference is that interfaces can have several "superinterfaces," which means they are not necessarily derived from one class.

5.5.3 Delphi Particularities

Properties

Properties are special attributes
A property is a special sort of an attribute. In addition to the value of an attribute, we can also define how the attribute should be read or written. The following source code fragment shows a property, name, of a class, Person.

```
Person = class (TObject)
  public
     property name: String read GetName write SetName;
     procedure GetName (): String;
     procedure SetName (s: String);
  . . .
end;
```

Property
Properties initiated by the keyword property can improve a program's readability. Using our preceding example, the attribute name would be set and read by the methods GetName and SetName. The source code piece

```
var p: Person; s: String;
. . .
p := Person.Create();
p.name := s;
WriteLn(p.name);
```

is converted as follows, based on properties and using the methods GetName and SetName:

```
var p: Person; s: String;
. . .
p := Person.Create();
p.SetName(s);
WriteLn(p.GetName());
```

However, better readability (an instruction is simply easier to understand than a method call) is not the only advantage of properties. A simple assignment is often not enough, such as when controls and similar things have to be executed. A corresponding method would have to be called in any event. The problem is that the user would have to be aware of this, so it would be necessary to study the class library. This can be avoided by using the property, and the user can do the assignment in the normal way.

In addition, properties can also be used so that read does not access a method but another attribute of the class.

Compiler Directives

As in COBOL, the Delphi compiler offers a large number of options we can use to influence the compiler's behavior, such as switching the control of array limits on and off. In Delphi, these options are available within the project. As an alternative, you could also control them in the source code and, for example, set other compiler options just for the translation of a few lines. These compiler directives are written in parentheses and always begin with a dollar sign—for example, {$B-}—to disable the shortcut evaluation (see Section 3.4.1).

Operator @

Converting into a pointer variable

The special operator @ can be used in Delphi to convert a normal variable into a pointer variable. The short source code fragment that follows explains this point:

```
var i: Integer; p: pointer to Integer;
. . .
p := @i;
```

Forward Declaration

Forward declaration is needed for interdependent classes

Forward declaration was described in Section 3.5.1. Interdependent classes must be declared in advance, just like procedures. Such a declaration is achieved by the type definition ClassName = class;. The following source code fragment shows an example:

```
type
    Postings = class; // forward declaration
    Account = class
```

```
      first: postings;
      . . .
    end;
    Postings = class // defining declaration
      k: Account;
      . . .
    end;
```

5.5.4 Java Particularities

Final Classes and Methods

Final classes and methods cannot be overwritten

Java also offers a way to mark classes and methods as final. No other classes can be derived from such classes. Similarly, final methods cannot be over-written. This is actually a contradiction to the basic rules of object-oriented programming, because it limits reusability. However, in certain situations, it may be meaningful for security reasons. A "final" class Class1 could be declared as follows:

```
final public class Class1 {
    int field1;
    public void show () {
        . . .
    }
}
```

Nested Classes

Nested classes are a way to improve the support of the information hiding principle (see Section 4.1). This means that we could define additional (quasi-inner) classes within the implementation of a class. Depending on whether this class was defined as public, these "inner" classes can be used generally or only locally. The following short source code fragment shows a local class that can be used only within the method proc.

```
public void proc () {
    class Local {
        int sum
        ...
```

```
    }
    ...
}
```

A special form of nested classes are the *anonymous* classes. These classes have no names and are defined directly within the new instruction. This instruction can be extended so that a class body can be written after the class identifier and the argument list. Anonymous classes are useful when we have to deal with small, one-time objects for simple tasks.

Static Data Elements and Static Methods

Static elements are not assigned to one object but to an entire class As described in Chapter 3, in addition to data elements, methods can be declared with the keyword static. These methods will then be assigned to the entire class and not to a single object.

```
public class StaticDemo {
    public static int x;
    public static void p () {
        . . .
    }
}
```

Assuming that we want to create different objects of this class, such as o1 and o2, the two fields o1.x and o2.x would be the same field, because they were assigned to the class and not to the single object. Any change to o1.x would automatically also change o2.x. This is why we cannot map global module variables, like those introduced in Section 3.6, with such static data elements.

The situation is similar with static methods, which are always assigned to the entire class; this is why they are called class methods. Such a method can be called even if no object was previously created. Class methods can be used in Java to simulate normal procedures, like those introduced in Section 3.3, but the call is written in method notation.

Garbage Collector

Naturally, one of the most important Java features is the Garbage Collector, which was briefly introduced in Section 3.7.4. We will have a closer look at it here.

Dynamic objects are created with new and then basically remain in memory, in contrast to normal variables, whose memory space is released automatically when the block is exited. For dynamic structures, the memory space does not have to be released until some event happens, such as when a delete operation like Delphi's dispose is invoked. This deletion is often not easy to implement and carries a risk of *memory leaks.*

Let's use an example to better explain this situation. Assume we have a head node to a linear list, and this head node is deleted, while the list elements themselves remain. The problem is that these elements can no longer be reached, because the reference to them was deleted. Unfortunately, it also means that we cannot delete them, and the memory space occupied cannot be reclaimed. If such a situation happens often with large lists, our memory may be exhausted sooner or later.

"Dangling pointers," which can occur when two pointers point to the same object, can pose a similar problem when dispose is invoked for one of them. The second pointer will still point to the deleted object that no longer exists. An attempt to access this object can lead to unexpected results.

Of course, these two risks are due to programming errors, but these errors can happen easily. To prevent them, Java does not offer an explicit delete function but instead the powerful concept of a Garbage Collector. The Garbage Collector builds on "memory leaks," because objects that can no longer be reached are useless and should be released. This is exactly what the Garbage Collector does.

To delete a list, all that needs to be done is to set the head pointer to null so that none of the single elements of this list is reachable any more. The Garbage Collector detects this and automatically frees the memory space taken by these elements. It relieves the programmer of this work and reduces a large error potential.

Of particular interest at this point is the method finalize inherited from the Object class in Java. In fact, other actions often have to be taken when deleting objects. These functions can be embedded in the method, because the Garbage Collector invokes the Finalizer automatically when it frees objects. For example, if a file must be closed before an object is removed, the finalize method could look like this:

```
protected void finalize () throws IO Exception {
   super.finalize();
   if (fd != null) {
```

```
        if (fd != fd.in) {
          close();
        }
    }
}
```

Reference Classes

Weak references are ignored by the Garbage Collector

Reference classes can be used in Java to simulate *weak* references. To better understand this point, we first need to recall the Garbage Collector definition from earlier. The Garbage Collector removes all objects from memory as soon as no more references point to them. Considering that we distinguish here between "strong" and "weak" references, the definition would have to read as follows: All objects that have no more "strong" references will be removed from memory. The Garbage Collector ignores the "weak" references introduced here.

Such reference classes are derived from the base class java.lang.ref.Reference. If we want to create a weak reference to an object, we have to pass the object to the constructor of the reference class:

```
Object o1 = new Object();
WeakReference ref = new WeakReference(o1);
```

5.5.5 Exercises

Task 1 (90 minutes): Exceptions

Consider the exercise in Section 5.4.5; adapt it to use meaningful exceptions. Your exceptions should be defined as types in the module and then be caught in the calling test program.

Task 2 (45 minutes): Interfaces

Find a way to best represent a class, HouseBoat, from House and Boat. The new class should inherit three meaningful methods each from House and Boat, where the definition is sufficient—that is, no implementation is necessary.

6

Object–Oriented Design

A big problem when working with object-oriented programming is to find the correct kind and number of classes. This chapter presents techniques to support this task.

6.1   Object–Oriented Design and UML

Abbot method, UML, CRC cards

This section deals with how to best divide a system into classes. The object-oriented design differs from the procedural design—the stepwise refinement discussed in Section 2.4. In this case, we will first work out the particularities of the design and then discuss the Abbot method. Moreover, this section introduces tools, such as the Unified Modeling Language (UML) and CRC cards. These issues will be completed with a few useful tips and warnings about frequent design errors.

6.1.1   Comparison with the Procedural Design

The question of what the system uses to do something is in the foreground

Stepwise refinement can be applied to work out clean program logic that is easy to use but also sensitive to changes and not very friendly toward reusability. In an object-oriented design, what the system uses to do something is the focal point. The results are classes, forming core components, and several procedures (or classes) building on the former.

Central things first

The general approach is to first work out the things central to the task—for example, in an accounting software, accounts, postings, or persons. Next, we consider what operations could be executed with these central things such as, creating an account, printing an account, or adding a posting entry. Also, we would have to think what information should be stored about an object—attributes such as account name, opening balance, current balance, and so on.

We have to think about more things, for example, whether there will be system-dependent details, such as disk controllers or input/output operations, because it would be useful to encapsulate them. Moreover, we should absolutely check for a potential risk of parts being modified. Finally, when you are designing a system, care should be taken that the impact of changes is kept to a minimum.

Consider reusability!

One of the important differences versus procedural designs is the reusability of existing classes. If we are faced with a problem that has been solved similarly in the past, a procedural design allows us to duplicate existing code and modify it to match the new task. In object-oriented design, it is possible to derive a new class from an existing one and then effect only those changes that are absolutely necessary for the new task. Of course, this facilitates maintainability, because errors do not have to be corrected more than once (both in the original code and in the duplicated code).

Building on these design principles, we can apply the Abbot method.

6.1.2 The Abbot Method

The Abbot method permits designing an object-oriented system

The method invented by Abbot [Abb83] serves to design an object-oriented system. It is easy to use. In a first step, we work out a textual specification; then we can read all nouns, verbs, and adjectives directly from this specification:

- Nouns are candidates for classes or attributes.

- Verbs are candidates for methods.

- Adjectives are candidates for attributes.

The preceding description is overly simplified to better illustrate the concepts. The words found are always just candidates and thus a starting point for decomposition that must not be realized blindly. It takes a lot of experience to achieve a good decomposition. Another major drawback of the method is that it always goes back to restart from zero—it does not consider existing classes that could be used as a basis. Again, considering such base classes is a matter of experience.

A short example shows how the Abbot method is applied. An account includes several postings. The sum of these postings produces the account balance. There should be a way to add a posting to the account. There should also be a way to print the account. Accounts can be divided into two groups, depending on whether they are OI-leading or not (that is, whether or not it is a leading account for open items).

Table 6.1 lists the most important nouns, verbs, and adjectives that occur in this example.

This list in Table 6.1 shows potential candidates for classes, methods, and attributes. The noun Account is easy. It is most likely a class. The verbs add and print are also straightforward, because two useful methods can be designed from them.

The nouns AccountBalance and Postings are a little more complicated. Postings will probably become an attribute of the new class to be constructed. To make a final decision on this issue, we will need more information, such as how these postings are to be structured. AccountBalance could be both an attribute of the class Account and a functional procedure. For efficiency, an attribute is probably the preferred use, while a method would be the preferred option for abstractions. Similarly, the adjective OI-leading will probably become an attribute of the class Account.

The important point is that everything a software object knows (state) or does (behavior) is expressed by attributes and methods within this object. Finally, everything an object should not know or do will not be included.

Which attributes and methods should be generally accessible? We need to determine the attributes and methods that should or should not be generally accessible. This will normally require a tradeoff between maximum security(export as little as possible) and maximum reusability (export as much as possible).

Table 6.1   Nouns, verbs, and adjectives of the account specification

Nouns	Verbs	Adjectives
Account	Add	OI-leading
Account balance (sum) Postings	Print	

6.1.3   CRC Cards

Easy representation methods for designed classes

CRC offers a simple method to represent classes as a kind of blueprint for designs. CRC stands for Class—Responsibilities—Collaborators. It uses small cards that can be created easily to note a class's most important properties. Figure 6.1 shows an example of a CRC card.

Such a card is created for each class and labeled with the class name. First, we define responsibilities and collaborators (that is, classes that have to cooperate). The responsibilities can initially be written in informal language and then refined to eventually develop them into methods with names. Often, only attributes emerge from such responsibilities.

One major advantage of CRC cards is that they can be produced easily in a large number of arrangements, making it possible to view many classes together. This makes them the ideal vehicle for brainstorming meetings. They also support the validation of object candidates. If no responsibilities and no attributes are found in a brainstorming meeting, they can generally be left out.

Another advantage of CRC cards is their limited size, which forces the developer to keep classes small.

6.1.4   Unified Modeling Language

UML offers a model to represent classes and their relationships

UML is an alternative form to represent a design with classes and their relationships. These classes, together with their attributes and methods, are mapped onto an object model. The word *model* indicates that we do not necessarily have to provide all details, at least not at this stage. In fact, the level of detail should be just sufficient to understand the representation.

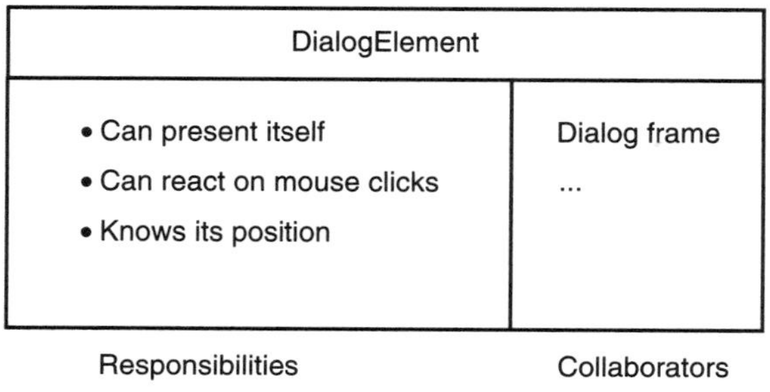

DialogElement	
• Can present itself • Can react on mouse clicks • Knows its position	Dialog frame ...
Responsibilities	Collaborators

Figure 6.1 Example of a CRC card.

For example, attribute types, method interfaces, and—most important—method implementations are optional.

UML is an international standard of OMG for representing class libraries and frameworks (more about these issues in Section 6.4). This section introduces UML; extensive information is available in [RBJ98].

The most important elements UML can represent are classes and their specific objects. Both are drawn as rectangles or diamonds. Rectangles representing specific objects have round edges. Within a class, the rectangle is divided into three parts, for names, attributes, and methods. The latter may have a small box attached to it to denote the implementation. For objects, the values of the individual attributes are represented. Figure 6.2 shows a class and an object side by side in UML representation.

We can see from Figure 6.2 that the class name for a specific object is given in parentheses. If UML representation shows an abstract class, it is also useful to write the class name and abstract methods in parentheses for easier understanding [Mös99].

In representing relationships between objects or between classes, three important relationships are worth mentioning:

Uses relationship

- **Association:** This is a simple *uses* relationship—a class is used in the implementation of another class. This relationship is identified by a plain line.

Has-a relationship

- **Aggregation:** This is a *has-a* relationship, which occurs when a class has an attribute with a type of another class. Such a relationship is denoted by a diamond at the beginning of the line.

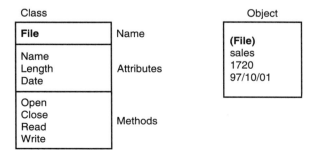

Figure 6.2 Class and specific object in UML representation.

Is-a relationship ■ **Generalization:** This derivation from one class to another is an *is-a* relationship. For graphical representation, the classes are drawn one on top of the other with a triangle on the line.

Figure 6.3 compares the three most important relationships. We return to these terms in connection with our description of databases in Section 7.2. There could also be cardinalities—how many objects relate to how many others. For example, an account may relate to an arbitrary number of postings. For this purpose, digits are written next to the objects; an asterisk denotes an arbitrary number.

6.1.5 Tips

Object-oriented design requires extensive experience   As mentioned, object-oriented design is not trivial and requires extensive experience. This section provides a few tips [Mös99, p. 159 ff.]. The most important thing is to be aware of common errors to avoid them.

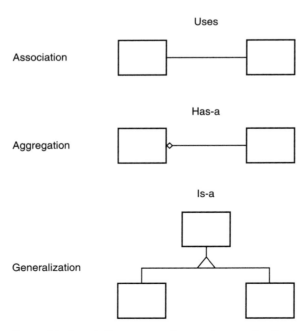

Figure 6.3 Association, aggregation, and generalization in UML representation.

Too Many Trivial Classes

Is this class really necessary? Would a standard type do the job?

One of the most frequent errors beginners make is to create too many classes. This makes an object-oriented system difficult to understand. For this reason, consider carefully whether a class is necessary, whether it may just be an attribute of a class, or whether a standard type (for example, integer) might be sufficient. A simple example is the balance of an account, which would hardly make a meaningful class; the standard type floating-point number is normally sufficient.

Variants with Identical Structure and Identical Behavior

Another risk, in addition to creating too many classes, is designing different classes only to satisfy a specific attribute, although both variants have basically the same structure and behavior. For example, the two classes RedRectangle and BlueRectangle could be derived from a base class Rectangle. If the red and the blue rectangles differ only in their colors and not in their behavior, or by different attributes, it would be better to add a new attribute, color, to the base class Rectangle; this attribute could then be set to the appropriate color.

Confusing Is-a and Has-a Relationships

Inheritance means is-a relationship

A new class should ideally be derived from an existing base class whenever it appears possible and meaningful. "Possible and meaningful" means that nothing should be derived at any cost. Often, this is meaningful only for an is-a relationship. For example, many tend to derive a class—say, Line—from a base class—say, Point. Deriving the former from the latter does not make sense because, although a line *has* two points, it *is* not a point. In the case of a has-a relationship, it is normally better to create a new class and use the existing class as an attribute.

Wrong Receiver Object

List.Remove (element) or Element.RemoveFrom (list)

Another area to watch for common errors is when designing methods. A method should always be defined in the correct class. A simple example is the design of a method to remove an element from a list. For this purpose, we could imagine implementing a method, List.Remove (element), but Element.RemoveFrom (list) would also be feasible. Naturally, we have to ask ourselves which would be the correct one. We can normally answer this question by considering the following principle: the receiver should be the object with data that will most likely change. In the previous example, we would certainly prefer the variant `List.Remove (element)`.

Class Hierarchies Are Too Deep or Too Flat

A class hierarchy should be well balanced. For this purpose, we can use the following rule of thumb: Derive many specific classes from one abstract class, but only few new abstract classes. In contrast, derive as few additional specific classes as possible from a specific class.

More Tips

- Although *super calls*—calls to methods of the base class—help avoid redundancies, they normally make the program more complex.

- A has-a relationship (the use of a class as an attribute) is often more flexible than an is-a relationship (the derivation from this class).

- Methods with many parameters should be decomposed into smaller methods.

- Ensure that others can use your classes as a basis in their development projects.

6.1.6 Exercises

Task 1 (180 minutes): Designing the Account Class

The Abbot method Apply the Abbot method to the following text. Basically, we distinguish between two types of accounts: personnel and inventory. Personnel accounts are characterized by being OI-leading and subject to turnover.

Both account types have a unique number, a name, and several postings. A posting consists of a posting date, an offset account, debit and credit identifiers, and a posting amount. The sum of these postings results in the account balance. It should be possible to add a posting entry to the account and to print a list of all postings of an account.

Apply the Abbot method to design the required classes. You should represent these classes both in UML and in an object-oriented programming language (Delphi or Java).

Design Patterns and Components

The following sections introduce design patterns and components, modern methods used in software development. We first describe *design patterns,* which can be thought of as descriptions, or blueprints, of proven solutions for recurring problems. Subsequently, we will introduce *components:* small, manageable, largely independent software pieces that can be easily developed and joined to form a larger application.

6.2.1 Design Patterns

Design patterns take the idea of class libraries a step further

Design patterns can be thought of as a continuation of the concept of class libraries. Classes and methods form a specific solution to a specific problem and can be extended but not changed. Design patterns provide solutions for frequent problems and can be adapted to specific problems. Such patterns identify and specify abstractions on a level above the level of classes and objects and above the level of entire components [GHJV94]. Accordingly, a pattern does not describe just a single class or method but several components, classes, or objects.

This section gives an overview of what such design patterns look like and provides a few examples. We recommend the following textbooks to readers interested in learning more about design patterns:

■ Gamma, Helm, et al., *Design Patterns* [GHJV94]: The seminal work on design patterns and object-oriented software development, this book presents a catalog of simple and precise solutions for recurring design problems. The four authors are often called the "gang of four" because of their international acceptance as experts in the field of object-oriented software development.

■ Pree, *Design Patterns for Object-Oriented Software Development* [Pre95]: In addition to the aforementioned seminal work of the "gang of four," this book is one of the most frequently quoted concerning design patterns. It contains many examples and real-world case studies that show how to achieve specific goals with design patterns.

■ Buschmann, Meunier, et al., *Pattern-oriented Software Architecture* [BMRS96]: This book contains a collection of patterns extending over several abstraction levels in the field of software design, ranging from basic architectural patterns to patterns for detailed system design to programming language–specific idioms. The authors also show how the patterns can be combined.

- Mössenböck, *Object-Oriented Programming in Oberon-2* [Mös99]: This book is an excellent introduction to object-oriented programming, based on Oberon-2, a programming language similar to Pascal. A full chapter is dedicated to patterns, including many not found in [GHJV94].

Design pattern: context, problem, and solution   A design pattern is always subject to a scheme, consisting of three parts [BMRS96, p. 8 ff.]: context, problem, and solution. The relationship between these parts can be represented as follows. *Context* is a situation in which the problem occurs for which a solution should be found. Therefore, a design pattern should include an exact description of the problem to be solved. For example, it should consider requirements, side conditions, and desirable properties. The relevant solution is often knowingly described in an abstract way, without dealing with implementation details. This allows us to use a pattern independently of a specific programming language.

Based on their use, design patterns can be distinguished as belonging to one of three categories [BMRS 96, p. 11 ff.]:

- **Architectural patterns:** These patterns reflect fundamental structural principles of software systems. Such a pattern describes a set of prede-fined subsystems and specifies their respective areas of competency. It also contains rules to organize the relationships between these subsystems.

- **Design patterns:** These patterns enable us to describe structures of communicating components that solve a general design problem in a special context.

- **Idioms:** In contrast to the other two pattern types, idioms are more specific to a programming language. As in a specific programming language, they can show special aspects of components or how to implement the relationships between them.

Regardless of the category to which a design pattern belongs, it must be represented in an appropriate form. Accordingly, it should have an intuitive name. Moreover, a significant example should be added to the problem description. The solution should be further illustrated by diagrams (for example, UML) and scenarios. A few design patterns are described in the following sections.

Constructor

A constructor [Mös99, p. 111] is an object-based construction pattern that encourages initialization of an object. This is a particular benefit in programming languages that do not have their own constructors, such as Delphi or Java, where they are part of the language.

The pattern will be explained by a simple example: a class T with an attribute a and a method InitT, which initializes the value of a. Figure 6.4 shows this structure.

Building on this basis, we can easily implement a procedure, NewT, which creates an object of class T and initializes it right away. Whenever such a T object is required, it can be created and initialized by calling the constructor NewT. This pattern can be easily transported to any class by using the respective class name (for example, NewAccount, NewBill) for T.

Factory

A *factory* [GHJV94, p. 107] offers an interface to create families of related objects, or objects that depend on each other.

A simple example will explain this pattern. We derive various kinds of accounts from an abstract class, Account. On one hand, a simple account, BasicAccount, provides the posting and output functions. On the other hand, a class, MightyAccount, offers additional functions, such as for bonus analysis. A financial accounting program could optionally work with these accounts by providing an attribute k of the abstract class Account. When creating such an accounting system, we have to decide whether the attribute k should store a BasicAccount or a MightyAccount. Exactly this problem can be solved with a factory pattern.

A factory object creates the account. For each account type, there is an independent factory class—BasicAccountFactory, MightyAccountFactory,

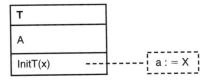

Figure 6.4 Structure of a constructor pattern.

and so on. All these classes are derived from an abstract class, resulting in the pattern shown in Figure 6.5.

During initialization of the accounting program, the desired factory class is assigned to the attribute factory, depending on whether the accounting system is to work with a BasicAccount or a MightyAccount object. The call k := factory.New() will supply the desired account type.

In summary, factory classes can be used to dynamically specify the component to be used at runtime.

Iterator

An *iterator* [GHJV94, p. 335] serves to enable sequential access to the elements of a dynamic data structure, such as a list or stack (see Section 4.2.2), without the need to disclose the underlying representation.

We briefly described methods such as PrintAll in the introduction of these data types. In many cases, clients of these data structures want not

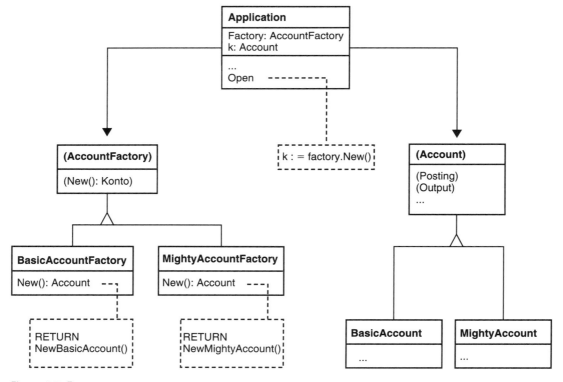

Figure 6.5 Factory pattern.

Figure 6.6 Iterator pattern.

only to print the individual elements but perhaps to do totally different operations on them. These could be operations not yet known when a data structure is implemented. Therefore, a solution of the kind PrintAll is not really satisfactory. Iterator classes would be more meaningful; Figure 6.6 shows their pattern. The important thing is that an iterator reduces the amount of information a client must know to be able to access the elements in the collection.

Such iterator classes are implemented in the same module as the data structure. These objects can be moved beyond the data structure. A simple interface is then available, offering the possibility of creating a loop that will iterate over the elements in the collection, regardless of whether the collection is a vector or a binary tree. It could work like this:

```
iterator := list.CreateIterator();
iterator.Start;
while not iterator.IsReady() do begin
   elem := iterator.CurrentElement();
      // work with elem
   iterator.Continue;
end;
```

Delphi particularity   In Delphi, the procedure variables frequently used in the examples of Chapter 4 could be used instead of the iterator pattern.

6.2.2 Components

Components are small, easily manageable, and largely independent of one another   The underlying principle of components is similar to that of a class library. It is based on the assumption of an existing solution to be embedded into a new application. However, components are always small and easily manageable software pieces that are largely independent of one another. Despite their small size, they can be joined to form extensive applications so that, in a certain way, they can be thought of as a kind of Lego system for software engineers.

This section provides a rough overview of what such components look like. We recommend the following books for readers interested in learning more:

■ Szyperski, *Component Software: Beyond Object-Oriented Programming* [Szy99]: This seminal work on components shows the way from object-oriented programming to component-oriented programming. It also discusses both Java beans and Active-X, the component model of Microsoft.

Java beans ■ Piemont, *Components in Java* [Pie99]: This book discusses mainly Java beans, the component model of Java. It presents many advanced issues, such as customizing, design patterns for beans, seralization, and the interplay between Java and Active-X. It also contains an overview of development tools and beans libraries and an introduction to component-oriented software development.

What Is a Component?

A component has no unique definition in software engineering, but most agree that it is an executable piece of software representing a self-sufficient construct with its own describable functionality and semantics at the application level. Components have a state, reflecting their property values, and this state is often stored beyond application borders (persistent components). Components are always accessed over a defined interface. In general, the access can be manipulated by events or directly by method calls.

Components are independent of both the programming language and the operating system   An important requirement of components is that they should be independent of any programming language or operating system. Typical examples for components are user interface elements—more specifically, Web browser components or model constructs of facts from corporate business processes. As usual in object-oriented programming, reusability is one of the main aspects of components. Unless they can be reused, components are too complex to be useful.

It seems intuitive to ask what the real differences are between a component and a class, because a class also meets many of the previous criteria. Both a component and a class follow the same goals and will coexist in the future. In general, however, a component has a larger functional extent than an object and can even be considered independent.

It is also important to note that the information-hiding concept is much stronger for components than for classes. In relation to components, information hiding is strict and could even go as far as not making the source code public, which is not the case with classes. Only a binary format is supplied, instead of disclosing the source code.

The following sections discuss component-based software development, where we basically have to distinguish between development of a single component and composition of a component-based application.

Development of a Single Component

Development of a single component is similar to object-oriented design. The most important point is that the interface should be clearly identified and cleanly specified (for properties, methods, and events). This interface will later serve as a contract, so to speak, which other objects will enter into with this component as soon as they want to use it. Also, components should be designed with utmost flexibility—ideally supplied within the environment situation at runtime and not before, to prevent strong interdependencies.

A component should offer a solution for general-purpose problems and not for a specific problem. This should be taken into account when developing components.

Composition of a Component-Based Application

Components are "composed" Building an application from many components is not a trivial activity. It can be considered a piece of art, so many like to use the expression "composition." Essentially, creating an application from many components involves several steps, repeated over and over:

1. Define the requirements of the application.

2. Select suitable components.

3. Adapt and configure the selected components.

4. Develop additional components, if required.

5. Create a framework and integrate the components into a complete software system.

6. Test the component-based application.

6.2.3 Exercises

This tutorial section was definitely not easy. Readers who still have problems with the two new terms, *design patterns* and *components*, will find this exercise helpful in deepening their knowledge of the subject. As a motivation, we should mention that few programmers really master these issues.

Task 1 (180 minutes): Literature Study

Study the online help of Delphi or Java and try to find terms such as Active-X (Delphi) or Beans (Java). Try to get an overview of the options behind these terms.

7

Databases

Whereas we have concentrated more on algorithms, methods, and activities in the previous parts of our OOP course, this chapter discusses databases. In most applications, such as billing software, working with data is at the center of activities. These data not only are input but also have to be stored and retrieved again and again (even many months later). Think only of the postings entered in a financial accounting program.

Similarly, almost every COBOL program in the traditional form requires data to be saved to files. Because this saving to files has a few drawbacks, which is discussed later, it is customary in object-oriented programming to use databases. This chapter deals with databases, although they are not really an object-oriented feature but rather state-of-the art, describing many issues, including SQL as the most important query language for databases.

7.1 Introduction and Differences from COBOL IS Files

COBOL, or at least traditional COBOL (more about this later), uses individual files to store data. A program works mainly with several files open at the same time. In contrast, a database can be thought of as a huge data repository that stores all data. This section describes the basic idea behind a database and then highlights the differences from COBOL. It also explains special database functions, such as recovery or concurrency, and introduces a new generation of object-oriented databases. Finally, this chapter describes the change from ISAM COBOL systems to an RDBMS (relational database management system) architecture.

7.1.1   The Basic Concept of a Database

The basic concept of a relational database, currently the most popular form of database, which is discussed in the following sections, is that data are stored in the form of usual tables. Table 7.1 shows an example.

Tables such as Table 7.1 always have a fixed structure, composed of rows and columns, which are defined once only. This definition is elaborated on the basis of a *normalization* (see also Section 7.2.2). The rows of such a table accommodate records, and the columns define various attributes. Such a record compares well with a conventional record or object.

Table rows are defined by a key

In general, each row is identified by a key, for example, a unique number, such as an account number. This key can be used to access a record directly, as in an index-sequential file, without the need to walk through the entire table. Similarly to COBOL, it is also possible to generate additional indexes to optimize access speed (see also Section 7.2.5).

Despite significant similarities, we can already identify a fundamental difference versus the file-based systems known from COBOL. The definition of tables is centralized, as opposed to the record structure of files in individual programs. In addition, databases assume other activities, offering various benefits versus file-based systems.

A database system offers more than fundamental tools for the following tasks:

Table 7.1   Example for a database table

Account number	Account name	Balance
2700	Cash	12,000
2800	Bank	40,000
4000	Earnings	12,999
. . .		

- Define a new table.

- Insert and remove records from these tables.

- Find data in these tables.

- Change individual data fields in these tables.

In fact, a database system supports additional activities, such as monitoring for unauthorized access, data security, or control of concurrent access attempts by several programs. In addition, database functions such as recovery or concurrency offer important benefits versus file-based systems.

A program is an interface between user and database

Normally, instead of a user communicating directly with the database, designers write a program, which serves in a way as an interface between the user and the database. These programs can be kept much shorter, compared with similar programs that work with file-based systems, because they can assume the activities mentioned previously from the database. The way these programs can look like will be described in Section 7.4.

However, although index-sequential files are mostly used in traditional COBOL programs to store data, newer COBOL versions are able to access relational databases by using embedded SQL statements and ODBC protocols, too.

7.1.2 SELECT: One Word—Two Meanings

Database SELECT and COBOL SELECT have different meanings

Our previous brief introduction already revealed fundamental differences from COBOL and its index-sequential files. Another important difference is the keyword SELECT. Whereas COBOL uses it to describe each file to be processed in a program, databases use this keyword to select specific columns from the entire data repository.

So, whereas a SELECT in COBOL could look like this:

```
SELECT POSTING FILE
    ASSIGN TO "D:POST.DAT"
    LOCK MODE EXCLUSIVE
    FILE STATUS IS POST-STAT
    ACCESS SEQUENTIAL
    ORGANIZATIONAL SEQUENTIAL.
```

a SELECT operated on a database could have the following form:
SELECT *

FROM POSTING
WHERE ACCOUNT = 4400

This database SELECT would select all postings made to account 4400 from the data repository. The instruction SELECT is the most important command of SQL (Structured Query Language; see also Section 7.3). This database query language can be used to do the following:

■ Write data to and delete it from a data repository.

■ Define the structure of a database.

■ Define queries to select data from the data repository.

SQL is similar to English and a uniform language. Despite the large number of programming languages, the database discipline reached a certain degree of standardization [DaDa97]. On the other hand, the databases available in the market have introduced different dialects of SQL. A special dialect, namely, *OQL (Object Query Language)* [CBB97], is used for object-oriented databases. Although object-oriented databases have not become really popular yet, we will describe them briefly in Section 7.1.8.

SQL is a strongly set-oriented language

Sections 7.3 and 7.4 concentrate on SQL, but we should mention here that SQL is strongly oriented to sets. This means that most of the single operations refer to data sets, as opposed to single records, as in COBOL. However, this also means that scrolling through records—something we are used to from COBOL (particularly scrolling up from an arbitrary record to the first record)—is not that easy in the object-oriented world.

7.1.3 Data Security, Data Protection, and Recovery

An important benefit of databases versus individual files is data security. This benefit is twofold. First, a database can be protected easily, because everything is centralized, so to speak, and one command is enough to protect things. Second, a database offers many options to protect data against unauthorized access. We can specify exactly which database and records users are allowed to access. Moreover, this function is permanently integrated into the database, so no special code has to be written.

For this purpose, a database normally offers a user management function, based on user names and passwords. Each user has to log on to the database, just like logging on to an operating system to obtain the right to access certain records and he or she cannot access any records not included in this access right. Although this sort of access protection is costly in file-based systems, requiring a high programming effort to solve it, it is virtually an automatic and integral feature of database systems.

Consider payroll accounting as a simple and typical application example. For this program, it is important to ensure that only selective users can see the salary information of all employees. For example, a department manager should see only the salary information of his or her employees but not those of other departments. Potential solutions to such problems are often one of the most important criteria when selecting software.

Recovery: no need to correct or reorganize programs

Another important advantage of databases is a mechanism called *recovery*. When an error occurs, such as a program crash, this mechanism ensures that the database maintains a consistent state. Let's look at this situation by using a short example. Think of a simple account to which postings can be added. The new balance of each account should be calculated automatically every time a transaction is posted.

If the program crashes between the time when we add a posting transaction and the time it takes to calculate the new account balance, the data status would be inconsistent, because the account balance stored in the database does not correspond with the actual account balance. Every COBOL programmer is aware of such situations, as many correction or reorganization programs have to be created exactly for this purpose.

A database solves this problem by the recovery mechanism. Required database changes of a program are grouped to form a transaction. In our example, this could be three actions together—insert a posting, calculate the account balance, and write this amount. Such a transaction is called "atomic," which means that this transaction is executed completely or not at all.

For example, if a program crashed in the middle of such a transaction, the database would restore the status it had before the transaction was initiated. In our example, this would mean undoing the insertion of a new transaction. Based on this capability, the programmer could use *commit instructions* to define the instructions belonging to one specific transaction.

7.1.4 Parallel Processing

Transactions can be executed either consecutively or concurrently

The transactions introduced in the previous section can be executed not only consecutively but also concurrently. However, it is important to pay careful attention to the order in either case. For instance, if two transactions access the same field (that is, one to duplicate it and the other to add a value of three), the sequence in which the two actions are executed plays an important role.

Also, in some situations, fields have to be locked. In the previous example, during the time when the account balance is read, the posting is entered, and the posting value is added to the account balance, the account balance must not change. This rule is known from file-based systems, where we normally also work with locking mechanisms, except that databases use an improved form.

We will explain this with a simple example. Table 7.2 shows two transactions, T1 and T2, which both access objects A, B, and C. The initial value of each object is 60.

We can see in Table 7.2 that the result from a quasi-concurrent (that is, parallel) execution is as follows: A = 55, B = 70, C = 80. The result would be different if the two transactions were executed consecutively. Table 7.3 shows this situation.

We can see that the result in Table 7.3 from the serial execution would be A = 55, B = 50, C = 80. Considering that these results differ, it is obvious

Table 7.2 Example for transactions: parallel execution

Transaction T1	A_{T1}	B_{T1}	C_{T1}	Transaction T2	A_{T2}	B_{T2}	C_{T2}	A_{file}	B_{file}	C_{file}
Read A	60							60	60	60
A := A 5	55									
				Read B		60				
Write A	55							55		
				B := B 20		40				
Read B		60								
				Write B		40			40	
B := B + 10		70								
				Read C			60			
Write B		70							70	
				C := C + 20			80			
				Write C			80			80

Table 7.3   Example for transactions: serial execution

Transaction T1	A_{T1}	B_{T1}	C_{T1}
Read A	60		
A := A 5	55		
Write A	55		
Read B		60	
B := B + 10		70	
Write B		70	
Transaction T2	A_{T2}	B_{T2}	C_{T2}
Read B		70	
B := B 20		50	
Write B		50	
Read C			60
C := C + 20			80
Write C			80

that these processes cannot be serialized. For this reason, we have to insert LOCK and UNLOCK operations in the appropriate places. Table 7.4 shows this approach, based on our previous example.

Beware of deadlocks!   When using such LOCK and UNLOCK operations, it is important to ensure that no deadlock situation can occur. This situation, which can also occur in COBOL, would in most cases be a programming error that occurs when two transactions lock each other forever. For example, if transaction T1 locks object A and then tries to access object B while T2 locks object B and tries to access A, T1 would wait for T2 to free object B. Naturally, this will never happen, because this transaction is waiting in turn for T1 to free object A.

It is possible that a deadlock cannot be prevented. Therefore, the database management system may abort a transaction if it detects a deadlock cycle.

7.1.5   Possibility for End Users

Databases allow end users to evaluate data themselves   Another advantage of databases is that, in addition to the program itself, the database query language can be used to access the data stock. Because the data definition is integrated in the database rather than distributed over

Table 7.4   Example for transactions: LOCK and UNLOCK
operations inserted

Transaction T1	Transaction T2
LOCK A	
Read A	
A := A 5	
	LOCK B
	Read B
Write A	
UNLOCK A	
	B := B 20
	Write B
	UNLOCK B
LOCK B	
Read B	
B := B + 10	
	LOCK C
	Read C
Write B	
UNLOCK B	
	C := C + 20
	Write C
	UNLOCK C

several programs or copies, any person other than the programmer can access the database. The simplicity of some databases, such as Microsoft Access, allows end users to evaluate the information stored in the database. Therefore, special database queries specified and developed by the customer make a program package much more attractive. This factor has become one of the major purchase decision criteria, so using databases can also mean a significant competitive edge.

However, as attractive as it may be for customers to be able to specify data queries themselves, it may be problematic, especially when a change to the records is effected in this way. For this reason, appropriate security mechanisms are recommended, such as granting only read access to specific data.

7.1.6 Requirements to a Relational Database

We can identify the following requirements to, or properties of, a relational database [Dat90]. Databases should do the following:

Properties of a relational database

- Provide a way to manipulate data.

- Avoid redundancy—each piece of information should be stored only once. However, we will see later that controlled redundancies may indeed be useful in some cases, for efficiency. Consequently, this requirement refers to uncontrolled and unnecessary redundancies.

- Offer universal usability—that is, in various fields of application.

- Be independent of the accessing program. A piece of information created by one program should be able to be read and modified by other programs. This holds true even for programs not known to the creating program.

- Be independent of any specific hardware and software environment.

- Provide functional integration, representing semantic data relationships so that they are transparent and usable.

- Have a flexible, modifiable data structure, for example, allowing a six-digit account number to be converted to a nine-digit number.

- Allow concurrent access by several users.

- Support access protection and data protection tasks.

- Guarantee data integrity. The information held in the database should be complete and semantically correct.

- Provide data security. The database should support backup and reconstruction processes.

7.1.7 Client/Server Solution

The term *client/server* is closely related to databases. It means that the application does not run on a single computer, as in conventional programming, but that tasks are shared between the front end and back end. *Front end* means the application program, running on the client's PC; *back end* means the database management system, running on the server. The client sends tasks and requests in the form of SQL instructions to the server, and the server serves these requests. In contrast to conventional programming, the client does not have direct access to the data. This offers two important advantages:

- The client has fewer tasks than the server, so the server must be a powerful engine, but a less powerful computer is sufficient for the client. This reduces the total hardware investment cost.

- In contrast to conventional file systems, the client and server exchange only requests and result sets, which means that the data volume transmitted is limited. This reduces the network load.

Two-tier and three-tier models   Figure 7.1 shows such a client/server system, often called *two-tier model*. Particularly for large applications, it may be useful to use a *three-tier model*, which results in the following distribution of tasks:

- Tier 1 forms the graphical interface—the application program.

- Tier 2 implements the program logistics.

- Tier 3 consists of the database system.

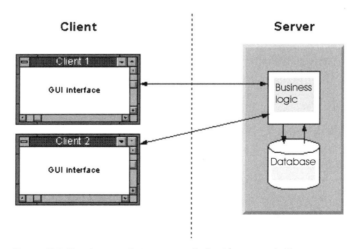

Figure 7.1 Fundamental structure of client/server solution.

7.1.8 Object-Oriented Databases

Object-oriented databases have not really become popular yet

Object-oriented databases are a new form of database currently in the research phase (see, for example, [Kna97]). Although some commercial products have been available since 1988, they have not yet gained a large market share. This is contrary to the situation in software engineering, where the advantages of object-oriented programming have led to conventional languages being gradually replaced. In the world of databases, this step has not been reached, which may be partly for psychological reasons (for example, tradition, not enough time for testing, not enough behavior). Nevertheless, it is useful to briefly discuss object-oriented databases.

In an object-oriented database, persistent objects are placed permanently onto a *persistent heap* while transient objects are located in a transient storage medium. Transient and persistent objects can have mutual access. Access to a persistent object causes this object to be loaded into transient storage. As soon as transient objects no longer reference it, this persistent object is written back to the persistent heap. A transient object becomes persistent as soon as it can be reached by a persistent root object, and any arbitrary object can become such a root object by using a special operation, such as `Persistent.SetRoot(obj, key)`, to register it.

OMG

The Object Database Management Group, a workgroup of OMG, defined an object-oriented standard to access database systems. This standard includes the following parts:

- The object model

- The Object Definition Language (ODL)

- The OQL query language, which is similar to the SQL query language introduced in Section 7.3

- Language integrating features for C++, Smalltalk, and Java

More information about object-oriented databases is available in [CBB97]. Although pure object-oriented databases have not yet reached a mature state, they will definitely be around in the near future, but in the form of object-relational databases, such as Oracle, DB2, and Sybase.

7.1.9   Changing from ISAM to RDBMS

ISAM vs. RDBMS   Many large organizations individually store gigabytes of mission-critical data in index-sequential files. Often, these environments have a variety of software applications (mostly built in-house or custom-made applications) that access and manipulate data in these files through the ISAM standard. As explained earlier, database systems have many advantages, so it appears useful to migrate to them. However, high barriers must be overcome. This section explains these barriers, because they clearly show the differences between data files and databases [Bor02].

The technical issues relevant to retargeting ISAM COBOL applications to RDBMS architecture can be categorized into two main groups: incompatibility arising from a shift of the programming model (cursor-based versus index-based) and a shift of the way you think about data (incompatible record structures and data types).

Structure of data files   One main difference between the two systems is COBOL's ability to define variables and the structure of data files. In COBOL, this action can be done in a single operation. You can also define multiple sets of a field within a single record (using the OCCURS clause), and a single record can be structured according to different rules (using the REDEFINE clause). RDBMS architecture does not support these "shortcuts.".

For example, we can have the following COBOL data structure:

```
01 customer-record.
   03 telephone-number.
      05 country-code pic 999.
      05 area-code pic 999.
      05 local-number.
         08 prefix pic 999.
         08 subscriber-number pic 9999.
```

OCCURS, REDEFINE   Such a data structure can be easily stored in a COBOL data file. A programmer could also write an instruction that accepts screen input and writes the telephone number directly to a variable. When using a relational database, we first have to flatten this data structure, because relational databases can use only a flat record buffer.

In the RDBMS philosophy, each field is an element in its own right, and fields cannot be split or grouped into a level that gives the data an aggregate meaning. Furthermore, an OCCURS is not directly supported. Extending the previous example to have `telephone-number occurs 3` would be simple when using data files. If we used a relational database, we would have to define a separate table for the type `TelephoneNumber`.

Another problem is redefinitions, which are impossible in an RDBMS architecture. They can be solved such that only one of the concurrently incompatible definitions is used as the master reference to construct a table.

Index-based vs. cursor-based program flow
The other important difference between ISAM and RDBMS is the index-based versus cursor-based program flow. In COBOL, the developer has a high degree of control and transparency over the physical location in data files from which data is read from or to which it is written. In contrast, with most RDBMS systems, developers are unable to find out where or how, physically, a record or any piece of information is stored on a disk.

Furthermore, in a database, queries are the only way to retrieve data. The concepts of *recordsets, fetching,* and *queries* are foreign to the ISAM mindset, and COBOL applications that are retargeted from ISAM to RDMBS have to introduce all of them somehow. Although technically this may be easy to achieve, it remains a challenge to ensure that these concepts can be implemented consistently and that the solution at all times assures acceptable levels of performance of the programs, once retargeted.

Hopping of indexes
These issues can get tricky—two of them come to mind. The first regards hopping of indexes (caused by two consecutive READs on different keys) or the reversal of their direction (caused by using consecutive READ PREVIOUS and READ NEXT operations). Although hopping or changing indexes in ISAM is easy, within the RDBMS mindset we are generally confronted with another cursor that must be active in another recordset each time a hop takes place. Any retargeting solution will have to provide a standardized answer to this so that performance is not too heavily affected or that the resulting code is not too cumbersome to maintain.

"Scrolling cursors"
In addition, when COBOL programs reverse the direction of their queries, for instance, by scrolling upward in the data file after having browsed downward, the choice of the target RDBMS system may influence how easily the cursor's ability to invert can be retargeted. Some modern RDBMS products implement "scrolling cursors" that can change direction within the recordset, but not all do. If the target RDBMS does not provide support for scrolling cursors, the solution may, in the worst case, have to rely on the definition of double recordsets in the database each time

a query is made. The cursors in these double recordsets will always scroll forward, but the order of the records in the recordset will have to be opposite.

The second issue, of course, regards the ability of the retargeting solution to reliably produce recordsets that are minimal in size. For instance, if a particular area of an application requires retrieving only one or two records from a large table, creating queries that include the full table of information in the recordset will cripple application performance. The solution will have to find some way to generate the appropriate "where" clauses in the resulting code that serve as the vertical qualification of the query. Where this is impossible (as it most often is), it will be necessary to devise a mechanism that allows full tables to be scanned without creating whopping recordsets.

When applications are reengineered, this change from ISAM to RDBMS can be automated with tools such as Anubex *(www.anubex.com)*.

7.1.10   Exercises

Task 1 (30 minutes): Simple Relation

Consider a part of your environment (perhaps your own video collection) and create a simple relational model with at least five tables.

Task 2 (10 minutes): Relations: A Matter of Understanding

By which points of view will the individual rows of a relation be arranged?

Task 3 (40 minutes): Transactions

To understand the problem of executing transactions in parallel, determine the result from the transactions listed in Table 7.5 from both parallel and serial executions. The initial value of each, A and B, is 40.

7.2   Data Modeling

Designing a database Data modeling means working out the design of a database. In particular, data modeling defines the tables a database should have and the fields

Table 7.5   Example for transactions

Transaction T1	Transaction T2
Read A	
	Read A
	A := 10
	Write A
A := A + 10	
Read B	
B := A * 2	
	Read B
	B := 10
	Write B
Write A	
Write B	

needed in these tables. It should also identify a key for each table. Considering that a database table can be compared with a single file in COBOL, it may seem intuitive to expect that data modeling is an important issue in COBOL too. The truth is that data modeling is more important in relational databases, because they are expected to offer a large number of functions that would have to be created individually when using independent files. These functions are normally usable only provided that relationality is maintained.

The following sections discuss data modeling. The first of these sections introduces a data modeling example. The next section discusses potential errors and a method to avoid these errors, based on this example. Finally, we present the ER model, a representation form for data models.

7.2.1   Introduction

To model a database, we first have to look at the objects. The word *model* in itself indicates that we are dealing with a way to map such objects. In simple examples, it is easy to represent such objects and derive the appropriate tables from them. Normally, however, we have to deal with more complex cases, so a disciplined approach is recommended to avoid errors.

We begin with a simple example and derive a model from it. It is important in the field of financial accounting to save an account together with its postings. This Account has a unique Number and a Name. This account has a set of postings, identified by a unique LedgerNumber. A ledger is a set of all postings.

The principle of double bookkeeping says that a transaction must always consist of two postings (one of the type Account and a second one on a mirror account, the *offset account*). Consequently, a Posting has an Amount and a short PostingText as well as the properties Account and OffsetAccount. Postings have another relationship: They also contain invoices and payments, and at least one Invoice belongs to each Payment. Of course, this also holds true in the opposite sense. Figure 7.2 shows tables modeling this situation.

There are three types of anomalies

At first glance, this model seems to have a perfect structure. However, more careful study is necessary to determine whether it contains errors. We distinguish three types of errors (anomalies):

- The **Insert** anomaly means that a record is inserted into the table more than once—for example, if account 4711 in Table 7.6 existed several times.

- The **Delete** anomaly occurs when data are not managed in neatly divided tables. In our example, a delete anomaly would occur if an account were deleted without deleting all the postings of this account.

Redundancy

- Before describing the **Update** anomaly, we have to mention another problem of poor database modeling: redundancy. This means that the same information exists several times, for example when an account name exists both in the account table and in the postings table. Such a redundancy is a drawback with regard to storage requirements. It can

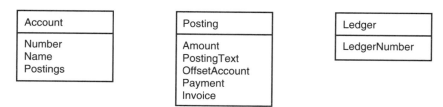

Figure 7.2 Modeling accounts.

Table 7.6   Example for an Insert anomaly

Account	Description
4000	Revenues
4711	First occurrence
4711	Second occurrence
. . .	. . .

also cause update anomalies when a change to a record is not effected in all occurrences, such as if a name is changed in the account table but not in the posting table.

None of these anomalies should arise when inserting, changing, and deleting records. To ensure that this will not happen, it is necessary to consider a special approach to the design of a data model: *normalization*.

7.2.2   Normalization

A data model is subject to several steps during its development: the *normalization steps*. Although the literature describes various approaches, the most popular are the *normalized forms*. These normalized forms are all required, because they build on each other.

The First Normalized Form

This first step lists all data elements to be included in the model. When the first normalized form is reached, all obvious redundancies should have been removed. Each data element should occur once and only once. Moreover, this first step identifies the keys for the respective data fields. These are the data elements that provide unique identification of an object, that is, an account number. Each table has a unique key, and it is common to compose keys from several fields. This unique key is also called the *primary key.*

To reach this state, we can use a simple table as our auxiliary tool. This table lists all data elements and dependencies between them. This will be an easy basis to determine the keys.

Table 7.7   Example for the first normalization

	1	2	3	4	5	6	7	8	9
1 Account number		X							
2 Account name									
3 Ledger number				X	X	X	X		
4 Posting text									
5 Posting amount									
6 Posting account									
7 Offset account									
8 Invoice number								X	X
9 Payment number								X	X

Table 7.7 shows how such a tool could look in our example. Both the rows and the columns of this table list data elements.

Each X in this table denotes a dependence between data elements. For example, the X in column 2 on the account number line means that the account name (2) depends on the account number (1).

Mutual dependence   When allocating invoices and payments, it is more complicated to find dependencies than when allocating fields of an account or posting. The reason is that there is no direct dependence, because we cannot find a unique invoice number from the payment number. Also, one payment may cover several invoices. On the other hand, we cannot find a unique payment number from an invoice number, because one invoice could be settled by more than one payment. Both fields depend on one another in a certain way.

This table meets the goals of the first normalized form. We found the data elements. Each data element occurs only once, and each one has a key.

The Second Normalized Form

Looking for dependencies within one table   This step creates unique dependencies within one table. In general, the data elements are divided into tables identified by dependencies. The rule of thumb is that all data elements that are not keys have to fully depend on a key, where emphasis is placed on "fully." No attribute can depend on a part of the key in terms of function.

The preceding steps produced the following tables:

- The table `Account` with the key field `AccountNumber` and the data field `AccountName`

- The table `Postings` with the key field `LedgerNumber` and the data fields `PostingText`, `PostingAmount`, `PostingAccount`, and `OffsetAccount`

- The table `Invoice/Payment` with the two key fields `InvoiceNumber` and `PaymentNumber`

Primary and foreign keys

If data fields occur more than once at this point, then this may not necessarily be due to redundancy. The second occurrence could be a foreign key to fields by the same name in other tables. The term *foreign key* denotes attributes of a table that are defined as primary keys in another table.

The Third Normalized Form

The third normalized form is aimed at dissolving any remaining (hidden) redundancies. This step checks whether a field depends on more than one key in a table. If so, the key and the field are moved to a separate table.

For example, if we want to save the persons working in a company in a table with the structure `StaffNumber`, `Name`, `DepartmentNumber`, and `DepartmentName`, this would not be the third normalized form, because `DepartmentName` depends not only on the key `StaffNumber` but also on `DepartmentNumber`. It would be necessary to remove this field from the table and create a separate table with the key `DepartmentNumber` and the field `DepartmentName`.

Our example with the accounts has no such dependencies, so it meets the criteria for the third normalized form.

Redundancy is often accepted for efficiency reasons

There are more normalized forms, but the third is normally sufficient. Additional normalized forms are found in theory rather than in practice. It may also be a good idea not to exaggerate the normalization process. In fact, it can often be useful to leave redundant data to ensure that processing speed is not unnecessarily slowed due to additional table accesses.

A simple example is the `Balance` of an account. If we inserted such a data field, it would be in conflict with the first normalized form. It would be redundant, because the balance can be determined from the sum of all posting amounts. Of course, it would also be inefficient, because all postings would have to be visited in this frequently occurring calculation.

The Benefits of Normalization

We summarize the benefits of normalization as follows:

- It reduces redundancy by swapping redundant information to separate tables.

- It reduces anomalies.

- It increases consistency.

- It saves storage space.

7.2.3 The Entity–Relationship Model

ER model represents the built model
During the modeling process, a graphical representation of the model is important. One possibility, UML, was presented in Section 6.1. This section presents another possibility often shown in the literature: the *entity-relationship model,* or *ER model* for short. This represents the model built during the normalization steps. Basically, the ER model maps objects (entities) to relationships (relations), or vice versa.

Objects and Relationships

The starting point is an object—in our example, Account or Posting. These objects can be represented by rectangles (Figure 7.3).

In general, these objects have relationships—for example, postings relate to an account, as Figure 7.4 shows.

Such a relationship could also be inverted: an account relates to postings. The solution is a matter of taste rather than of correctness.

I : I, I : N, N : M
With regard to relationships, we also have to determine their degree. We normally distinguish among three degrees of entity-relationships:

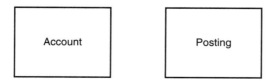

Figure 7.3 The Account and Posting objects.

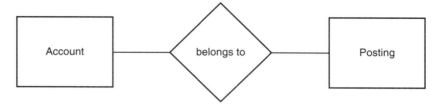

Figure 7.4 Relationship between Account and Posting.

- **1:1 (one-to-one):** This relationship denotes a unique allocation. In our case, this would mean that an account relates to exactly one posting, and one posting relates to exactly one account. Of course, this is not the case in the real world. A simple example would be where the relation "manages" two objects, say, an employee and a project: Exactly one employee manages exactly one project. It is important that *zero relationships*—employees who do not manage any project—not violate this rule.

- **1:N (one-to-many):** This allocation is present in our example, because one posting always relates exactly to one account (the posting account), while on the other hand, several postings relate to one account.

- **N:M (many-to-many):** This relationship can best be explained by an example based on the relationship "processes" between the objects "employee" and "project." An employee can work on several projects, and a project can be handled by several employees.

The degree of a relationship is registered in the ER model. The relationship that an account can consist of N postings and a posting can be allocated to exactly one account (based on the posting account) can be represented as shown in Figure 7.5.

In addition to these fundamental relationships, we can identify two special relationships: the is-a relationship and the has-a relationship. Also called *generalization* and *aggregation,* respectively, these were introduced in Section 6.1 in connection with object-oriented design. They play an important role in the design of databases.

Generalization

Generalization is synonymous for an is-a relationship, which means that one object is a specialization of another. In object-oriented design, this

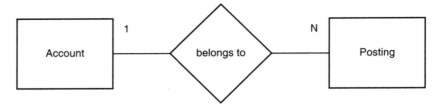

Figure 7.5 Representation of a 1:N relationship.

means that one class is derived from another. Figure 7.6 shows how generalization can be represented in the ER model.

Aggregation

Aggregation is synonymous for a has-a relationship; it occurs when an object is virtually a property of another. In object-oriented design, this is an attribute. Figure 7.7 shows how aggregation can be represented in the ER model.

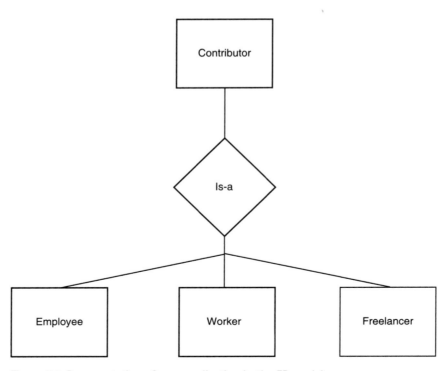

Figure 7.6 Representation of a generalization in the ER model.

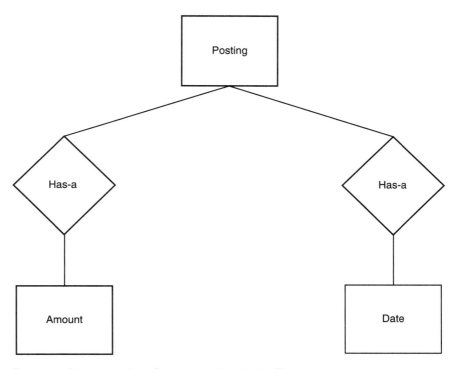

Figure 7.7 Representation of an aggregation in the ER model.

It is worth mentioning that UML (see Section 6.1.4) has been more popular recently than the ER model to represent a database model.

7.2.4   Views

Views allow us to focus on specific parts of a relationship

Views are a concept used to see specific parts of a relationship instead of the entire relationship. Views are a virtual dynamic table, containing a choice of records from other tables. This selection is done when a relevant view is accessed, so the user always works with the current values of relationships stored in the database. The major benefits of views are as follows:

- They simplify complex data structures and the database programming job itself, because they allow division into simpler parts.

- They represent data under different points of view; for example, columns of basic tables can be renamed without the need to change the definition of that basic table.

- They protect data within tables, because they limit the access to specific rows and columns of a table. This can be configured so that a user is authorized to access a specific view but not the basic table.

7.2.5 Other Particularities

NULL Values

NULL stands for an undefined value

A NULL value is a special value, or a sort of empty attribute, that can be permitted for a column. This could be useful, for example, for a record that lacks information about an attribute, such as when a person is added to a table and the phone number is unknown. In this case, the column can be filled with a NULL value. However, this is possible only if the column is configured during database design to accept NULL values (see also Section 7.3.1).

In the database query language we introduce in Section 7.3, the keyword NULL can be used to test for a value.

Index

An index increases execution speed

How fast a data value (that is, a single row in a table) can be accessed depends largely on whether access is by a key. Using a key to access a data value, such as an account number, is generally fast. The same access using a nonkey attribute, such as by account name, can take much longer, because all records have to be read before the result is output, similar to unsorted lists.

This problem can be avoided by creating an index to this attribute (or to the attribute combination). Such indexes are created similarly to index-sequential files in COBOL (*.idx). This affects only the efficiency, not the query structure. In contrast to COBOL, additional indexes can be created as needed, even after the fact.

Surrogate

Examples for surrogates: ISBN, EAN

A *surrogate* is the solution for searching by an appropriate key. As we know, each table should have a key, and this key should be short and easy to understand. Unfortunately, this is not always the case. In fact, we often have to build keys from a combination of several attributes to ensure unique access.

In this case, it an artificial key, or *surrogate,* is useful. Such a surrogate can be something as simple as the sequential numbering of objects. An international standard book number (ISBN) or European article number (EAN) are examples of such surrogates.

7.2.6 Exercises

Task 1 (100 minutes): Normalization

Create an ER model for the following task. Assume a payroll accounting system calculates salaries for the staff of a company. Each employee has a unique number, a name, and various other general information, including date of birth and so on. Moreover, the employees are divided into five categories, determined by their salaries. For example, the employees of category 1 are paid $2000 and those of category 2 are paid $2500. In addition, each employee is assigned to exactly one department, identified by a unique number.

Solve this task based on the normalization steps introduced earlier in this chapter and define the attributes for which an index should be created.

7.3 Introduction to SQL

SQL: Structured Query Language

Structured Query Language, or SQL, is a set-oriented language used to work with databases. This language is divided into three parts, according to various tasks:

- Data definition (DDL = Data Definition Language)

- Data manipulation and queries (DML = Data Manipulation Language)

- Data control and data security (DCL = Data Control Language)

This section describes the most important commands of the language, based on the data model created in the previous sections. First, we discuss how tables are created and how values are inserted. Then we describe instructions, such as SELECT, to evaluate such tables. Finally, we see how this job can be optimized by creating an index or a view.

7.3.1 Creating Tables

CREATE TABLE   To create a table, we use the CREATE TABLE instruction. Subsequently, we state a name for the table and then the data elements within parentheses. For each data element, we also state the type (as in a normal record definition). Table 7.8 lists the available data types, but they depend on the selected database. Special data types, such as image or sound, are important for Internet applications.

Keys must be We also specify keys and add them to our table definition. The keyword **defined** PRIMARY KEY (list of attributes) is used to define the attributes that will serve as primary keys. Furthermore, we can specify that an attribute should serve as a foreign key. This is useful because it allows the database to check whether the value actually occurs as a key in the foreign table.

In this case, we have to use the definition FOREIGN KEY (list of attributes) REFERENCES TableName. TableName stands for the name of that table, where the foreign key is used as a primary key. In our example, the table Posting contains PostingAccount and OffsetAccount as foreign keys, which are used as primary keys in the table Account. To ensure that an attribute is not allowed to take a value of NULL, we have to use the keyword NOT NULL and add it to the end of the attribute definition.

Accordingly, the tables designed in Section 7.2.2 could be defined as follows:

Table 7.8   The most important data types (using Oracle as an example)

Data type	Description
VARCHAR2 (size)	String with variable length and a maximum length specified by size (size <2000)
CHAR (size)	String with maximum length of 255 but a fixed length specified by size
LONG	String with variable length of $2^{31} - 1$ characters (for text)
CHAR	One character
NUMBER (p, s)	Number with maximum p digits, including s places before the decimal point
NUMBER (p)	Integer with p places
DATE	Date
RAW (size)	Binary data with a byte length specified by size (size <256)

```
CREATE TABLE Account (
   AccountNumber NUMBER (9) NOT NULL,
   AccountName CHAR (30),
   PRIMARY KEY (AccountNumber)
);

CREATE TABLE Postings (
   LedgerNnumber NUMBER (9) NOT NULL,
   PostingText CHAR (30),
   PostingAmount NUMBER (18, 2),
   PostingAccount NUMBER (9),
   OffsetAccount NUMBER (9),
   PRIMARY KEY (Number),
   FOREIGN KEY (PostingAccount) REFERENCES Account,
   FOREIGN KEY (OffsetAccount) REFERENCES Account,
);

CREATE TABLE NoOfInv (
   InvoiceNumber NUMBER (9) NOT NULL,
   PaymentNumber NUMBER (9) NOT NULL,
   PRIMARY KEY (InvoiceNumber, PaymentNumber),
   FOREIGN KEY (InvoiceNumber) REFERENCES Postings,
   FOREIGN KEY (PaymentNumber) REFERENCES Postings
);
```

Tables can be modified after the fact   It is also possible to modify tables or delete them later. More specifically, we can use ALTER TABLE TableName ADD (ColumnName Type) to add a new column or ALTER TABLE TableName MODIFY (ColumnName Type) to add a new column or modify an existing column. Adding columns is normally easy, but we have to pay attention to the existing values when modifying the type of a column. We can delete an entire table by using DROP TABLE TableName.

7.3.2 Inserting and Deleting Records

The instructions INSERT and DELETE can be used to insert or delete values, respectively. The use of these commands is easy:

```
INSERT INTO Account VALUES (2700, "CASH")
INSERT INTO Account VALUES (2800, "BANK")
INSERT INTO Account VALUES (4000, "REVENUES")
```

```
INSERT INTO Account VALUES (2500, "TAX")
INSERT INTO Posting VALUES (1, "test posting", 1000, 4000, 2700)
INSERT INTO Posting VALUES (2, "tax", 5030, 2500, 2700)
INSERT INTO Posting VALUES (3, "revenues", 27000, 4000, 2700)
INSERT INTO Posting VALUES (4, "tax", 5030, 2500, 2700)
DELETE FROM Account WHERE number = 2800
```

We can also use SELECT instructions to insert several objects, such as a part from another table. As mentioned earlier, SELECT generally selects a set of records from the data repository. This issue is discussed in the following sections.

7.3.3 Functions

SQL allows you to use various predefined functions, such as to calculate the sum of a column or an average value. Table 7.9 shows these functions.

The average value of the sum of all postings could be calculated by using AVG (amount). These expressions could also be used within other SQL instructions; for example, SELECT * FROM Posting WHERE Amount > AVG (amount) determines all postings with a posting amount larger than the average.

In addition to these operations that can be applied to table columns, numerous other functions are available. Table 7.10 explains the most important ones.

Also, all expressions known from Delphi or Java can be created. Besides the arithmetic operations mentioned earlier, Boolean expressions, such as

Table 7.9   Predefined SQL functions

Function	Meaning
COUNT	Number of values
SUM	Sum of values
AVG	Average value
MAX	Largest value
MIN	Smallest value
VARIANCE	Variance
STDDEV	Standard deviation

Table 7.10   More useful functions

Function	Meaning
+ - * /	Basic arithmetic operations
POWER (M, N)	Calculating powers
ABS (N)	Absolute value
SQRT (N)	Square root
LOWER (S)	Convert to lowercase letters
UPPER (S)	Convert to uppercase letters
SUBSTR (S1, S, N)	Substring function
SYSDATE	Current date and time
USER	User name

the comparative operations (=, <>, <, >, <=, >=) or logical operators (NOT, AND, OR), can also be used.

IN and BETWEEN   The operators IN and BETWEEN are designed to work with sets. IN (list of values) can be used to check whether a value is present in a certain set: AccountNumber IN (4000, 4020, 4060). BETWEEN ComparativeValue1 AND ComparativeValue2 can be used to check whether a value is within a certain range: AccountNumber BETWEEN 4000 AND 4050.

LIKE   A comparative operator, LIKE, compares against *patterns;* it is particularly useful for strings. A pattern is a character string, where the characters "%" and "_" have a special meaning. "%" stands for a string composed of an arbitrary number of characters that may include an empty sequence of any characters, whereas "_" stands for a single character. This allows us to formulate comparisons such as "MARKUS" LIKE "M%" or "MARKUS" LIKE "MAR_U%". Both comparisons would return a true result.

7.3.4   SELECT Instruction

As mentioned earlier, this instruction serves to read data from the database. The result is a set of data structured like a table. We will explain this step by step in the following section.

A Simple SELECT Instruction

The simplest form of a SELECT instruction could look like this:

```
SELECT * FROM Account
```

The result will return the table of all accounts, which means that all records and all fields will be selected. This result can be limited both in terms of records and in terms of fields. If we list one or several attributes instead of an asterisk, a table containing only those columns would be created. The code line

```
SELECT postingText, postingAmount FROM posting
```

would return the result shown in Table 7.11.

DISTINCT   To avoid having lines with the same contents occur more than once, such as "Tax", 5030 in this example, we can use the keyword DISTINCT:

```
SELECT DISTINCT PostingText, PostingAmount FROM Posting
```

However, the SELECT instruction can be used to select not only attributes of a table but also other values, for example, calculations such as the double of an amount (PostingAmount * 2). Such "virtual" columns can also be output by a replacement or alias name, using the keyword AS. This name can then be addressed in subsequent clauses. Such a definition could look as follows:

```
SELECT DISTINCT PostingText, PostingAmount * 2 AS DAmount FROM Posting
```

The WHERE Clause

Continuing on this basis, we can show more possibilities for selecting specific records. For example, WHERE can be used to select rows—records that meet a certain criterion, such as

Table 7.11   Result from a SELECT instruction with a column limitation

PostingText	PostingAmount
Test posting	1000
Tax	5030
Revenues	27000
Tax	5030

Table 7.12   Result from a SELECT instruction with WHERE clause

PostingText	PostingAmount
Tax	5030
Revenues	27000

```
SELECT DISTINCT PostingText, PostingAmount FROM Posting
        WHERE PostingAmount > 5000
```

would supply the result shown in Table 7.12.

Only the attributes Text and Amount would be displayed for postings with a PostingAmount larger than 5000.

All functions and operators discussed in Section 7.3.3 could be used in this WHERE clause.

The ORDER BY Clause

Sorting records   Another advantage of databases is that the selected data can be easily sorted by appending the ORDER BY clause. In this case, the resulting set is determined by the given criteria in sorted order. The syntax is ORDER BY AttributeName. If the values of the attribute should not be unique, several attributes, separated by commas, can be specified. The sort order can be by the first attribute in case of equality. To sort in descending order, we can write the keyword DESC at the end. Sorting accounts by AccountName could look like this:

```
SELECT * FROM Account ORDER BY AccountName
```

The GROUP BY Clause

Grouping with   The GROUP BY clause can be used to group the result by attributes. As a
GROUP BY   simple example, the postings could be grouped by PostingAccount:

```
SELECT PostingAccount, MAX (PostingAmount), COUNT (*)
   FROM Posting
   GROUP BY PostingAccount
```

The result is grouped by the criterion PostingAccount. The output also includes the maximum posting amount per group and the number of postings per group. Table 7.13 shows the result.

Table 7.13   Result from the GROUP BY clause

PostingText	MAX (PostingAmount)	COUNT (*)
Tax	5030	2
Revenues	27000	2

The HAVING Clause

HAVING Similar to the WHERE clause, which can be used to limit the query result to lines that meet a certain condition, we can limit a selection of groups by using the HAVING clause. This ensures that only groups meeting this condition are included in the resulting set. For our example, the group with a maximum amount of 27000 will be excluded if we use the following SELECT instruction:

```
SELECT PostingAccount, MAX (PostingAmount), COUNT (*)
   FROM Posting
   GROUP BY PostingAccount
   HAVING MAX (PostingAmount) < 27000
```

We could also arbitrarily combine the clauses; the following instruction would be feasible:

```
SELECT PostingAccount, MAX (PostingAmount), COUNT (*)
   FROM Posting
   WHERE PostingAmount < 20000
   GROUP BY PostingAccount
   ORDER BY MAX (PostingAmount)
```

7.3.5 Set Operations

Joining tables As mentioned in the introduction, SQL is a set-oriented query language, so set operations obviously play a major role. The most important operation is a *join*, which joins various tables (or one table to itself). Essentially, this operation maps the Cartesian product of these tables: all combinations possible according to the query will form the resulting set. A join operation can be formulated by means of a SELECT instruction, but the FROM clause will list several tables, separated by commas. For instance, the tables Posting and Account could be joined as follows:

```
SELECT Account.AccountNumber, AccountName, PostingAmount, OffsetAccount
   FROM Account, Posting
```

In the preceding example, with equally named attributes from different relationships, we can apply the dot notation—TableName.AttributeName—to create uniqueness, just as in a conventional programming language. Table 7.14 shows the result.

Such a join operation is useful particularly when only table rows that somehow relate to each other are joined, as in the following SELECT instruction:

```
SELECT Account.AccountNumber, AccountName, PostingAmount, OffsetAccount
   FROM Account, Posting
   WHERE Account.AccountNumber = PostingAccount
```

This example joins only accounts with postings that have an Account.AccountNumber equal to PostingAccount. PostingAccount from the table Posting is the foreign key. Table 7.15 shows the result.

Outer join   A special type of join is the *outer join*. To implement an outer join, we select not only all records of both tables that meet the WHERE clause but additional records, depending on the outer join used:

Table 7.14   Result from a simple join

Account.AccountNumber	AccountName	PostingAmount	OffsetAccount
2700	CASH	1000	2700
2700	CASH	5030	2700
2700	CASH	27000	2700
2700	CASH	5030	2700
4000	REVENUES	1000	2700
4000	REVENUES	5030	2700
4000	REVENUES	27000	2700
4000	REVENUES	5030	2700
2500	TAX	1000	2700
2500	TAX	5030	2700
2500	TAX	27000	2700
2500	TAX	5030	2700

Table 7.15　Result from a join using PostingAccount as the secondary key

Account.AccountNumber	AccountName	PostingAmount	OffsetAccount
4000	REVENUES	1000	2700
4000	REVENUES	27000	2700
2500	TAX	5030	2700
2500	TAX	5030	2700

- LEFT OUTER JOIN: All records of the left table are evaluated, even if this means that some records may not be linked with the right table.

- RIGHT OUTER JOIN: Same as LEFT OUTER JOIN, except that all records of the right table are evaluated.

- FULL OUTER JOIN: All records of both tables are evaluated, regardless of whether the links between the tables can be resolved.

Unfortunately, various database systems use different notations for outer joins, so we will not describe this approach in detail.

Set operations　Finally, we should note that all usual set operations are available:

- Unifying sets: UNION

- Calculating the intersection of sets: INTERSECT

- Calculating the difference of sets: MINUS

7.3.6　The UPDATE Instruction

UPDATE can be used to modify specific lines of a table　This section begins a new issue within our brief SQL introduction, describing how single lines in a table can be modified. More specifically, the column values of the entire table or selected lines can be set to a new value if they meet a specific criterion. For this purpose, we use the UPDATE instruction. This instruction has the following basic structure: UPDATE TableName SET ColumnName = Value. If only selected lines are to be modified, this can be specified by using a WHERE clause. For example, we could set the PostingAccount of all postings that include the text "Tax" to a value of 5040 with the following UPDATE instruction:

```
UPDATE Posting
   SET PostingAccount = 5040
   WHERE TEXT = "Tax"
```

7.3.7   Other Instructions

Views

Views focus on a selected part
We introduced views in Section 7.2.4; such views can be defined by using access operations. For example, the following instruction implements a view:

```
CREATE VIEW ViewName AS SELECT instruction
```

This means that all the options of the SELECT instruction are available. For example, to create a view, SelectPosting, that displays only the fields PostingText and PostingAmount of all postings with a PostingAmount larger than 5000, we can write the following instruction:

```
CREATE VIEW SelectPosting AS
   SELECT DISTINCT PostingText, PostingAmount FROM Posting
   WHERE PostingAmount > 5000
```

This view can then be used to continue working as if we were using a normal table, except for data manipulation operations. Operations that manipulate data would be possible only if the records of the view to be modified (insert or delete records) can be mapped onto a basic table. In this case, the view is not allowed to contain any constructs such as joins, set operators, GROUP BY clauses, aggregation functions, or the DISTINCT operator.

Index

CREATE INDEX
The meaning of an index in a database was explained in Section 7.2.5. This section introduces the CREATE INDEX instruction, which is used to create such an index. Although this instruction is not included in the SQL standard, most databases use it more or less the same way. An index, name, is defined in a table, tab, with columns, listOfColumns, by the following instruction: CREATE INDEX name ON tab (listOfColumns). For example, creating an index name to the account name could look like this:

```
CREATE INDEX name ON Account (AccountName)
```

Unique key is identified by UNIQUE

If the attribute is a unique key, instead of using `CREATE INDEX`, we can use the keyword `CREATE UNIQUE INDEX` to achieve additional optimization. We can append the keywords ASC or DESC to sort the index in ascending or descending order. This is important for sorted data output where the sort criterion begins with the index column. Such an index can be removed later by specifying `DROP INDEX name`.

Granting Privileges

GRANT instruction

As mentioned in the introduction of this chapter, a major advantage of databases is that they facilitate configuration of privileges for users to access tables. This ensures that unauthorized users cannot access data. Such privileges can be configured exactly so that a certain user can evaluate certain data, for example, but cannot create new records (has only read access).

The user who creates a table has full access capabilities to that table. If other users are authorized to access that table, then we have to specifically grant appropriate privileges. Such privileges are granted by the `GRANT` instruction. More specifically, these privileges can be granted both on tables and on views. The instruction can be written in the form `GRANT privilege ON tab TO user`. Table 7.16 shows the capabilities a user will obtain from the `privilege` option.

For example, the following `GRANT` instruction grants a user identified by the user name MHK001 read privileges for the table Account:

```
GRANT SELECT ON Account TO MHK001
```

Table 7.16   Common privileges

Privileges	Grants the right to
SELECT	Select records
INSERT	Insert new records
UPDATE	Modify columns in a table
DELETE	Delete records
ALTER	Change the structure of a table
INDEX	Create an index
ALL	Global access (sum of all privileges)

Privileges can be passed on to other users   By appending the keywords `WITH GRANT OPTION`, we authorize this user to grant his or her privileges to other users. Of course, previously granted privileges can be revoked: `REVOKE privilege ON tab TO user`.

7.3.8 Exercises

Task 1 (20 minutes): Creating Tables

Use the solution from task 1 in Section 7.2.6 to formulate SQL instructions that define the required tables.

Task 2 (100 minutes): Creating Queries

Using the tables you created in task 1, formulate SQL instructions to supply the following results:

1. A list of all employees

2. All employees, including number, name, and date of birth, sorted by name

3. All employees of department number 10

4. All employees of department number 10, sorted by date of birth

5. All employees, including number, name, and salary

6. The highest, lowest, and average salaries of all employees

7. The highest salary of department number 10

8. All employees of department number 10, sorted by salary in descending order

9. A list of all employees whose names begin with "Kn"

10. All employees whose date of birth is not known

11. The highest salary category for each department

12. All departments where the pay is at least salary category 3

13. An index to the name of an employee

SQL: Program Access

Embedded SQL This section shows how we can access a database from within a program. As already mentioned, many organizations use relational databases rather than index-sequential files to store data. Following this trend, new versions of COBOL also offer SQL program access, where SQL is "embedded" in traditional COBOL code using syntax-specific database operations. We present a simple COBOL SQL example, followed by sections showing how Delphi and Java manage the SQL program access.

```
. . .
DETAIL-LINE
05 DL-NAME PIC X(20).
05 DL-NUMBER PIC 9(9).

* defining variables from the table
EXEC SQL BEGIN DECLARE SECTION END-EXEC.
01 HV-NAME PIC X(20).
01 HV-NUMBER PIC 9(9).
EXEC SQL END DECLARE SECTION END-EXEC.
EXEC SQL INCLUDE SQLCA END-EXEC.
PROCEDURE DIVISON.
MAIN CONTROL.

* declaring cursor for holding a set of data from the table
EXEC SQL DECLARE C CURSOR FOR
   SELECT NAME, NUMBER FROM ACCOUNT
END EXEC.

* open the cursor
EXEC SQL OPEN C END-EXEC.

* read the data
PERFORM UNTIL SQLCODE NOT = 0
  EXEC SQL FETCH C
     INTO :HV-NAME, :HV-NUMBER
  END EXEC
  MOVE HV-NAME TO DL-NAME
  MOVE HV-NUMBER TO DL-NUMBER
  DISPLAY DETAIL-LINE
END-PERFORM.
```

```
EXEC SQL CLOSE C END-EXEC.
STOP RUN.
```

Because database access is an important issue, class libraries normally provide appropriate functions for this purpose. Using these functions, it is relatively easy to embed the SQL instructions presented in the previous sections in a program. Because they are embedded, we often speak of "embedded SQL."

Delphi: DBTables   In Delphi, to be able to use SQL functions, we have to use the unit DBTables.

Java: java.sql   In Java, to be able to use SQL functions, we have to import the package java.sql.

Access to a database from within a program is based on the following scheme:

1. Set up a connection to the database.

2. Send an SQL instruction to the database.

3. Allocate the returned result to local variables, which can then be evaluated.

The next three sections are built on this general scheme, describing each in more detail.

7.4.1   Setting Up a Connection

Database drivers   In the first step, a database driver is used to establish a connection to an existing database. The result is a pointer to this database, which can be accessed from within the program at any time. The structure of this connection is simple but depends largely on the class library used. We briefly describe our two Delphi and Java examples.

Delphi   In Delphi, an object of the class TDatabase must be used to connect to a database. This object must be created by using Create, where the global variable session, supplied by the unit DBTables, can be passed as a parameter. Otherwise, we would have to set up a separate database session (object of the class TSession).

The Intrabase database is available on the book CD   Subsequently, a few attributes of this object have to be initialized. The most important attributes are databaseName and driverName, where databaseName defines the name of the database. This is necessary because names are needed for later queries on this database. driverName defines the type of database (Oracle, Intrabase, Sybase, and so on) In the case of Intrabase, we have to use a driver called INTRBASE.

To prevent the program execution from being interrupted by a database login, we have to set the attribute loginPrompt to FALSE. But first, we have to specify the user and password information that should be supplied to access the database.

For this purpose, we can use Params.Add(s) to set the required parameters, where s means that a character string has to be passed, as we can see in the following source code fragment. Similarly, we have to set a parameter, SERVER NAME, to specify where the database is located—in our example, in the file FinAcct. Finally, we need to set the attribute connected to TRUE to ensure that the database connection is active. These steps can be seen in the following source code fragment:

```
var db: TDatabase;
. . .
db := TDatabase.Create(session);
db.driverName := 'INTRBASE';
db.name := 'FinAcct';
db.databaseName := 'FinAcct';
db.Params.Add('USER NAME=SYSDBA'); // Attention: no blanks!!
db.Params.Add('PASSWORD=masterkey');
db.Params.Add('SERVER NAME=FinAcct');
db.loginPrompt := false;
db.connected := true;
```

Java   In Java, a connection of the type Connection can be created simply by calling the method DriverManager.GetConnection (name, user, pwd), where name is the name of the database. This should have a structure similar to jdbc:borland:local:DatabaseName. The first part, jdbc:borland:local, denotes the protocol and subprotocol used to establish the connection. Naturally, we first have to install the desired driver, so we use a call of the type Class.forName "com.borland.datastore.jdbc.DataStoreDriver") up front.

This example uses a database driver for DataStore. If the database is not present locally in the client but is on a database server, as is normally the case, then instead of jdbc:borland:dslocal, we would use the start

URL jdbc:borland:dsremote, followed by the file name and the computer name. We could also use other database drivers, for example, oracle.jdbc.driver.OracleDriver for Oracle.

Because databases support an extensive system for granting and revoking user privileges, the user name user, to obtain access to the database, and the password pwd should also be specified. The following example shows how this could look:

```
Class.forName("com.borland.datastore.jdbc.DataStoreDriver");
String file = "FINACCT.jds";
String url = "jdbc:borland:dslocal:" + file;
Connection db;
db = DriverManager.getConnection(url, "SYSDBA", "masterkey");
```

When the user finishes the session, the database connection could then be closed as follows:

Delphi   To indicate in Delphi that the connection to the database is no longer used, the attribute connected is set to FALSE. Subsequently, the database object can be released by calling the destructor Free.

Java   In Java, the connection to the database can be closed by calling the method close: dbConn.close().

7.4.2 Sending SQL Instructions to the Database

SQL instruction is a parameter of a method   When executing an SQL instruction, it is necessary to call a method in which a character string that includes the SQL instruction is passed as a parameter. In general, class libraries offer various options for this purpose, and we introduce the most important ones in this section. First, it is important to distinguish whether an SQL instruction returns a result. If it does, this result has to be loaded in separate result variables and evaluated.

Delphi: Execute   If the SQL instruction to be executed does not return a result, such as an INSERT instruction, this can be implemented by calling the method Execute (statement, nil, false, nil), where statement passes the desired SQL instruction as a character string. The other parameters specified in this statement to accept nil or false can be used to create a cache or to pass other properties. This is normally not necessary; see your Delphi documentation for further details.

As an alternative, we can use an object of the class TQuery. These objects are able to encapsulate a query and are created by Create(nil). For a Windows application (see Chapter 8), we can pass the relevant component instead of nil. To specify the database used, the attribute databaseName has to be set accordingly, where the name is the one given when the connection to an object of the class TDatabase was established.

In this respect, it is important to ensure that the attribute sql contains the query itself. First, this attribute has to be initialized by using the method Clear; subsequently, we can use the method Add(s) to pass a character string, s, which contains the query.

When we are done with this preparation, we can run the SQL query. Depending on whether (for example, a SELECT instruction) or not (for example, an INSERT instruction) a result set is calculated during that query, either the method Open or ExecSQL has to be called for that purpose. We can see an example for the former case in the following source code fragment:

```
var s: String; q: TQuery;
 . . .
s := 'SELECT * FROM ACCOUNT';
q := TQuery.Create(nil);
q.databaseName := 'FINACCT';
q.sql.Clear; // initialize
q.sql.Add(s);
q.Open; // execute, if Select; otherwise ExecSQL
```

Java: Statement   To run an SQL query in Java, we have to create an object of the class Statement. We can do this by calling the functional method db.createStatement(), where db identifies the database to be queried. To run the query, we call the method executeQuery(s) or executeUpdate(s), where s is a character string containing the SQL query. Which method we use depends on whether the query will produce a result, that is, whether a SELECT instruction is executed or not, such as with an INSERT or DELETE instruction.

The former case runs executeQuery and returns an object of the type ResultSet. This type is discussed in the next section. If no result is expected, executeUpdate is executed, which returns an integer value for the number of lines in the result. The following source code fragment shows an example for the former case:

```
String s = "SELECT * FROM ACCOUNT";
Statement q = db.createStatement();
ResultSet res = q.executeQuery(s);
```

7.4.3 Evaluating the Result

The result set has to be read from beginning to end

For queries that produce a result set—an SQL statement—it is intuitively understood that one will want to process and use this result. Normally, this requires reading the result set from beginning to end. The most difficult part of this is how to access one element in this result set, because we normally deal with a wide range of data types (account, posting, and so forth) A simple variant reads column by column, where each column value is loaded into a special type-independent object, which is then converted into the required type for further processing.

Delphi

The query object q we created in the previous section can now be evaluated. The entire resulting data set is iterated by setting a virtual pointer to the first object. This virtual pointer is set by calling the method First. As long as the end of the data set is not reached (in this case, this would happen when the attribute eof is TRUE), the record can always be evaluated, and the method Next can set the virtual pointer to the next object.

At this point, the problem mentioned earlier regarding evaluation of the record arises, because it could be an arbitrary object with any data structure. One solution is to do a conversion, and an even simpler solution is to read the individual attributes. The method FieldByName ('AttributeName') can be used to maintain the column value in an object of the class TField. This is a special class that can accept an arbitrary column value and convert it to a standard type by calling methods such as AsInteger() or AsString(). The following source code fragment shows how the result set can be output line by line:

```
q.First;
while not q.eof do begin
  Write(q.FieldByName('Number').AsInteger());
  Write(' ');
  WriteLn(q.FieldByName('Name').AsString());
  q.Next; // eof is true, if Next fails
end;
```

If the names of the attributes—of the columns—are not known during development, because they will be finalized at runtime, a list of attributes can be created by calling the method GetFieldNames(list). list has the type TStrings, which is a list of character strings offered by the Delphi class library. Subsequently, the individual character strings can be accessed by accessing the attribute strings, a simple array (starting with index 0). The attribute count denotes the number of strings.

Java   In Java, the result set yielded in the previous section, res, can easily be evaluated by iterating line by line. At the beginning, a virtual pointer is placed immediately before the first line. The method next() will then jump to the next line (which is the first in the first call). This method returns the value FALSE as soon as no more iteration is possible.

As mentioned earlier, another problem can arise when evaluating a record, because the record could be any object with an arbitrary data structure. One solution would be a conversion, and an even simpler solution would be to read the attributes one by one. By calling methods such as getInt(s) or getString(s), we can obtain a column value, where the column name has to be passed in s. However, instead of the column name, we could also pass the column index (Attention! It begins with 1).

This is possible because these methods were overwritten, and they can process integer values as parameters. Depending on the expected data type, we have to call the desired get method. For example, the following source code fragment shows how the result set can be output line by line:

```
while (res.next()) {
    System.out.print(res.getInt("NUMBER"));
    System.out.print(" ");
    System.out.println(res.getString("NAME"));
}
```

ResultSetMetaData   If column names are not known at development time, then a Result-SetMetaData object with the number of columns, data types, and other properties can be created by calling the method getMetaData(). Detailed information about the structure of this data type is included in the Java class library documentation.

7.4.4 Summarizing Example

Listings 7.1 and 7.2 show the full Delphi and the Java examples.

Both the database object and the query object have to be released to complete the example.

Listing 7.1.
Example for
the Delphi
Implementation
of a Database
Access

```
program ExampleAccount;
uses
   Forms, DBTables, SysUtils;
var
   ch: Char;
   s: String;
   db: TDatabase;
   q: TQuery;
begin
   // --- connect to database
   db := TDatabase.Create(session);
   db.driverName := 'INTRBASE';
   db.databasename := 'FINACCT';
   db.Params.Add('USER NAME=SYSDBA'); // Attention: no blanks!!
   db.Params.Add('PASSWORD=masterkey');
   db.Params.Add('SERVER NAME=finacct');
   db.loginPrompt := false;
   db.connected := true;
   // --- execute SELECT instruction
   s := 'SELECT * FROM ACCOUNT';
   q := TQuery.Create(nil);
   q.databaseName := 'FINACCT';
   q.Sql.Clear; // initialize
   q.Sql.Add(s);
   q.Open; // execute, if Select; otherwise ExecSQL
   // --- evaluate result set
   q.First;
   while not q.eof do begin
      Write(q.FieldByName('Number').AsInteger);
      Write(' ');
      WriteLn(q.FieldByName('Name').AsString);
      q.Next; // eof is true, if Next fails
   end;
```

```
    // --- finalizing actions
    q.Close;
    q.Free;
    db.connected := FALSE;
    db.Free;
    ReadLn(ch); // to ensure that the result screen is not deleted
end.
```

Potential Java exceptions must be caught, as explained in Section 5.5.1.

```
import java.io.*;
import java.sql.*;
class ExampleAccount {
  public static void main (String args[]) {
    try {
      // --- connect to database
      Class.forName("com.borland.datastore.jdbc.DataStoreDriver");
      String file = "FINACCT.jds";
      String url = "jdbc:borland:dslocal:" + file;
      Connection db
      db = DriverManager.getConnection(url, "SYSDBA", "masterkey");
      // --- execute SELECT instruction
      String s = "SELECT * FROM ACCOUNT";
      Statement q = db.createStatement();
      ResultSet res = q.executeQuery(s);
      // --- evaluate result set
      while (res.next()) {
        System.out.print(res.getInt("NUMBER"));
        System.out.print(" ");
        System.out.println(res.getString("NAME"));
      }
      q.close();
      db.close();
    }
    catch (SQLException e) {
      System.out.println("Exception: " + e.getMessage());
      e.printStackTrace(); // outputs detailed information
    }
    catch (ClassNotFoundException e) {
```

```
        e.printStackTrace();
      }
    }
}
```

7.4.5 Exercises

Task 1 (90 minutes): Creating a Database

The Intrabase database system is available on the book CD   Read the corresponding instruction part of your database system documentation and create a database, including the tables designed for task 1 in Section 7.2.6.

Task 2 (90 minutes): Accessing the Database

Write a program that accesses the database designed in task 1. Your program should read a SELECT instruction and output the results.

8

Graphical User Interfaces

Textual vs. graphical user interfaces The previous chapters introduced the world of object-oriented programming and databases. In closing this part, we will briefly discuss graphical user interfaces, because they are an absolute must for new programs today. In contrast, older COBOL programs have mostly the conventional textual interface, because they have a terminal origin.

This chapter shows that the difference between the two types of user interfaces is that event-oriented programming requires not only more complex programming and the use of some classes but a totally different approach. Newer COBOL programs have such Windows and HTML interfaces too. However, for the large number of programmers engaged in maintaining processes for the past years, it would be useful to cover this topic too.

8.1 Structure of a Graphical User Interface

A graphical user interface (GUI) differs from a textual interface not only in looking "friendlier" but that the user has many different input options and is not limited to a menu displayed on the screen. These options include the following:

- Selecting a menu option

- Clicking the mouse on an object

- Entering text

- Copying and pasting an object through the clipboard

- Changing the window size

Each action offers inputs for a program; even more options are available, depending on the structure of the graphical user interface. Figure 8.1 shows an example of such a mighty graphical user interface.

Such a graphical user interface must first be designed. Depending on the programming environment, the details of this design can differ a lot. Normally, we use a so-called empty form—an empty program window. To start, we insert control elements into this window form. The size and position of these elements can be defined by using the mouse. Table 8.1 shows a selection of the most common control elements. The object-oriented structure allows us to program and add new control elements without having to change anything in the existing system.

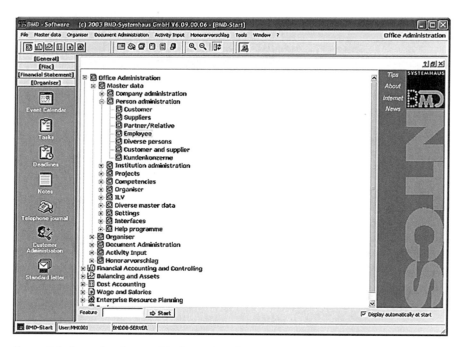

Figure 8.1 Example of a graphical user interface.

Core of an application

Once created, such a form, is the core of the application. This means that it is no longer necessary to program individual control elements, because their functions are part of the class library. In other words, we do not have to write any code stating how a button should change its visual appearance when the user clicks it. The program has only to respond to the event when the button is clicked. This is discussed further in Section 8.2.

Text input is easy to implement

Similarly, a text input is just as simple, because the selected control element will do the work, such as positioning the cursor correctly or running a certain error check. These are exactly the points that are difficult to program for a textual user interface. For example, with inputs of the type ReadLn, we cannot do much to influence things like the length of the text

Table 8.1 Popular control elements

Element	Mapping	Description
Button	Button	A small clickable square or rectangle linked with a certain action, activated by clicking the mouse on the button
Checkbox	☑	A selectable field that can take one of two states: checked (selected) or not checked (deselected)
Label	Label	A static piece of text that appears in the screen window but cannot be edited by the user
Text	Text	Defines an input field, so the user can enter a single line of text or several text lines
Radio button	◉ RadioButton	Similar to a checkbox, except that it is normally round, serving to select one option out of several, where normally no multichoice is possible
Listbox	ListBox 1.Zeile ListBox 2.Zeile	Displays a list of elements, from which the user can select
Combobox	ComboBox ▼	Similar to a listbox, except that it has an additional editing field, which can be used to search the list or enter an additional value
Bitmap	BMJ	Represents various images on the graphical user interface

read or whether certain characters are not permitted. Using ReadLn, an error message can be output only after an error is made, but the faulty input itself cannot be prevented.

Control elements are objects with attributes

The control elements introduced previously are objects that can be accessed by a program in the usual way. This means that existing control elements can be removed, new ones can be inserted, or their properties can be changed. This can be done by setting attributes, but these attributes differ a great deal, depending on the control element. Essentially, the most common attributes are as follows:

- **caption:** text displayed on the control element

- **font:** the font in which this text is displayed

- **height:** the height of the control element

- **width:** the width of the control element

- **name:** a name used within the application to access the control element

By setting the caption property of a button, we can modify the text that appears on the button at runtime. However, initial values for these attributes can be selected when we create the form.

Only one form can be active at a time, and only one control element can be in focus

We could create several forms. At runtime, an input or another action could display another form, which then serves as the new core of the application. The *focus* determines the control element currently active, because only one control element can be active at a time. Whether a control element is active is normally denoted by highlighting it, as by a darker font or dashed line. This control element receives the keystrokes typed by the user. The focus must be unique to a single control element in the form, and only one form can be active at a time.

8.2 Event-Oriented Programming

The basic programming flow is different

In contrast to a traditional command-line–oriented text interface, a GUI is based on a different programming flow. This kind of interface is event-controlled—special program parts are executed for different user actions, such as pressing a key, selecting a menu item, or clicking the mouse on a control element. Figure 8.2 shows this event-controlled process.

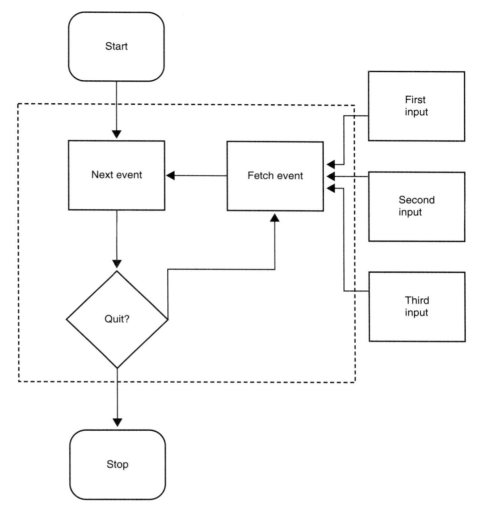

Figure 8.2 Example of an event-controlled processing sequence.

The fundamental concept is that each event must have an appropriate response: For example, if the user presses a button, execute Method1, or types some text, execute Method2, or if the user selects a checkbox, execute Method3, and so on. The following short code fragment in algorithmic notation shows this principle more formally:

```
HandleEvent (ev: Event)
begin
  case ev.kind of
    keyDown: HandleKey(ev)
    mouseDown: HandleClick(ev)

    . . .
  end;
end;
```

The procedure HandleEvent is the main program. The application uses it to catch each event and process all of them by calling methods. HandleEvent is not exited before the program terminates. This could look as follows:

```
GetEvent(ev)
while ev.kind <> endEvent do
  HandleEvent(ev);
  GetEvent(ev);
end;
```

8.3   Short Overview of Class Libraries

Creating a user interface and working with such an interface depends largely on the class library. The development environment also plays an important role. We already mentioned in Chapter 1 that it is possible in Delphi, for instance, to create a simple application with a few mouse clicks. This textbook is aimed at providing a general introduction to object-oriented programming, so a detailed presentation of these functions would definitely go beyond its scope. We limit ourselves to the most important issues in the following sections.

Probably the best example is a simple Windows application, HelloWorld, which has some static text, s1, and a button, but. When the button is clicked, the text "button clicked" appears on the button. This screen is shown in Figure 8.3, before the button was clicked.

Delphi   In Delphi, for the form itself, we have to define an independent class derived from TForm, an empty window, and a container for dialog elements. The two control elements, s1 and but, are attributes embedded in this

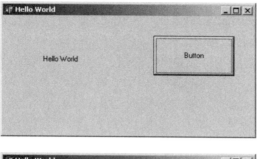

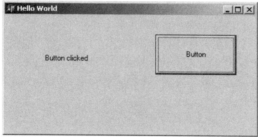

Figure 8.3 The "Hello World" screen.

class. The standard properties of these control elements are not set in the program itself but in a special tool by the name of Object Inspector (Figure 8.4). Using this tool, we can define many different things—for example, the attribute caption for the button but: the text displayed inside the button should be set to the value button.

The Object Inspector is the connection between your application's visual appearance and the code that makes your application run. The Object Inspector enables you to do the following:

- Set design-time properties for components you have placed on a form (or for the form itself).

- Create and help you navigate through event handlers.

- Filter visible properties and events.

To support you, the Object Inspector has two pages: the Properties page and the Events page. The Properties page enables you to set design-time

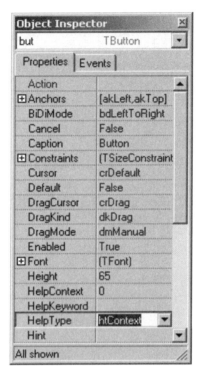

Figure 8.4 Object Inspector: setting properties.

properties for components on your form and for the form itself. By setting properties at design time, you are defining the initial state of a component. You can set runtime properties by writing source code within event handlers.

The Events page enables you to connect forms and components to program events. To generate a default event handler for an event, double-click the right column. The product creates the event handler and switches focus to the Code editor. In the Code editor, you write the event handlers that specify how a component or form responds to a particular event. The majority of new development environments offer tools like the Object Inspector.

Let us go back to our example. The type required for the screen shown in Figure 8.3, TMyForm, could look like this:

```
type
   TMyForm = class(TForm)
      s1: TLabel;
      but: TButton;
   end;
var
   myForm: TMyForm;
```

The rest is easy—we just have to declare a variable of that type. However, we don't have to write the entire source code given in this example. Instead, it is generated automatically by the Delphi development environment. Also, it is fairly easy to respond to each event. When the user clicks the button, the text of s1 should change to read "button clicked." For this purpose, we can write a method, such as ChangeText, of the class TMyForm, which will set the attribute caption of s1 accordingly.

```
procedure TMyForm.ChangeText (sender: TObject);
begin
   s1.caption := 'button clicked';
end;
```

The parameter sender identifies the control element that triggered this event. The button is passed to the method as a parameter and can then be accessed by this method. However, to ensure that the method ChangeText is executed when the button is clicked, we have to specify in the Object Inspector that this method is called when a mouse click (OnClick) occurs. Figure 8.5 shows this scenario.

We can see in this figure that methods can also be set for other events, such as when the mouse is dragged over the button. In this case, the Object Inspector generates the event handler automatically, not even visible to the programmer.

Listing 8.1 contains the entire source code for this program. Standard behavior, such as closing the application by clicking the cross in the top right corner, is naturally inherited from the base class TForm, and does not have to be specifically implemented.

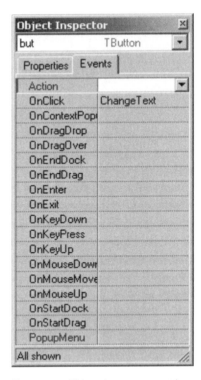

Figure 8.5 Object Inspector: setting events.

Listing 8.1. Delphi
Solution for
HelloWorld

```
unit HelloWorld;
interface
uses Windows, Messages, SysUtils, Classes, Graphics, Controls,
     Forms, Dialogs, StdCtrls;

type
  TMyForm = class(TForm)
     s1: TLabel;
     but: TButton;
     procedure ChangeText (sender: TObject);
  end;

var
  myForm: TMyForm;
```

```
implementation

procedure TMyForm.ChangeText (sender: TObject);
begin
   s1.caption := 'button clicked';
end;
end.
```

The previous example program is surprisingly short, because the Object Inspector defines both the standard settings of the control elements and the definition of methods to be called upon specific events. As comfortable as this may sound, it is not necessarily beneficial in all cases. When problems occur, we have to check not only the source code but also various entries in the Object Inspector, which could indeed be cumbersome and hard to reproduce.

In Java, for the form itself, we have to implement a separate class, derived from JFrame. In this class, we have to embed a panel (class: JPanel), a special container that can accommodate the control elements. We also have to define how these control elements are arranged in this panel. The most common and normally suitable arrangement is XYLayout—defining the coordinates of a corner point. Moreover, the two control elements, s1 and but, have to be embedded in this type. The basic structure of this type, at least as far as the attributes are concerned, looks like this:

```
public class Frame1 extends JFrame {
   JPanel contentPane;
   XYLayout xYLayout1 = new XYLayout();
   JLabel s1 = new JLabel();
   JButton but = new JButton();
   . . .
}
```

Subsequently, we have to write a constructor, defining the choice of standard settings: the text to appear on the button or the position of the control elements. This constructor also controls how to respond to various events that may arise. Generally in Java, we have to define events that could actually arise. For this purpose, we call the method enableEvents(ev), where ev carries those kinds of events that should be activated. The events that can actually be activated are specified in the class AWTEvent.

Next, to be able to properly respond to each of these events, we have to register *listener classes*. There is a separate listener class for each event (for example, mouse event, key event, or window event). More specifically, a mouse listener has to be registered by means of the function addMouseListener. This goal is achieved by deriving the class java.awt.event.MouseAdapter. As a response to the mouse click, the appropriate method has to be called.

The entire construction is implemented in a try block to catch exceptions. The following source code fragment shows the constructor:

```java
// build the frame
public Frame1 () {
  enableEvents(AWTEvent.WINDOW_EVENT_MASK);
  try {
    jbInit();
  }
  catch(Exception e) {
    e.printStackTrace();
  }
}
// initialize the components
private void jbInit () throws Exception {
  contentPane = (JPanel) this.getContentPane();
  contentPane.setLayout(xYLayout1);
  // . . . set properties
  but.addMouseListener(new java.awt.event.MouseAdapter() {
    public void mouseClicked (MouseEvent e) {
      but_mouseClicked(e);
    }
  });
  contentPane.add(s1, new XYConstraints(21, 50, 138, 36));
  contentPane.add(but, new XYConstraints(246, 48, 81, 31));
}
```

Listing 8.2 includes the entire program. This code also shows how the window event WINDOW_CLOSING is properly processed to ensure that the application terminates.

```java
package helloworld;
import java.awt.*;
import java.awt.event.*;
import javax.swing.*;
import com.borland.jbcl.layout.*;
public class Frame1 extends JFrame {
   JPanel contentPane;
   XYLayout xYLayout1 = new XYLayout();
   JLabel s1 = new JLabel();
   JButton but = new JButton();
   // build the frame

   public Frame1 () {
      enableEvents(AWTEvent.WINDOW_EVENT_MASK);
      try {
         jbInit();
      }
      catch(Exception e) {
         e.printStackTrace();
      }
   }
   // initialize the components
   private void jbInit () throws Exception {
      s1.setText("Hello World");
      contentPane = (JPanel) this.getContentPane();
      contentPane.setLayout(xYLayout1);
      this.setSize(new Dimension(400, 300));
      this.setTitle("frame title");
      but.setText("button");
      but.addMouseListener(new java.awt.event.MouseAdapter() {
         public void mouseClicked (MouseEvent e) {
            but_mouseClicked(e);
         }
      });
      contentPane.add(s1, new XYConstraints(21, 50, 138, 36));
      contentPane.add(but, new XYConstraints(246, 48, 81, 31));
   }
   // Overwritten, so we can terminate
   // when the window is closed.
```

```
protected void processWindowEvent (WindowEvent e) {
  super.processWindowEvent(e);
  if (e.getID() == WindowEvent.WINDOW_CLOSING) {
    System.exit(0);
  }
}

void but_mouseClicked (MouseEvent e) {
  s1.setText("button clicked");
}
}
```

<table>
<tr><td>8.4</td></tr>
</table>

Tips for Designing a User Interface

Programs are written for the user, not for the programmer!

We could continue writing a lot more about these things. However, considering that creating a user interface depends largely on the programming environment we select, as mentioned earlier, and because most of this material is extensively covered in the relevant documentation, we limit this description to what we have explained so far. In closing this chapter, we provide tips for designing GUIs:

- **User-oriented:** Always design your program for easiest use.

- **Look and feel:** Control objects should not be presented randomly on the screen but in a clear arrangement—neatly aligned buttons are easier to use and understand.

- **Consistency:** Represent similar things in a similar way and different things in a different way.

- **Fault tolerance:** A good program should be tolerant of user errors, behave nicely, and output an error message users can understand. User errors should never cause the program to crash.

- **Feedback:** Results from operations should be displayed immediately.

- **Keyboard users:** As comfortable as computer input devices, such as a mouse, may be, many users prefer the keyboard. A user interface should be built so that users can use either one.

- **Function keys:** Assign function keys with care, because each operating system makes different use of these keys by standard (for example, all

Windows applications use F1 to activate the online help system). Use function keys consistently in new applications.

- **Simplicity:** Observe the slogan "As simple as possible" in all your programming work.

Online Applications

Especially during the past years, online applications (applications executed over the Internet) have become increasingly important. They reached a new dimension under the name application service provider (ASP). The motivation behind this technology is that people no longer buy software but instead rent it. In this constellation, the software is installed on a server on the Internet while the user sits at an Internet terminal (usually a PC and modem) and runs this software on an Internet browser. The main benefit is doubtless a distribution of cost, based on the rental variant, particularly when usage is brief (for example, using a piece of software for only a few months), but it has additional benefits:

- Each software product requires a certain input and cost for maintenance, such as for updates. This input is done centrally and does not have to be provided by the user.

- One of the most important points when working on the PC is to save your work regularly. Unfortunately, many forget to save their work. In ASP operation, the software operator saves your work for you.

- ASP operation enables much better helpdesk services, because the helpdesk staff can connect to the ASP server and look at the problem in detail.

- A user can log in to the server and run the software from any Internet terminal anywhere in the world, for example, while on vacation.

Software operated over the Internet does not necessarily have to be different from conventional software. In fact, ASP operation is generally based on the guidelines outlined previously. In addition, the control elements available are the same, such as a Java program that generally runs in a browser—on the Internet.

On the other hand, consider execution speed, because each data transmission requires a certain amount of time. Things like filling in a form on the Internet should be planned. Say you first fill out the entire form, wait for a Save click, and finally transfer the entire work to the server. Input errors will be transferred together with the entire job in the form of a protocol. A "traditional" program would check field after field and output an error message if you made a wrong entry.

9

COBOL to OOP in Practice

Congratulations to all of you who made it to this point! You have acquired a solid knowledge of object-oriented programming and learned more about new techniques, such as databases and writing user interfaces.

9.1 Summary

OOP course in catchwords

This chapter provides a summary of the major issues covered in the previous chapters. This summary is in the form of catchwords, and we recommend that you think about each catchword. If you are not sure you understood an issue denoted by one of these catchwords, it would be helpful to repeat the relevant section and, have another look or two at the relevant exercises. The previous chapters of this book dealt with the following issues:

- **Basics:** symbols, standard types, declarations, value assignment, if instruction, multiple branching, loops, procedures, parameters, local names, functions, recursion, arrays, strings, records, stepwise refinement, open-array parameter, procedure variables, Java Virtual Machine, modules, export, import, modularization, pointers, creating and deleting objects

- **Dynamic data structures:** abstraction, ADS, ADT, linear lists, stacks, queues, trees, binary trees, logical delete, traversing, balanced trees, algorithms, heaps, graphs, hashing, sort algorithms

- **True OOP:** class definition, creating and releasing objects, instances, methods, constructors, destructors, inheritance, dynamic binding, abstract classes, access classes, overloading, generic components, replaceable behavior, extensible components, heterogeneous data structures, class libraries, TObject, exceptions, interfaces, properties

- **Object-oriented design:** The Abbot method, CRC cards, UML, design pattern, factory, iterator, components

- **Databases:** fundamental concept, data security, data protection, recovery, transactions, commit, deadlock, client/server solution, object-oriented databases, data modeling, normalization, ER model, generalization, aggregation, views, index, surrogates, SQL, creating tables, inserting and deleting records, functions, SELECT instruction, set operations, UPDATE instruction, privileges, embedded SQL, database drivers, sending an SQL instruction to the database, evaluating the results

- **Graphical user interfaces (GUIs):** building a GUI, control elements, event-oriented programming, HandleEvent, the Object Inspector, forms, tips for the design of user interfaces

Mastering the complexity
One of the major topics has been in the foreground: mastering the complexity! Object-oriented programming is complex. Therefore, the following order should be maintained in each software development project:

- Build the model: Programming means understanding!

- Implement the program by using a class library.

- Design the user interface.

The OOP course in this book was structured to ensure that these steps can be performed successfully. Exactly this stepwise structure, based on the order described earlier, distinguishes this OOP course from most other courses, many of which begin with the design of a user interface and deal with programming of methods as a secondary matter. This book places programming at the center!

As simple as possible

You should take home two important principles from this course: "As simple as possible" and "Programming means understanding!" Remember them when working in object-oriented programming or design. To find understandable solutions, it is important to understand even complex situations and be able to represent them in an easily understandable way. This art can be understood and learned from [BGP00], to mention one good source.

9.2 Changing to OOP in Practice

BMD

As mentioned in Chapter 1, this OOP course was applied at BMD Systemhaus GmbH, Austria's leading producer of business software [Kna99]. BMD has a software development department with more than 50 employees; I have been managing this department since 1997. Forty of these developers were—and some still are—busy maintaining and improving a COBOL product. This internal development effort at BMD—an integrated software package for all business areas—is installed at more than 12,000 customer sites, including Austria's leading tax advisors and some of the largest Austrian companies. More recently, BMD has expanded to the international market and now has customers in Germany, Hungary, Switzerland, and Czechia.

Thirty years' experience: NTCS

This COBOL product has been used for more than 30 years. It has been reimplemented using two major object-oriented programming languages, Delphi and Java, to form a new type of accounting software called BMD NTCS (New Technology Commercial Software). This combines the benefits of the BMD software and the Windows operating system. This section outlines the project's progress and some experiences as a result of it, which will be particularly helpful for programmers who plan to implement COBOL projects in OOP.

9.2.1 Main Tasks

The first project phase entailed two major tasks. First, we had to implement the required tools—the class library. Second, COBOL programmers had to be "converted" into object-oriented programmers. Building on these important preparatory steps, we were able to reimplement the individual program packages by use of the object-oriented class library.

9.2.2 Implementing the Required Windows Tools

Selecting a suitable development environment

Implementing the required Windows tools essential, because it forms the basis for the entire project. One of the first steps involved the selection of a suitable development environment. Although it would have been feasible to use a newer version of our COBOL compiler, this was not desirable, as mentioned in Section 1.5. Various tools based on different programming languages (for example, Java, C++, Visual Basic, Object-Pascal) had been studied, but the bigger the choice, the more difficult such a selection is.

Eventually, we selected Delphi, for two reasons. First, the Delphi class library is mighty and supports database accesses that occur frequently in accounting software. Second, Delphi is based on Pascal, which is an easily readable language making it easy for COBOL programmers to learn.

A class library for efficient input options

Using this new development environment, we designed a class library, focusing on efficient input possibilities and integration of all packages. Moreover, we tried to implement as many things as we possibly could into the class library, because this normally helps significantly reduce development time. This approach has not only the advantage that the product will be ready for market earlier but also reduces the period for double maintenance. This was required because the existing product still had to be maintained while we were working on the new object-oriented implementation.

Other parts of the class library are special input forms, report generators, Internet components, formula generators, capabilities management (user privileges), and SQL assistants, among others.

9.2.3 Retraining COBOL Programmers

To develop the class library, we hired several new programmers with academic backgrounds who were optimally trained for object-oriented programming. This team was completed by several other developers who had several years of experience with the COBOL product and mastered object-oriented programming at the same time.

Experience in OOP retraining

The remaining programmers had excellent COBOL knowledge but little or no experience in object-oriented programming. However, we found their strengths in their experience with the existing software—they knew exactly what functionality the new product would have to offer and how this could look. I am convinced that this combined knowledge is imperative and harder to learn than OOP. For this reason, we decided to retrain these programmers for object-oriented programming.

Exercises were
walked through
and corrected

This retraining effort took place on the basis of the OOP course presented in this book. Each of the tutorial sections was held weekly, and the exercises were all practiced and corrected. However, these exercises were not corrected to give scores but to learn about the progress of each participant and avoid misunderstandings.

9.2.4 Experiences

All have to pull
in the same
direction!

BMD NTCS is a large project, at least for Austrian dimensions, with a duration of more than 5 years and a budget of approximately 10 million Euros. With such projects, it is important for everyone to support the project. Therefore, it was necessary to "sell" the project to every single member of the development team, which was not easy, because some feared losing their jobs. These worries were not substantiated, because the retraining effort was conducted by the company, and everybody who attended this course successfully was assured of being taken on for the new project. This activity helped convince the team of the NTCS project.

Strategies for
double
maintenance

Another important aspect of such a project—when an old product is replaced by a new one—is the period when the team has to work on both products at the same time. Two strategies are feasible: Have two separate development teams work on one project—one for the old product and one for the new—or have a team work on both at the same time.

The first solution would mean doubling the number of developers. In addition, it would be difficult to find programmers for the "old" project, because they would fear falling behind in their careers or similar drawbacks. The second solution could mean that both projects would get less than their fair share.

These reasons encouraged BMD to opt for the "golden" middle course. We hired a new crew to develop the basis for the new project—the class library. The existing programmers were entrusted with the tasks of maintaining the existing program and developing the specific parts (but only parts) of the new project. This approach is possible only because of the major advantage of object-oriented programming: modularization.

9.3 Career Switch to OOP in Practice

View of the
people behind
the object

Having presented managements view of this change, this section concentrates on the people behind this project. It is important to see their knowledge, their human backgrounds and, of course, their problems [Kna02].

9.3.1 Knowledge

Programmers at BMD Steyr have sufficient COBOL knowledge, which is probably one of the most important contributions to our current product's success. Another important factor, essential for the production of accounting software, is an above-average knowledge of and experience with domains. I believe that this domain knowledge and experience in implementing such a software product are far more important than the programming knowledge itself. Who, other than these programmers, could extend the strengths hidden in the intensive contents and parameters of our program? It was precisely these strengths that made this software so successful.

Domain knowledge is necessary

Before the object-oriented programming course at BMD Steyr began, programmers were familiar with COBOL and its concepts, such as records, arrays, and procedures. They were competent in structured programming and, clearly enough, avoided GOTO statements. However, their COBOL compiler did not support a variety of essential programming features, such as call by reference parameters, local variables, and pointers. Because of this, most were unfamiliar with or rarely used algorithms for binary trees, hash tables, and/or heaps.

9.3.2 Human Background

Most of these programmers have been working at BMD for more than 10 years, some for more than 25 years. Many were shocked to hear that they would have to learn object-oriented programming. Employees may have doubts about whether they can become skilled at new techniques and may also fear that fewer programmers will be needed as a result of increased productivity.

Older COBOL programmers are still afraid of losing their jobs

This is a false conclusion. Demand is proportional to productivity and grows with an increase in output. Yet older COBOL programmers are still afraid of losing their jobs. It is not easy for older employees to find an adequate position in this business.

It is up to the project manager to provide his or her staff with the necessary motivation and sense of security. Security is important—insecure employees are not only less productive but are easy prey for headhunters. Rumors spread; gossip, such as that every other employee will be made redundant, is not uncommon when working on projects of this kind. This must be dealt with immediately.

Learning leads to progress

Most of our programmers were aware that NTCS was not only an opportunity for the company to grow but for them too. Their interest in programming and ambition to learn inspired them to gain knowledge of the new technology. Profit-sharing as the company prospered was another motivation.

9.3.3 Problems

While learning object-oriented programming, the programmers naturally had some problems—not just technical but psychological.

Technical Problems

Pointers

Following the concepts presented previously, most members of the staff were able to learn object-oriented programming within a reasonable time. However, they were sometimes faced with difficulty in understanding object-oriented concepts predominantly relating to dynamic objects. This is absolutely new terrain for traditional COBOL programmers, because COBOL does not use pointers. The most relevant example was the one about the difference between two different objects and pointers. We often had to refer to this example, with the objective of making participants aware and helping them understand the principal difference.

Inheritance and dynamic binding

Because there are no counterparts in the COBOL language, after having overcome this problem, the next step was to introduce *inheritance* and *dynamic binding*. Inheritance was basically explained as being a type extension. A subclass is an extension of a base type: It *inherits* the fields and methods of the base type and may declare additional fields and methods of its own.

The explanation of dynamic binding was trickier, but based on the clarification of inheritance, we were able to make apparent that the compatibility between a subclass and its base class enables a variable at runtime to contain objects of diverse types that react differently to a message.

COBOL programmers found it hard to identify with certain other points, such as runtime errors when using a wrong type or a wrong array index, which do not exist in COBOL (the return value is just zero). An appealing feature is that the COBOL environment we use (MICROFOCUS COBOL) is powerful and prevails over the Delphi debugger, especially the COBOL animator. We therefore had to elucidate additional static test methods to support the programmers when searching for bugs.

We conclude with a few recommendations to successfully coach object-oriented programming:

■ Begin with programming, then train object-oriented programming. Data abstraction and writing well-structured programs should be the first lessons, mainly because it is easier to explicate object-oriented programming based on knowledge of data abstraction.

■ Try to avoid academic terms (such as *ontology*) that might be misinterpreted.

■ Use as many examples as possible. A simple example can say more than a hundred words.

■ When introducing object-oriented programming in a company, use the initial products of inexperienced programmers with caution, because they are likely to contain errors.

Psychological Problems

One psychological problem, as already mentioned, is the feeling of uncertainty apparent in new component programmers and users. If components can easily be replaced, why not software engineers? [Chr02]

Most programmers handled the change with ease—they mastered the art of learning. Many spent their free time reading and studying books; others have written short projects. They preferred working on the new projects to programming in COBOL for maintenance or customer requests.

Using the new possibilities? However, some programmers had difficulty adapting to OOP. They were not able to increase productivity because they did not make appropriate use of the new possibilities put at their disposal. This is relevant: for many years, programmers have written their own code, with negligible inspection or supervision. They are now expected to use components structured by other programmers.

And why not? After all, it saves time and increases productivity. It is now no longer necessary to write tedious programs—it is enough for them to produce components that make sense to themselves and others. It is important to keep documentation of the components, a task often ignored in most COBOL programs. A possible motivation could be a further bonus for documented components usable by other programmers rather than for the quantity of code delivered.

Objective thinking Objective thinking was another point our programmers seemed to have difficulty with. Object-oriented programming is not just a new kind of programming, it is a method of design, programming, and also testing—all requiring objective judgment. The ability to assess objectively is an instinctive talent and advantage for those who enter the world of object-oriented programming over other, more experienced programmers who were always expected to think sequentially when working with COBOL. The latter were expected to abruptly alter their manner of thinking, and sometimes, they understandably slipped back to their old patterns.

Slips of this kind can be minimized by applying object-oriented design methods, starting with the first step of each project, for example, by means of the Abbott method [Abb83] or CRC cards, which can also be used for each class to present names, responsibilities, and partners. They are easy to produce, understand, and discard. Multiple cards can be laid out on a large table to spawn effective discussions [Mös99]. The results should be consolidated using UML and not by means of relational techniques such as ER diagrams.

Components also enhance teamwork. A certain level of teamwork existed in COBOL programming—for example, teams for bookkeeping, salary administration, and CRM software. Yet each team worked independently of the other, and work within each team was not always a group product.

OOP teams use components written by other teams, and the social value increases, because the members of different teams get together. Formal and informal discussions—coffee-break chats—present new components, and productivity increases. The better team players mix and trade information; the less effective ones are generally unwilling to communicate and inadvertently conceal new and helpful components. After all, it goes against the principle of most COBOL programmers to use information generated by others. Back in their schooling days, "copycat" versions were considered a fraudulent way to attain results [Chr02]. Although component-oriented programming need not increase individual productivity, it unquestionably improves the collective output.

Programmers who performed poorly with COBOL usually also ended up struggling to achieve the desired expectations in the new language. It is often the case that some programmers would solve a problem in a matter of hours, whereas others would need weeks or more.

A third group of programmers is normally also evident: programmers who are unable to learn anything new, not because they are not prepared to but because of other valid reasons. It is usually wiser to place this workforce in positions that most suit their capabilities rather than force them to do something they do not want. This is especially important for companies dealing with projects on the market that must react promptly to errors or individual requests.

9.3.4   Results

Freshly trained OOP programmers performed surprisingly well after having completed their course and a few practical projects. Needless to say, their performance could not match that of programmers who already had a few years of OOP experience. Practice makes perfect, which is why we sincerely believe that new programmers should be entrusted more frequently with larger projects.

9.4   Accompanying Activities

More novelties can be realized

An entry into the world of object-oriented programming is often a good chance to realize other novelties in the field of software development. This could be seen as an accompanying activity—for example, ISO 9001 certification, automatic tests, or version management.

9.4.1   ISO 9001

ISO certification improves quality and competitiveness

A switch from COBOL to object-oriented programming requires changing the entire development process. This switch could be usefully accompanied by an introduction of the ISO 9001 standard. This is a quality assurance model used mainly in disciplines such as design, development, production, assembly, and maintenance. The core consists of about 20 elements whose substance must be met:

- Commitment and responsibility of the corporate management

- Quality assurance system

- Internal audits

- Correction of errors and faults

- Contract verification

- Definition of the principals' requirements

- Development planning

- Quality assurance planning

- Design and implementation

- Test and validation

- Acceptance test

- Reproduction, commissioning, and installation

- Configuration management

- Documentation control

- Quality reporting

- Measurements

- Rules, practices, agreements

- Tools and techniques

- Purchasing and procurement

- Third-party software

- Training

Quality manual   Documentation, the so-called quality manual, is created and used to define exactly who is in charge for these elements, and in what way. Such a model is likely to be present in every company, although it is often not fully documented or observed. The meaning of ISO certification is to document everything, gradually creating a complete manual to improve the quality of everyday company processes. The certification also foresees that a third party, called a certification commission, checks for observance of the quality standards. Details about ISO standard 9001 are found in [Hoy01], to mention one good source. (Information can also be found on their website: *www.iso.ch*.)

In addition to improving quality, this kind of certification offers a competitive edge, because many customers prefer to do business with certified vendors. Some (especially governmental organizations) even require their suppliers to have this certification.

9.4.2　Automatic Tests

Test cases are recorded and repeated as often as needed

The automatic test method, which is also used at BMD, enables efficient implementation of all required tests. Test tools (for example, QACenter of Compuware [Com98]) record test cases and run them anytime they are needed. Test cases created internally—*test scripts*—can be implemented by using a macro language. QACenter can also be used to maintain test scripts, manipulate test data, and run load tests.

This sort of test tool can be introduced by a three-step principle:

1. Install the tools and train the testing department staff. This step is relatively easy and can be completed in a few days. The most difficult task is to convince the staff of the project's importance, which requires some psychological work, because words such as "automation" have a negative effect on many employees.

2. Build a test series. At BMD, for example, the basic strategy was to create an accounting system, run a few special posting cases, close the accounts, and print a balance sheet. This test series is done after each change—daily—at the development location. The next task of this step is then to check—automatically—that the printouts are identical.

   The most important aspect of this task is to find test cases that should be integrated into the test series. Such a test series ensures that the program will work even after several changes so that even major changes produce only minor problems.

3. See if these automatic tests can be "optimized." We could embed special controls—for example, to test for the following cases. In the BMD software, the user sees the current result of a company after each posting. A simple control that monitors the display of such results could be added to the test series. The use of such controls could help improve the quality of automatic tests significantly.

Although such a control script can be implemented relatively easily, those who test the software are normally end users rather than programmers. For this reason, it appears useful to assign the implementation of such controls to a programmer.

9.4.3 Version Management

The ideal time to think about introducing source management or version management is when programs—source code—are written from scratch.

Creation process is meticulously documented

This sort of software tool documents every detail of the creation process and can reconstruct all activities back to version 1.0. Also, an arbitrary number of programmers can work on the sources, because the tool prevents inadvertent overwriting of code.

Sources have to be checked before being used

All source code files have to be stored in a central location and are write-protected. If a change has to be made to a file, the developer has to obtain a request for change, including a description of the desired change. This request, which may indeed be issued by the same developer, entitles him or her to edit the relevant source code. For this purpose, the version management tool is used to "check out" the source code; subsequently, the source code can be edited locally.

From this point, all other developers have only read access to this source code. As soon as the change is readily implemented, this source code file can be "checked in" again so that it is available to all developers. The version management tool registers all changes, including the relevant requests, so that it is possible to return to an older source version or view changes between two versions in detail at any time.

Another developer could now effect changes to this file, but only after making an appropriate request to do so and checking the file out and back in again.

Implementing such a version management system requires great discipline, but it significantly improves quality (see also Section 9.3.1) and facilitates troubleshooting. Version management tools are effective support tools in a parallel development project.

9.5   Stick to COBOL All the Same?

Want to try your luck as a crossopterygian?

Although we made a huge step toward object-oriented programming in working our way through this book, some readers may feel they want to stick to COBOL. As mentioned in our crossopterygian example in Chapter 1, they may even be successful. Working our way through this book, with particular focus on Chapters 2, 3, and 4, has certainly helped improve general programming capabilities so that neither those interested in a career switch nor crossopterygian-minded readers wasted any of their time.

Furthermore, object-oriented COBOL might be worth a closer look. In fact, this book provides an excellent framework for a course on modern COBOL: (1) COBOL with Windows and/or HTML user interfaces incorporating JAVA script and JAVA beans; (2) with object application layers that make use of Object COBOL's class library, especially the Collection Classes; and (3) with embedded SQL to access relational databases via ODBC protocols. Most of our examples in Delphi and C++ could be rewritten in object-oriented COBOL.

9.6 One Last Word

The devil must have invented software, because hardware is almost perfect!

We close this book with a statement attributed to Professor Zemanek, an Austrian computer pioneer: "The devil must have invented software, because hardware is almost perfect!" We use his words as a good reason to emphasize our principle one last time: Object-oriented programming is complex and can be mastered only by applying a gradual approach and orderly modularization.

Appendix A

Using the Development Environments

Delphi and Jbuilder This appendix gives a short introduction to the development environments included on the book CD, explaining a few important basics so that you can use them to work on the exercises. Each of the two development environments is illustrated by a simple example, dealing mainly with input and output operations. All programs should be designed on the basis of the following sample.

A.1 Delphi

Start the Delphi system. From the File menu, select Open. In the dialog box that appears next, select the path Delphi\SampleProject on your CD and select the file Sample.

Sample project   A new input window appears, showing an empty Pascal program frame. The first step is to save the project under a new name. To do this, select Save As . . . from the File menu. Select a meaningful name, such as Exercise0, and save the file to a directory of your choice.

Now you are ready for programming. A short demo program could look like this:

```
// Markus Knasmüller, 8.1.2003
// This program reads two numbers and outputs the sum;
// it serves as a demo program (Exercise0)
program Exercise0;
var
   a, b, sum: Integer;
   dummy: Char;
begin
   Write('Please enter the first value:'); ReadLn(a);
   Write('Please enter the second value:'); ReadLn(b);
   sum := a + b;
   Write('The result is:');
   WriteLn(sum); // an alternative would be WriteLn(a + b);
   Read(dummy); // required to keep the result
end.
```

Compiling and starting the program

Fill the sample frame according to this source code. The next step is to compile and start this program. To start the program in Delphi, select Run from the Run menu (or press function key F9). This function compiles the program and runs it if no errors are found during compilation.

Compiler error messages and warnings

Errors found during translation will be displayed on the screen in the form of an error message. Delphi displays the input window in two panes. The top pane shows the source code you entered, and the bottom pane displays error messages. The line where an error was found is highlighted in red in the upper pane. (Careful: The compiler may find an error on one line but display red highlighting on the line below—for example, if you forgot a semicolon.)

Correct the error and proceed with your code. If several errors occurred, you can use the mouse in the lower pane to move the cursor to each error and correct it. When done with your corrections, select the Run again to continue. Warning messages output by the compiler can be ignored.

While the program is executing, an additional text window shows the message Please enter the first value:. Enter a value (say, 5) and press Enter. A second message, Please enter the second value: appears. Enter a value (say, 3) and press Enter. The program outputs the result: The result is: 8. Press any key to exit the program.

As you can see in the program code, Read and ReadLn allow you to read arbitrary values, which are output by Write or WriteLn, respectively. The appended Ln causes a line feed.

To print the source code, select Print from the File menu.

Units   If you want to use modules (see Section 3.6) in addition to your program, use New from the File menu to add them. In the dialog box that appears next, select the Unit icon.

A.2   Java

New project   Start the JBuilder system. Select New Project . . . from the File menu. In the dialog box that appears, select the desired directory path—for example, d:\ExerciseProject—and enter a different project name, such as Exercise0.

Select Add Files/Package from the Project menu. Enter the file name Exercise0.java and type "Yes" when asked whether you want to create this file. The name of the new file is displayed in the left frame. Double-click the file name to open the file.

You are now ready for programming. A short demo program could look like this:

```java
// Markus Knasmüller, 8.1.2003
// This program reads two numbers and outputs the sum;
// it serves as a demo program (Exercise0)
class Exercise0 {

  public static String readName () { // auxiliary procedure
    String s = "";
    try {
      s = new java.io.DataInputStream(System.in).readLine();
    }
    catch(java.io.IOException e) {}
    return s.trim();
  }

  public static int readInt () { // auxiliary procedure
    String s = "";
    try {
      s = new java.io.DataInputStream(System.in).readLine();
    }
    catch (java.io.IOException e) {}
    return java.lang.Integer.parseInt(s);
  }
```

```java
public static void main (String args[]) {
    int a, b, sum;
    System.out.print("Please enter the first value:");
    a = readInt();
    System.out.print("Please enter the second value:");
    b = readInt();
    sum = a + b;
    System.out.print("The result is:");
    System.out.println(sum);
    // an alternative would be System.out.println(a + b);
  }
}
```

Compiling and starting the program

Type this source code. The next step is to compile and start the program. In Java, select Run Project from the Run menu (or press function key F9) to compile and start a program. This menu item compiles your program and runs it if no error occurred during compilation process. Before the program can be executed, you have to set the main class. In this dialog box type Exercise0.

Compiler error messages and warnings

Errors found during compilation will be displayed in the form of an error message. Java splits the input window into two panes. The upper pane displays the source code you typed, and the lower pane shows error messages. A faulty line is highlighted in red in the upper pane. Correct the error. If several errors were found, you can use the mouse to move the cursor to each error and correct it. When you are done with your corrections, select Run again to proceed. Warning messages output by the compiler can be ignored.

While the program is executing, the message Please enter the first value: is displayed on the screen. Enter a value (say, 5) and press Enter. Then the second message, Please enter the second value:, appears. Enter a value (say, 3) and press Enter. The result is displayed: The result is: 8.

As you can see in the program code, readInt allows you to read any numbers, and readName allows you to read any character string. You could copy the source code fragment for readInt and readName to each of your programs that requires inputs. Use System.out.print or System.out.println to output arbitrary values. The appended ln causes a line feed.

To print the source code, select Print from the File menu.

Modules

If you want to use modules (see Section 3.6) in addition to your program, select Add Files/Packages from the Project menu.

Appendix B

Sample Solutions

This appendix contains sample solutions for the tasks from the tutorial sections. To stay within the limits of this book, this chapter contains only selected solutions, mostly in one programming language. The CD to this book includes all solutions, both in Delphi and Java code.

All sample solutions in this chapter are intended to serve as examples, showing how a problem could be solved. There may be other—more efficient—solutions. The following sample solutions are intended to provide basic concepts, to serve as a reference, and to encourage you to work out different solutions to similar problems.

B.1 Solutions to Chapter 3

B.1.1 Exercises in Section 3.1.5

Task 1 (20 minutes): Declarations

Delphi
```
1. accountNumber: Integer;

2. accountBalance: Real;

3. ch: Char;

4. short: Shortint;

5. exactValue: Double;
```

Java

1. `int accountNumber;`

2. `float accountBalance;`

3. `char ch;`

4. `byte short;`

5. `double exactValue;`

Task 2 (30 minutes): Boolean Expressions

1. (x < z) and (y < z) and (x < y) or (x >= z) and (x < y) ⇔
   ((x < z) and (y < z) and (x < y)) or ((x >= z) and (x < y)) ⇔
   ((y < z) and (x < y)) or ((x >= z) and (x < y)) ⇔
   (x < y) and ((y < z) or (x >= z))
   x = 3, y = 5, z = 7 ⇒ TRUE
   x = 5, y = 3, z = 7 ⇒ FALSE
   x = 5, y = 7, z = 3 ⇒ TRUE

2. Formulate expressions that give a TRUE result if
   a. ch is a letter or a digit:
      (ch >= 'a') and (ch <= 'z') or (ch >= 'A') and (ch <= 'Z') or
      (ch >= '0') and (ch <= '9')
   b. x, y, z all contain different values:
      (x <> y) and (y <> z) and (x <> z)

3. Simplify the following expression:
   (x <> y) or not ((y = z) and (y = x)) ⇔
   (x <> y) or (not(y = z) or not(y = x)) ⇔
   (x <> y) or (y <> z) or (y <> x) ⇔ **(x <> y) or (y <> z)**

B.1.2   Exercises in Section 3.2.7

Task 1 (60 minutes): Fibonacci Numbers

Delphi

```
program PgmFibonacci;
var
  n, i: Integer;
  fib1, fib2, res: Integer; // Fib(n - 1), Fib(n - 2), Fib(n)
```

```
begin
  ReadLn(n);
  while (n >= 0) do begin
    res := 1;
    fib1 := 1; // initialize Fib(n-1)
    fib2 := 1; // initialize Fib(n-2)
    for i := 2 to n do begin
      res := fib1 + fib2; // Fib(n) = Fib(n-1) + Fib(n-2)
      fib2 := fib1; // new Fib(n-2)
      fib1 := res; // new Fib(n-1)
    end;
    WriteLn('The ', n, '. number is:', res );
    ReadLn(n);
  end;
end.
```

Task 2 (60 minutes): Book Price

Java

```java
import java.io.*;
class PgmBookPrice {
  static int readInt () {
    String s = "";
    try {
      s = new java.io.DataInputStream(System.in).readLine();
    }
    catch (java.io.IOException e) {}
    return java.lang.Integer.parseInt(s);
  }
  public static void main (String args[]) {
    int number, days, quality;
    final int PAPERBACK = 300;
    final int HARDCOVER = 400;
    double price = 0;
    double factor;
    quality = readInt();
    while (quality > 0) {
      number = readInt();
      days = readInt();
      factor = 1;
```

```
        switch (quality) {
          case 1:
            if (number > 300) {factor = 0.9;}
            else {
             if (number > 200) {factor = 0.95;}
            }
            price = PAPERBACK * number * factor;
            break;
          case 2:
            if (number > 200) {
             if (number > 300) {factor = 0.85;}
             else {factor = 0.9;}
            }
            else {
             if (number > 100) {factor = 0.95;}
            }
            price = HARDCOVER * number * factor;
        }
        if (days < 10){
          switch (quality) {
            case 1:
            if (days < 5) {factor = 0.97;} else {factor = 0.99;}
             break;
            case 2:
             if (days < 5) {factor = 0.95;} else {factor = 0.97;}
          }
          price = price * factor;
        }
        System.out.print("The price is: ");
        System.out.println(price);
        quality = readInt();
      }
    }
  }
```

Table B.1   Desk test

Program line	x	y
P(x, x);	5	5
y:= 2 * x;	10	10
y:= y * x;	100	100

B.1.3   Exercises in Section 3.3.7

Task 1 (15 minutes): Simplifications

These source code fragments can be simplified as follows:

```
i := j; // Subtask A
a := a * b + 2 * c; // Subtask B
if a < b then begin // Subtask C
   c := a; a := b; b := c;
end;
```

Task 2 (5 minutes): Desk Test

Table B.1 shows how the variables change as they are processed. The parameters x and y occupy the same storage space, because x is used twice.

B.1.4   Exercises in Section 3.6.5

Task 1 (180 minutes): Priority Queue

Array Because the task says that the line will never have more than 100 people, you can use a regular array to implement this queue. It would be useful to distinguish among three arrays, depending on the category kind, which means that three queues—one for each category of people waiting—would be managed internally. Such a solution could look like this:

Delphi
```
unit PriorityQueue;

interface
   const UNPLEASANT = 1; NORMAL = 2; PLEASANT = 3;
   procedure Add (name: String; k: Integer);
   (* adds a new person - type k - to the queue *)
   procedure GetNext (var name: String);
```

```
      (* supplies the name of the next person and removes it *)
      function Count (): Integer;
      (* supplies the number of persons *)
implementation
  type
     PersonArr = array[0..99] of String;
  var
     queues: array[UNPLEASANT..PLEASANT] of PersonArr;
     index: array[UNPLEASANT..PLEASANT] of Integer;

  procedure Add (name: String; k: Integer);
  begin
     queues[k, index[k]] := name;
     Inc(index[k]);
  end;

  procedure GetNext (var name: String);
     var i, j: Integer;
  begin
     if index[PLEASANT] > 0 then i := PLEASANT
     else begin
        if index[NORMAL] > 0 then i := NORMAL
        else i := UNPLEASANT;
     end;
     if index[i] = 0 then name := ""
     else begin
        Dec(index[i]);
        name := queues[i, 0];
        for j := 0 to index[i] do begin
           queues[i, j] := queues[i, j + 1];
        end;
     end;
  end;
  function Count (): Integer;
  begin
     result := index[UNPLEASANT] + index[NORMAL]
        + index[PLEASANT];
  end;
initialization
  index[UNPLEASANT] := 0; index[NORMAL] := 0;
```

```
      index[PLEASANT] := 0;
end.
```

B.1.5 Exercises in Section 3.7.6

Task 1 (170 minutes): Priority Queue

Pointers have to be used here

In contrast to the previous task, this task does not limit the number of persons, so you cannot use an array. Instead, this solution implements a dynamic list. Insertion and deletion operations are simple, so it is unnecessary to split the list into three category-specific lists. This kind of solution could look as follows:

Java

```java
package Priority;
class Person {
   String name;
   int kind;
   Person next;
}
public class PriorityQueue {
   public final int UNPLEASANT = 1;
   public final int NORMAL = 2;
   public final int PLEASANT = 3;
   static int nrOfElems;
   static Person head;

   public static void add (String name, int k) {
      Person p1, p2;
      nrOfElems++;
      if ((head == null) || (head.kind < k)) {
         // new element becomes new head
         p1 = head;
         head = new Person();
         head.name = name; head.kind = k; head.next = p1;
      }
      else {
         p1 = head; p2 = head;
         while ((p1 != null) && (p1.kind >= k)) {
            p2 = p1; p1 = p1.next;
         }
```

```
            p1 = new Person();
            p1.name = name; p1.kind = k; p1.next = p2.next;
            p2.next = p1;
        }
    }

    public static String getNext () {
        String n;
        if (head != null) {
            n = head.name;
            head = head.next;
            nrOfElems-;
            return n;
        }
        else {
            return "";
        }
    }

    public static int count () {
        return nrOfElems;
    }

    static {
        nrOfElems = 0;
        head = null;
    }
}
```

Task 2 (10 minutes): Troubleshooting

**A created object
is never accessed**
The problem is that new(p) creates an object, but this object is never accessed, so the instruction is meaningless. Because of the next instruction, p := nil, the allocated storage block can no longer be reached. Delphi does not have a Garbage Collector, so such blocks have to be released explicitly. In this situation, we cannot free the block, because it cannot be reached. The result is that this storage space is unused and wasted.

B.2.1   Exercises in Section 4.1.4

Task 1 (170 minutes): Relations

Delphi

```
unit Relations;

interface
  type
    Item = ^ItemDesc;
    ItemDesc = record
      oid: String;
      adr: Integer;
      q: Boolean;
      next: Item;
    end;
    Relation = ^RelationDesc;
    RelationDesc = record
      head: Item;
      n: Integer;
    end;
  function Adr (r: Relation; oid: String): Integer;
  procedure Delete (r: Relation; oid: String);
  function Entries (r: Relation): Integer;
  procedure Insert (r: Relation; oid: String; adr: Integer; q: Boolean);
  function Quality (r: Relation; oid: String): Boolean;
  procedure Init (var r: Relation);
  var err: Boolean;

implementation
  procedure Search (r: Relation; oid: String; var prev, elem: Item);
  begin
    prev := nil; elem := r.head;
    while (elem <> nil) and (elem.oid <> oid) do begin
      prev := elem; elem := elem.next;
    end;
  end;

  function Adr (r: Relation; oid: String): Integer;
    var prev, elem: Item;
```

```
begin
  err := false;
  Search(r, oid, prev, elem);
  if elem <> nil then result := elem.adr
  else begin
    err := true;
    result := 0;
  end;
end;

procedure Delete (r: Relation; oid: String);
  var prev, elem: Item;
begin
  err := false;
  Search(r, oid, prev, elem);
  if elem <> nil then begin
    Dec(r.n);
    if prev = nil then begin
      r.head := elem.next;
    end
    else begin
      prev.next := elem.next;
    end;
  end
  else begin
    err := true;
  end;
end;

procedure Insert (r: Relation; oid: String; adr: Integer; q: Boolean);
  var elem: Item;
begin
  err := false;
  New(elem); elem.adr := adr; elem.oid := oid; elem.q := q;
  elem.next := r.head;
  r.head := elem;
  Inc(r.n);
end;

function Quality (r: Relation; oid: String): Boolean;
  var prev, elem: Item;
begin
```

```
      err := false;
      Search(r, oid, prev, elem);
      if elem <> nil then result := elem.q
      else begin
         err := true;
         result := false;
      end;
   end;

   function Entries (r: Relation): Integer;
   begin
      err := false; result := r.n;
   end;

   procedure Init (var r: Relation);
   begin
      New(r);
      r.n := 0; r.head := nil;
      err := false;
   end;
end.
```

Task 2 (10 minutes): Abstract Data Type

Converting from ADS to ADT Converting an abstract data structure to an abstract data type always requires the following changes:

- Embedding the global variables within an exported type

- Adding a parameter of this type to all procedures

- Adding an init procedure, which assumes the functions of the module body

Accordingly, the result looks like this:

```
unit Lists;
interface
   type
      ListItem = record
         x: Integer;
      end;
      List = record
```

```
        l: array [0..30] of ListItem;
        n: Integer;
      end;
  procedure Enter (var l: List; item: ListItem);
  procedure Print (l: List);
  procedure Init (var l: List);
implementation
  procedure Enter (var l: List; item: ListItem);
  begin
    l.l[l.n].x := item;
    Inc(l.n);
  end;

  procedure Print (l: List);
    var i: Integer;
  begin
    for i := 0 to l.n - 1 do begin
      WriteLn(l.l[i].x);
    end;
  end;

  procedure Init (var l: List);
  begin
    l.n := 0;
  end;
end.
```

B.2.2   Exercises in Section 4.2.4

Task 1 (200 minutes): Queue

Delphi

```
unit Queues;

interface
  type
    Proc = Procedure (x: Integer);
    Node = ^NodeDesc;
    NodeDesc = record
      val: Integer;
      next: Node;
    end;
```

```
    Queue = record
       n: Integer; // number of elements
       top: Node;
    end;
  procedure EnQueue (var q: Queue; val: Integer);
  procedure DeQueue (var q: Queue; var val: Integer);
  procedure NewQueue (var q: Queue);
  function NrOfElems (q: Queue): Integer;
  function Full (q: Queue): Boolean;
  function Empty (q: Queue): Boolean;
  procedure Iterate (q: Queue; p: Proc);
implementation
  procedure EnQueue (var q: Queue; val: Integer);
    var x, cur: Node;
  begin
    New(x); x.val := val; x.next := nil; // create element
    Inc(q.n);
    if q.top = nil then begin
      q.top := x;
    end
    else begin
      cur := q.top;
      while cur.next <> nil do cur := cur.next;
      cur.next := x;
    end;
  end;
  procedure DeQueue (var q: Queue; var val: Integer);
    var h: Node;
  begin
    if q.top = nil then begin val := -1; exit; end;
    h := q.top; // to free the storage space
    val := q.top.val;
    q.top := q.top.next; // second element becomes first
    Dispose(h);
    Dec(q.n);
  end;
  procedure NewQueue (var q: Queue);
  begin
```

```
      q.top := nil; q.n := 0;
   end;
   function NrOfElems (q: Queue): Integer;
   begin
      result := q.n;
   end;
   function Full (q: Queue): Boolean;
   begin
      result := false; // never full, because data type is dynamic
   end;
   function Empty (q: Queue): Boolean;
   begin
      result := q.n = 0;
   end;
   procedure Iterate (q: Queue; p: Proc);
      var h: Node;
   begin
      h := q.top;
      while h <> nil do begin
         p(h.val);
         h := h.next;
      end;
   end;
end.
```

Task 2 (20 minutes): Discussion

When comparing dynamic and static data types, we can identify the following differences (from the dynamic type's view):

- The exact storage space required for the inserted number of elements is reserved.

- The queue can grow to an arbitrary size—that is, the function Full never returns TRUE. The case where the main memory would be insufficient is unlikely, so this case can be neglected.

- For the insert and delete operations, only single pointers have to be moved, without affecting the rest of the list. However, these operations are not always transparent.

- An element requires only slightly more storage space for the pointer.

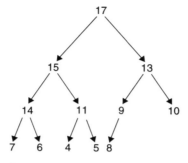

Figure B.1 A heap in tree representation.

B.2.3 Exercises in Section 4.4.5

Task 1 (10 minutes): Heap

Heap order This task concerns a heap, because the heap order applies. This means that the father of a[i] should be determined by a[i div 2], and the sons should be determined by a[2 * i] and a[2 * i + 1]. The father must always be larger than both sons, as Figure B.1 shows.

B.3 Solutions to Chapter 5

B.3.1 Exercises in Section 5.1.6

Task 1 (180 minutes): Queue

Delphi
```
unit Queues;

interface
  type
    Proc = Procedure (x: Integer);
    Node = ^NodeDesc;
    NodeDesc = record
      val: Integer;
      next: Node;
    end;
    Queue = class (TObject)
      private
        n: Integer; // number of elements
        top: Node;
      public
```

```
        constructor Create;
        procedure EnQueue (val: Integer);
        procedure DeQueue (var val: Integer);
        function NrOfElems (): Integer;
        function Full (): Boolean;
        function Empty (): Boolean;
        procedure Iterate (p: Proc);
    end;

implementation

  constructor Queue.Create;
  begin
    top := nil; n := 0;
  end;

  procedure Queue.EnQueue (val: Integer);
    var x, cur: Node;
  begin
    New(x); x.val := val; x.next := nil; // create element
    Inc(n);
    if top = nil then begin
      top := x;
    end
    else begin
      cur := top;
      while cur.next <> nil do cur := cur.next;
      cur.next := x;
    end;
  end;

  procedure Queue.DeQueue (var val: Integer);
    var h: Node;
  begin
    if top = nil then begin val := -1; Exit; end;
    h := top; // to free storage space
    val := top.val;
    top := top.next; // second element becomes first
    Dispose(h);
    Dec(n);
  end;
```

```
function Queue.NrOfElems (): Integer;
begin
  result := n;
end;

function Queue.Full (): Boolean;
begin
  result := false;
end;

function Queue.Empty (): Boolean;
begin
  result := n = 0;
end;

procedure Queue.Iterate (p: Proc);
  var h: Node;
begin
  h := top;
  while h <> nil do begin
    p(h.val);
    h := h.next;
  end;
end;
end.
```

Java

```
package Q;
class Node {
  int val;
  Node next;
}

public class Queue {
  Node top;
  int n; // number of elements
  public Queue () {
    top = null;
    n = 0;
  }
```

```
public void enqueue (int val) {
   Node x, cur;
   x = new Node(); x.val = val; x.next = null; // create element
   n++;
   if (top == null) {top = x;}
   else {
      cur = top;
      while (cur.next != null) {cur = cur.next;}
      cur.next = x;
   }
}

public int dequeue () {
   int val;
   if (top == null) {return -1;}
   val = top.val;
   top = top.next; // second element becomes first
   n-;
   return val;
}

public int nrOfElems () {
   return n;
}

public boolean full () {
   return false;
}

public boolean empty () {
   return n == 0;
}

public void print () {
   Node h;
   h = top;
   while (h != null) {
      System.out.println(h.val);
      h = h.next;
   }
}
}
```

B.4 Solutions to Chapter 6

B.4.1 Exercises in Section 6.1.6

Task 1 (180 minutes): Designing the Account Class

Table B.2 shows the important nouns, verbs, and adjectives occurring in this short example.

The list in Table B.2 shows potential candidates for classes, methods, and attributes. As a first step, we can form a class, Account, with the attributes Number, Name, and AccountBalance. This class also has two methods, PrintPostings and AddPosting. From this class, we can derive two other classes, PersonnelAccount and InventoryAccount, and the class PersonnelAccount has an additional attribute, Turnover. The adjective "OI-leading" represents only additional information and does not produce an attribute.

In addition, there is the class Posting, with the properties PostingDate, OffsetAccount, debitCreditId, and PostingAmount. Moreover, each account has a list of postings.

Figure B.2 shows the relevant UML representation.

Table B.2   Nouns, verbs, and adjectives of the Account specification

Nouns	Verbs	Adjectives
Account	Print postings	OI-leading
Personnel account	Add posting	
Inventory account		
Turnover		
Name		
Posting		
Posting date		
Offset account		
Debit/credit identifier		
Posting amount		
Account balance		

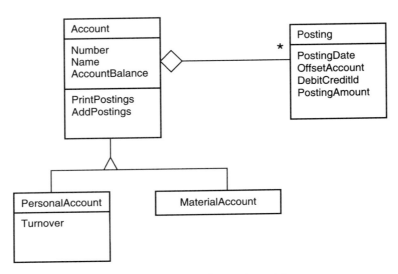

Figure B.2 UML representation of the Account model.

B.5 Solutions to Chapter 7

B.5.1 Exercises in Section 7.1.10

Task 2 (10 minutes): Relations

Admittedly, this is a sneaky question, but the answer is relatively easy: relations are not sorted.

Task 3 (40 minutes): Transactions

Table B.3 shows the result from parallel execution, and Table B.4 shows the result from serial execution.

Consequently, parallel execution produces the result $A = 50$, $B = 100$.

The serial execution produces a result of 10 each. It is easy to see that the two transactions cannot be serialized.

B.5.2 Exercises in Section 7.2.6

Task 1 (100 minutes): Normalization

The first step lists the data elements occurring in the model. Table B.5 shows this list.

Table B.3   Result from parallel execution

Transactions T1	A_{T1}	B_{T1}	Transactions T2	A_{T2}	B_{T2}	A_{file}	B_{file}
Read A	40					40	40
			Read A	40			
			A := 10	10			
			Write A	10		10	
A := A + 10	50						
Read B		40					
B := A * 2		100					
			Read B		40		
			B := 10		10		
			Write B		10		10
Write A	50					50	
Write B		100					100

Table B.4   Result from serial execution

Transaction T1	A_{T1}	B_{T1}
Read A	40	
A := A + 10	50	
Read B		40
B := A * 2		100
Write A	50	
Write B		100

Transaction T2	A_{T2}	B_{T2}
Read A	50	
A := 10	10	
Write A	10	
Read B		100
B := 10		10
Write B		10

Table B.5   First normalized form

	1	2	3	4	5	6	7
1 Number		X	X	X	X	X	X
2 Name							
3 Date of birth							
4 Salary							
5 Salary category of employee							
6 Department name							
7 Department number							

The result from this first normalized form is only one table. This division can be maintained even when considering the rules for the second normalized form, because so far, no attribute depends functionally on a part of the key.

In the next step, you have to determine whether data elements that are not keys depend on the key. You also have to ensure that they will not depend on any other data element.

At this point, you are confronted with a few problems, because DepartmentName depends on DepartmentNumber, and Salary depends on SalaryCategory. For this reason, you should swap these values to separate tables.

Tables in third normalized form

The result is the following tables in the third normalized form:

- The table Employees with the key field EmployeeNumber and the data fields Name, DateOfBirth, SalaryCategory, and DepartmentNumber

- The table Salary with the key field SalaryCategory and the data field Amount

- The table Department with the key field DepartmentNumber and the data field DepartmentName

It also appears useful to create an index pointing to the data field Name in the table Employees, because frequent evaluations in alphabetical order have to be expected. Additional index objects could be taken into consideration and would depend on the desired applications. Figure B.3 shows the ER representation of this model.

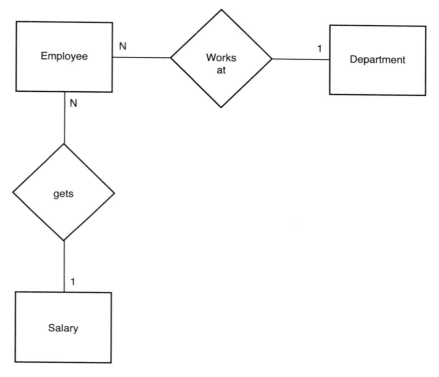

Figure B.3 ER model for payroll accounting.

This task may also produce other intermediate results. However, the final result should be similar to the sample solution.

B.5.3 Exercises in Section 7.3.8

Task 1 (20 minutes): Creating Tables

```
CREATE TABLE Employees (
    Number NUMBER (6) NOT NULL,
    Name CHAR (30),
    DateOfBirth DATE,
    SalaryCategory NUMBER (4) NOT NULL,
    DepartmentNumber NUMBER (4) NOT NULL,
    PRIMARY KEY (Number),
    FOREIGN KEY (SalaryCategory) REFERENCES salary,
    FOREIGN KEY (DepartmentNumber) REFERENCES department
);
```

```
CREATE TABLE Salary (
  Category NUMBER (4) NOT NULL,
  Amount NUMBER (18, 2),
  PRIMARY KEY (Category)
);
CREATE TABLE Department (
  Number NUMBER (4) NOT NULL,
  Name CHAR (30),
  PRIMARY KEY (Number)
);
```

Task 2 (100 minutes): Creating Queries

1. SELECT * FROM Employees
2. SELECT Number, Name, DateOfBirth FROM Employees ORDER BY Name
3. SELECT * FROM Employees WHERE DepartmentNumber = 10
4. SELECT * FROM Employees WHERE DepartmentNumber = 10 ORDER BY DateOfBirth
5. SELECT Number, Name, Amount FROM Employees, Salary WHERE SalaryCategory = Category
6. SELECT MIN(Amount), MAX(Amount), AVG(Amount) FROM Employees, Salary WHERE SalaryCategory = Category
7. SELECT MAX(Amount) FROM Employees, Salary WHERE DepartmentNumber = 10 AND SalaryCategory = Category
8. SELECT Number, Name, Amount FROM Employees EM, Salary SA WHERE EM.SalaryCategory = SA.Category AND DepartmentNumber = 10 ORDER BY Amount DESC
9. SELECT * FROM Employees WHERE Name LIKE "Kn%"
10. SELECT * FROM Employees WHERE DateOfBirth = NULL
11. SELECT DepartmentNumber, MAX(SalaryCategory) FROM Employees GROUP BY DepartmentNumber
12. SELECT DepartmentNumber, MIN(SalaryCategory) FROM Employees GROUP BY DepartmentNumber HAVING MIN (SalaryCategory) > 2
13. CREATE INDEX MyInd ON Employees(Name)

Appendix C

Glossary

abstract class This type of class typically consists of nothing but method headers, without implementation. Such a class is never used in an application but serves merely as an artificial superclass.

Abstract Data Structure (ADS) A data structure that can be used by an arbitrary client by accessing well-defined procedures but that has an open implementation.

Abstract Data Type (ADT) A data structure that presents itself like a data type to the outside.

aggregation Composition of several objects as parts of a new object.

anomalies Unexpected results incurred during an insert, delete, or modify operation, caused by an error in the database design.

assignment compatibility The right expression of an assignment can be assigned to the left part without the need to convert between types.

association A relationship between two objects.

attribute The describing properties of an entity type, such as a customer number, a name, or a phone number.

balanced tree This is a special type of tree that cannot degenerate into a linear list. The height of the tree increases only if it is absolutely necessary.

base class A class serving as a superclass for other classes; the base class itself is not derived from any other class—for example, TObject in Delphi.

binary tree A special type of tree with each node having a maximum of two sons (one on the left and one on the right).

class A class can be thought of as an abstract data type—one for which variables can be declared, which then dispose of attributes and operations (methods).

class library A collection of classes that can be reused.

client/server The client/server paradigm, or processing, divides an application into two parts. The front end represents and processes data on a workstation; the back end stores, retrieves, and protects data.

commit A commit operation terminates a transaction irrevocably.

compiler A compiler translates program code into executable code. An interpreter translates code during each runtime, but a compiler translates the code in advance, and only once.

concurrency A special database property in which several programs can access the same data at the same time.

constructor A special method used to create and initialize an object.

data abstraction A data abstraction hides data from the user behind an interface; the data can be accessed only from this interface.

database driver Independent software that establishes a connection between a program and a database.

deadlock Mutual blocking by two transactions that block the same objects while waiting for each other to release the blocked objects.

debugger A special tool used to run a program step by step while displaying the current values of the local variables in each step. Another term used in COBOL is *animator*.

destructor Destructors release objects and allow completion of actions currently running, such as the zeroing of a counter.

dynamic data structure A data structure that is normally created dynamically—only during runtime—so that it can have an arbitrary size.

entity An identifiable object from the real world. Each entity has specific properties, called *attributes*.

event In this context, an event is an action that can occur in connection with a graphical user interface. Examples are mouse movements or keyboard inputs.

exception Exceptions are objects signaling an exceptional or fault condition. They can be triggered by a `raise` or `throw` statement and caught by `try` blocks.

focus This term is important in connection with graphical user interfaces. Only one component can possess the focus, or be active, so keyboard inputs are forwarded to it.

Garbage Collection An automatic mechanism to remove objects that are no longer required from the storage location. Java offers this functionality, but not Delphi.

generalization A larger, comprehensive structure, as in the case of a superclass representing a generalized form of the derived class.

HTML (hypertext markup language) A language in which to code World Wide Web pages.

index An index in a database allows quick access to a desired row. Specific columns can be defined as index columns, and an index can be defined for each of them.

information hiding A technique that causes data to be hidden from the outside; closely related to *data abstraction*.

inheritance A type extension applied to achieve specialization of a class.

instance Alternative term for an object, in the sense that an object is instantiated by its class.

interpreter A tool used to translate program code into executable code at runtime. A compiler translates the code in advance, and only once, but an interpreter translates code every time at runtime.

ISO (International Organization for Standardization) The standards organization best known for having proposed the seven-layer reference model early in the history of data networking.

Java An object-oriented programming language, similar to C++, originally developed by Sun Microsystems. Now used mainly to create active World

Wide Web documents. This language has had the highest growth rate, driven by the explosive growth of the Internet.

javadoc A documentation generator that generates HTML pages based on Java source text. These pages contain the respective classes, interfaces, methods, constructors, and variables.

join A join operation connects two relations, similar to the Cartesian product.

key An attribute combination for unique identification of all instances of a class (relation).

leaf A node within a tree that no longer has any **sons**.

LOCK An instruction allowing a data object to be modified to lock to protect it from modification by other database operations.

message A means used to request an object to execute a specific method.

method An operation offered by a class.

multiple inheritance Given when a class is derived from several base classes.

normalization Dividing data into relations that are free from redundancies and that avoid anomalies.

NULL value A special value in a database indicating that the value is unknown or cannot be determined.

Oberon-2 An efficient and elegantly structured object-oriented programming language, considered the successor of Pascal.

object An item of a class.

object-oriented database A special form of database that uses and stores objects instead of tables.

OQL (Object Query Language) A query language for object-oriented databases defined by ODMG (Object Database Management Group).

package A grouping for classes in Java.

primary key A data element used for unique identification of an object, such as an account number.

profiler A special tool used to measure how long it takes to execute a program. It allows the user to determine how often each code line was iterated and how much time it took.

QACenter A tool developed by Compuware, used for automatic tests.

recovery In this context, to restore a consistent database state, even in case of total system failure.

recursion Occurs when a procedure calls itself again, directly or indirectly.

relationship Defines how individual objects relate to each other. In a database, this can be done by referencing to a key.

request A request for an object—a dynamically bound procedure call.

runtime error A critical program error that emerges only at runtime (that is, not during compilation)—for example, division by zero or an attempt to access a nonexistent dynamic data structure. Unless this type of error is caught by an **exception**, it will cause the program to exit.

secondary key A data element referring to a primary key. The value applies to the entire record in the table to which it refers. In contrast to the primary key, the values in a secondary key can occur more than once.

shortcut evaluation Given when, in Boolean queries of type A or B, A is evaluated first, and B is evaluated only if this is not already true. Similarly, for A and B, A is evaluated first, and B is evaluated only if this is true; otherwise, the result is already given. This is important to know, because if, for example, B is a functional procedure, it might not be called.

specialization A smaller, more particular structure, as in a subclass representing a special form of its superclass. For example, "clerk" is a specialized form of "employees."

SQL (Structured Query Language) A structured query language for relational databases.

static data structure A data structure the size of which is already known prior to executing the program. It is also independent of data input. The data structure is created based on the declaration and can neither grow nor shrink at runtime.

surrogate An artificial key, such as an ISBN.

transaction A set of instructions, where either all or none are executed.

tree A special data structure with a root at the top and a specific number of nodes—**sons**—underneath. Each son, in turn, is a root of a subtree. A node that no longer has sons is called a *leaf*.

UML (Unified Modeling Language) A notation used to represent object-oriented models.

Unicode A standardized, 16-bit character set used, for example, by Java. It supports a huge space of character sets, including Japanese and other non-Latin special characters.

URL (Uniform Resource Locator) A standardized method to represent Internet addresses.

view A logical view or perspective of one or several relations.

Y2K problem A problem incurred during the millennium change from 1999 to 2000. Many programs store only the last two digits of the year, so when the year 99 changed to 00, among other things, this made temporal sorting impossible.

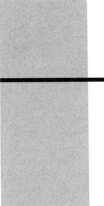

Appendix D

References

[Abb83] Abbott. *Program Design by Informal English Descriptions.* Communications of the ACM 26 (11), 1983.

[ArCo96] Arranga and Coyle. *Object-Oriented COBOL.* SIGS Publications, 1996.

[BGP00] Böszörményi, Gutknecht, and Pomberger. *The School of Niklaus Wirth.* dpunkt, 2000.

[BMRS96] Buschmann, Meunier, Rohnert, Sommerlad, and Stal. *Pattern-Oriented Software Architecture.* Wiley, 1996.

[Bor02] Borstlap. "Understanding the Technical Barriers of Retargeting ISAM to RDBMS." *www.anubex.com/anugenio!technicalbarriers1.asp,* Anubex, 2002.

[Bud02] Budd. *Object-Oriented Programming,* 3rd ed. Addison-Wesley, 2002.

[CaWa01] Campione and Walrath. *The Java Tutorial,* 3rd ed. Addison-Wesley, 2001.

[CBB97] Cattell, Barry, and Bartels. *The Object Database Standard.* Morgan Kaufmann, 1997.

[Chr02] Chroust. "Motivational Issues in Component-Based Software Development," *Proceedings of the Sixteenth European Meeting on Cybernetics and System Research* (EMCSR 2002), 2002.

[CLR01] Cormen, Leiserson, and Rivest. *Introduction to Algorithms,* 2nd ed. MIT Press, 2001.

[Com98] Compuware Corporation. *Compuware: QARun—Language Reference Manual.* Compuware Corporation, 1998.

[DaDa97] Date and Darwen. *A Guide to SQL Standard,* 4th ed. Addison-Wesley, 1997.

[Dat90] Date. *An Introduction to Database Systems,* Vol. 1, 5th ed. Addison-Wesley, 1990.

[GHJV94] Gamma, Helm, Johnson, and Vlissides. *Design Patterns.* Addison-Wesley, 1994.

[Hoy01] Hoyle. *ISO 9000 Quality Systems Handbook.* 4th ed. Butterworth-Heinemann, 2001.

[JeWi74] Jensen and Wirth. *Pascal User Manual and Report.* Springer, 1974.

[Kna97] Knasmüller. *Oberon-D: On Adding Database Functionality to an Object-Oriented Development Environment.* Trauner, 1997.

[Kna99] Knasmüller: "Quo Vadis, BMD? Research Projects at BMD Steyr—An Experience Report." *Proceedings of European Software Day,* Milan. Austrian Computer Society, 1999, 145–152.

[Kna01] Knasmüller: "How to Manage the Change from COBOL to OOP." *ACM OOPSLA Tutorial Notes.* ACM, 2001

[Kna02] Knasmüller. "Human Problems When Changing from COBOL to OOP," *Proceedings of the Sixteenth European Meeting on Cybernetics and System Research* (EMCSR 2002), 2002, 171–176.

[Knu84] Knuth. "Literate Programming." *Computer Journal,* 27 (2), 1984.

[Mös99] Mössenböck. *Object-Oriented Programming in Oberon-2.* Springer, 1999.

[Par72] Parnas. "On the Criteria to be Used in Decomposing Systems into Modules." *Communications of the ACM,* 15 (12), 1972.

[Pie99] Piemont. *Components in Java.* dpunkt, 1999.

[PoBl97] Pomberger and Blaschek. *Software Engineering.* Hanser, 1997.

[Pre95] Pree. *Design Patterns for Object-Oriented Software Development.* ACM Press, Addison-Wesley, 1995.

[RBJ98] Rumbaugh, Booch, and Jacobson: *Unified Modeling Language Reference Manual.* Addison-Wesley, 1998.

[Sed88] Sedgewick. *Algorithms.* Addison-Wesley, 1988.

[Szy99] Szyperski. *Component Software: Beyond Object-Oriented Programming.* ACM Press, Addison-Wesley, 1999.

[Wir71] Wirth. "Program Development by Stepwise Refinement." *Communications of the ACM,* 14 (4), 1971.

[Wir85] Wirth: *Algorithms + Data Structures = Programs.* Prentice Hall, 1985.

Index

Limited Warranty

The Publisher warrants the media on which the software is furnished to be free from defects in materials and workmanship under normal use for 30 days from the date that you obtain the Product. The warranty set forth above is the exclusive warranty pertaining to the Product, and the Publisher disclaims all other warranties, express or implied, including, but not limited to, implied warranties of merchantability and fitness for a particular purpose, even if the Publisher has been advised of the possibility of such purpose. Some jurisdictions do not allow limitations on an implied warranty's duration; therefore the above limitations may not apply to you.

Limitation of Liability

Your exclusive remedy for breach of this warranty will be the repair or replacement of the Product at no charge to you or the refund of the applicable purchase price paid upon the return of the Product, as determined by the Publisher in its discretion. In no event will the Publisher, and its directors, officers, employees, and agents, or anyone else who has been involved in the creation, production, or delivery of this software be liable for indirect, special, consequential, or exemplary damages, including, without limitation, for lost profits, business interruption, lost or damaged data, or loss of goodwill, even if the Publisher or an authorized dealer or distributor or supplier has been advised of the possibility of such damages. Some jurisdictions do not allow the exclusion or limitation of indirect, special, consequential, or exemplary damages or the limitation of liability to specified amounts; therefore the above limitations or exclusions may not apply to you.